The Long Civil War

The Long Civil War

New Explorations of America's Enduring Conflict

Edited by
John David Smith and Raymond Arsenault

UNIVERSITY PRESS OF KENTUCKY

Scholarly publisher for the Commonwealth,
serving Bellarmine University, Berea College, Centre College of Kentucky, Eastern Kentucky University, The Filson Historical Society, Georgetown College, Kentucky Historical Society, Kentucky State University, Morehead State University, Murray State University, Northern Kentucky University, Spalding University, Transylvania University, University of Kentucky, University of Louisville, and Western Kentucky University.

Editorial and Sales Offices: The University Press of Kentucky
663 South Limestone Street, Lexington, Kentucky 40508-4008
www.kentuckypress.com

Library of Congress Cataloging-in-Publication Data

Names: Smith, John David, 1949– editor. | Arsenault, Raymond, editor.
Title: The long Civil War : new explorations of America's enduring conflict / edited by John David Smith and Raymond Arsenault.
Description: Lexington, Kentucky : The University Press of Kentucky, [2021] | Series: New directions in Southern history | Includes index.
Identifiers: LCCN 2021006479 | ISBN 9780813181301 (hardcover) | ISBN 9780813181318 (pdf) | ISBN 9780813181325 (epub)
Subjects: LCSH: United States—History—Civil War, 1861–1865—Influence. | United States—History—Civil War, 1861–1865—Social aspects. | United States—History—Civil War, 1861–1865—Historiography.
Classification: LCC E468.9 .L65 2021 | DDC 973.7/1—dc23
LC record available at https://lccn.loc.gov/2021006479

This book is printed on acid-free paper meeting the requirements of the American National Standard for Permanence in Paper for Printed Library Materials.

Manufactured in the United States of America.

Member of the Association of University Presses

The contributors dedicate this book to Professor Randall M. Miller of St. Joseph's University—scholar, teacher, mentor, friend. His unfailing generosity and uncommon wisdom have touched all of our lives.

Contents

Introduction

In 1873, four years before what historians consider the official end of Reconstruction, Mark Twain wrote that the Civil War era already had become a historical perennial. "History," Twain wrote, "is never done with inquiring of these years, and summoning witnesses about them and trying to understand their significance." The nine years between South Carolina's secession in 1860 and the election of Ulysses S. Grant as president in 1868 signified a watershed in American history. Twain, who served the Confederacy briefly in the Marion Rangers, a ragtag unit of the Missouri State Guard, recalled that the war "uprooted institutions that were centuries old, changed the politics of a people, transformed the social life of half the country, and wrought so profoundly upon the entire national character that the influence cannot be measured short of two or three generations."[1] In fact, long after the passing of these generations the Civil War continues to grasp the national psyche with an almost religious intensity. One historian explains correctly that it took almost nine decades to eradicate slavery; and its direful legacies endure painfully alive today.[2] The "Long Civil War" remains, according to another scholar, "an unfinished process," "The Undead War."[3]

Contemporary historians and literary scholars continually expand the geographic, temporal, and thematic dimensions of the Civil War era, what an earlier generation of scholars termed the "Middle Period" of American history.[4] No longer do they limit the Civil War's meaning and range of impact to the antebellum decades, or from 1861 to 1865, or define the so-called Reconstruction period as covering the dozen years from 1865 to 1877. Rather, today's scholars increasingly follow Eric W. Hobsbawm's lead in lengthening chronological boundaries, most notably his famous conceptualization of the "long nineteenth century" ranging backward and forward across time.[5] Writing in 1975, in *The Age of Capital, 1848–1875,* Hobsbawm advised historians to frame the past within the context of their day. But they also should benefit from "the wisdom of hindsight," which Hobsbawm considered the historian's "most powerful asset, for which any betting man and investor would give his eye-teeth, namely the knowledge of what actually happened later."[6]

Heeding Hobsbawm's advice, students of the so-called Long Civil War probe widely, deeply, and expansively, identifying progressions of subjects, themes, topics, and tropes that emerged decades before the secession crisis of 1860–1861 and lingered long after the last federal troops left the less-than-reconstructed South. Kevin Gannon has advocated expanding the "historical periodization" of the Civil War and its consequences. By doing so, he explains, "It allows us to see the larger ways in which racial and racist ideologies shaped not only the pitched warfare of 1861–1865, but the violent struggles for mastery of much of North America in the surrounding decades."[7] Similarly, in assessing nineteenth-century American literature, Cody Marrs has implored scholars to reconsider "the 1865 divide" that locks them in "chronological segmentation" and to reassess the writings of "transbellum" canonical authors whose "periodic fluidity" assists in explaining their connection to the Civil War and thereby "recast[s] the historicity" of the conflict.[8] More recently Marrs has remarked that "If we have learned anything from the recent waves of Americanist scholarship, it is that the borders that long organized literary-historical inquiry are far more unsettled than anyone knew."[9]

In 2011 Aaron Sheehan-Dean sounded the call for an extended Civil War historiography. He implored scholars to broaden their focus, both temporally and spatially. "For too long, Civil War historians have been justly criticized for writing within a deep but narrow and disconnected part of the larger community of scholars studying the United States." Sheehan-Dean proposes that much like those who study the "Long Civil Rights Movement," students of the Civil War should reorient their historical vision, considering origins, sources, and "evolutionary time scales" that contribute to "the dynamism of history." Doing so, he insists, would introduce "more human stories that restore a crucial sense of contingency to the past and connects the pivotal changes of the era . . . to the broader flow of human thought and action surrounding it."[10]

Linking Civil War–era subjects to past and future projects broadens the importance of historians' work. Subjects generally identified with the Civil War era, including nationalism, federalism, states' rights, sovereignty, slavery, race, reconciliation, and proscription, resonate with Americans today who ponder such questions as reparations for slavery, racial injustice and violence, representation, ethnicity, national identity, and retaining or removing such controversial symbols of the American past as Confederate monuments and other signifiers. The Long Civil War thus enables twenty-first-century Americans to reflect on what in 1782 the French naturalized citizen J. Hector St. John Crèvecoeur asked rhetorically, "What then is the American . . . ?"[11] In 1961, during the Civil War centennial, Robert Penn Warren, formerly US poet laureate, went so far as to assert that "the imaginative appeal of the Civil War . . . may be, in fact, the very ritual of being American."[12]

By expanding the contours of the Civil War's reach, historians add new frameworks for assessing continuity and change and identifying similarities and differences among regions, peoples, and ideas. They chart the variety of uses of the Civil War in contemporary culture, including as analogy and as metaphor. Such analyses contribute in diverse ways to broadening the meaning of America's bloodiest war. Paradoxically, although the war accounted for approximately 750,000 deaths and countless shattered lives, communities, families, and individual dreams, Americans incontrovertibly "love" this horrible conflict with a passion. They enthusiastically purchase books on the topic, visit restored battlefields, join Civil War Roundtables, and watch documentaries on the topic. According to estimates, upward of thirty thousand men and women reenact aspects of the war as hobbyists. And courses on the Civil War and Reconstruction continue to be extremely popular at colleges and universities, north and south.

Beyond the war's broad appeal and its pathos of death and destruction, it led to the emancipation of 4 million persons of color and, during Reconstruction, to landmark constitutional amendments that eradicated slavery, established equal protection and birthright citizenship, and excised racial discrimination in voting. Union victory also enabled the freed men and women to reconstruct their families and establish new communities with schools, churches, and civic organizations.[13] Today historians emphasize the Civil War's broad imprint long after Yankees and Rebels heard their last tattoos. Victoria E. Bynum's *The Long Shadow of the Civil War: Southern Dissent and Its Legacies* (2010) includes as part of the war's heritage southern Unionists who, in the postwar decades, "evolved into New South populists and socialists and multiracial communities, such as the one in Mississippi, which emerged from anti-Confederate collaboration between blacks and whites." In her judgment, "truly, these are living histories that connect past and present."[14] So too, as Nina Silber has documented in her history of the Civil War as a source of American ideals and national identity in New Deal

America, Americans across the political spectrum have invoked the war's memory during times of national crisis.[15]

In terms of American culture, the ongoing Civil War appears most conspicuously in what Melvyn Stokes terms "the birth, growth and dissemination of the 'Lost Cause,' a romantic myth revolving around the 'Old South' and the way in which it fought the Civil War." According to this powerful cultural battleground and political trope, this time around the Rebels proved triumphant against the Yankees because they allegedly fought a more honorable fight to protect states' rights and their proverbial "southern way of life," predicated by gentility and advanced civilization. Trained historians, north and south, have long dismissed the phrase "southern way of life" as a crude euphemism for defenses by white southerners for the alleged golden age of the antebellum South, for the so-called paternalism of African American slavery, and for the maintenance of a benign white supremacy following emancipation.[16]

Memories of the war and its consequences not only have remained powerful, but they die hard, as David Goldfield has explained in his *Still Fighting the Civil War: The American South and Southern History* (2002). In Goldfield's assessment, the Civil War remains very much alive in the minds of Americans, especially white southerners, in memory and society, due largely to the convergence of decades-old racial assumptions about persons of color and the reinforcing influence of race on fundamentalist Christianity. It resembles "a ghost that has not yet made its peace and roams the land seeking solace, retribution, or vindication. It continues to exist, an event without temporal boundaries, an interminable struggle that has generated perhaps as many casualties since its alleged end in 1865." To a significant degree, postbellum white southerners have triumphed in the memory war of the Civil War and Reconstruction.[17] They remain so mired in their history, Goldfield argued in a later book, that they came "to define themselves, their religion, and their region by their past, and contrary perspectives threatened the community, for if their myth proved untrue, who, then, were they?"[18] According to one critic, Goldfield exaggerates the importance of the Civil War to southern history by transforming the Lost Cause into the "first cause," diminishing "all historical memory in the South to redactions of the Civil War." Such an interpretation, Bruce Baker writes, "impoverishes our understanding of the many things Southerners have considered worth remembering about their past."[19]

Nevertheless, many on both sides of the Mason-Dixon Line concur with Warren, who remarked in 1961 that "The Civil War is for the American imagination the great single event of our history." "Without too much wrenching," he added, "it may, in fact, be said to *be* American history." Warren went on to allege that "The Civil War is our only 'felt' history—history lived in the national imagination." He insisted that the fact that persons, north and south, oftentimes held divergent opinions about the war's meaning, actually strengthened his argument. Disagreements about the Civil War, Warren averred, provide "an index to the very complexity, massiveness and fundamental significance of the event." In Warren's opinion, the internecine conflict provides "an overwhelming and vital image of human, and national experience."[20] It remained, according to contemporary cultural critic Adam Gopnik, "this country's central moral drama."[21] In their collection of essays, *The World the Civil War Made* (2015), Gregory P. Downs and Kate Masur have examined what they term "the enduring illiberal and chaotic qualities of life in the postwar United States not as imperfections in a consolidating liberal nation, but as central to the American experience."[22] This insight exemplifies the expansion of the thematic and chronological boundaries of traditional topics in American history and the maturation of its historiography.[23]

The essays in *The Long Civil War* contribute to this emerging and expanding new scholarship. This collection of ten essays begins with two studies that connect antebellum racial questions with those that preoccupied Civil War–era Americans during and long after emancipation in 1865: the merits of repatriating freed slaves to West Africa, and the complex tactics of initiating political racial reform in Congress.

In "West African Missions, Colonies, and Imperial Anxieties in the United States, 1834–1865," Daniel Kilbride explains how for three decades before the Civil War colonizationists espoused the return of African Americans to "benighted Africa" on several grounds, although often disagreeing on particulars. In the 1830s and 1840s some proponents of colonization openly criticized the alleged benefits of repatriation for the Africans themselves. By the 1850s, however, most agreed that colonization would civilize and Christianize the Africans, halt the African slave trade, benefit American commerce, and reduce racial tensions at home. Kilbride investigates two southern-born white missionaries who interpreted the fruits of repatriation differently—J. Leighton Wilson, who served in Liberia from 1834 to 1852, and Thomas Jefferson Bowen, who served in present-day Nigeria from 1850 to 1856. Wilson's experiences in Liberia led him to become a severe critic of colonies and empire because he believed that the white settlers threatened to annihilate the indigenous population in what amounted to no less than a race war. Bowen saw things differently, enthusiastically promoting an American-led empire in Africa that would westernize the continent. In his opinion, colonization worked best when missionaries proselytized religion along with commerce and cultural penetration—equal parts of an incipient American imperialist enterprise.

Stanley Harrold's "The Abolition Lobby: Its Development, Successes, and Disintegration, 1836–1845," brings to light the so-called abolition lobby—abolitionist activists, clergymen, and journalists determined to mobilize the caucus of northern Whig congressmen to propose antislavery legislation during the decade before the Mexican-American War. These politicians generally sought to excise slavery in the nation's capital, opposed the annexation of the slaveholding Republic of Texas and the admission of the Florida Territory as a slave state, and insisted on the right to present antislavery petitions and to speak before Congress on antislavery topics. But they also tried to maintain ties to their southern Whig colleagues and favored compromise whenever possible on sectional disputes. Focusing on the relationships between the abolitionist lobbyists and antislavery Whigs, Harrold dates the formation of the lobby earlier than previous historians who have identified its rise with that of the Liberty Party in the early 1840s. The lobby reached its greatest strength in 1842 and declined three years later, the result of counter tactics adopted by proslavery congressmen. It died because slavery's defenders became less aggressive, less insistent on enforcing the Gag rule. Former lobbyists looked to the Liberty Party for electoral victories, hoping to destroy slavery root and branch.

The next two essays in *The Long Civil War* document how the Civil War itself complicated the lives of individual participants, both in the ranks and in hitherto unknown ways. These contributions treat numerous topics with longstanding implications for Civil War scholars, how disabled federal troops found ways to serve the Union in the Veteran Reserve Corps (VRC) during and after the war, and the broad political, social, and literary rhetoric of suicide in the Civil War–era South.

Paul A. Cimbala's "Officers of the US Army Veteran Reserve Corps: Motivation and Expectations of Veteran Soldiers during the Civil War and Reconstruction," explains why disabled Union officers sought service in the Veteran Reserve Corps (VRC) while and after the Civil War raged. The army established the VRC in April 1863 to boost its manpower shortage, utilizing disabled veterans to maintain order in northern towns and other rear echelon assignments. Eventually fifty-seven thousand enlisted men served in the Corps. Cimbala identifies various motives for wounded and camp-sick officers seeking commissions in the VRC. They were determined to stay in the army, fearful that their injuries would prevent them from returning to their prewar occupations, but also deeply patriotic. Officers hoping to join the VRC expected the US government to honor their past service and suffering, not to provide charity. Unfortunately, because following Appomattox the government moved to a smaller, less expensive army, positions for officers in the VRC became scarce. Many disabled veterans then applied for positions in the Freedmen's Bureau in the occupied South. Cimbala concludes that a considerable number of the disabled officers who served in the bureau sympathized with the freedpeople and themselves were subjected to violent acts by disgruntled and racist white southerners.

In her essay Diane Miller Sommerville unearths how before and after secession, as well as following Confederate defeat, northerners and southerners employed "the language of self-destruction," "the political rhetoric of suicide," to accentuate the severity of the political crisis that befell them. Americans above and below the Mason-Dixon Line had long considered suicide abhorrent. During the secession crisis they identified disunion as a self-inflicted and unforgivable death blow to the republic that the Founders had established. Over time, however, as Sommerville shows through her close reading of numerous texts, especially newspapers, a competing version of suicide emerged in the post–Civil War South. "Confederates, enveloped in extreme emotional, psychological and material suffering during and then after the Civil War, had become more familiar with incidents of suicide." White southerners came to identify metaphorical national suicide, as well as cases of self-immolation, as evidence not only of a heroic crusade, but also of individual courageous acts. Sommerville cites the postwar suicide of Edmund Ruffin (1794–1865), the Virginia planter, agricultural reformer, and rabid champion of states' rights and secession, as a case in point. He preferred suicide and death to life under dreaded "Yankee rule." Other ex-Confederates, instead of owning up to their treason against the Union of their forefathers, and the death and destruction that devastated their land, redefined state and individual suicide as honorable, manly, reasonable, and respectable. According to Sommerville, this new ideology of suicide helped to establish and energize the Lost Cause cult that followed Appomattox. It contributed to Bourbon ascendancy and then to hegemony over the region and, ultimately, to Jim Crow's triumph.

The next two essays, biographical analyses of Emory Upton, a New Yorker, and Ulrich Bonnell Phillips, a Georgian, suggest the ways, directly and indirectly, how the Civil War influenced the life and labor of two intellectuals who contributed significantly to late-nineteenth- and early twentieth-century American military and racial thought, respectively.

"Warrior Turned Reformer: Emory Upton and the Modernization of the American Army" is James R. Hedtke's analysis of Upton's unwavering commitment to reforming the US Army from his days as an ambitious junior officer in 1861 until his suicide in 1881. Born in 1839, Upton distinguished himself in combat during the Civil War in numerous campaigns, including First Bull Run, the Peninsula, Antietam, Fredericksburg, Gettysburg, and, most significantly, at the Wilderness, where he introduced the tactic of massing infantry at isolated elements of the enemy's line. He gained renown during the war for serving in three branches of the Union forces—the artillery, infantry, and cavalry. In the war's aftermath, he served in the Department of the Cumberland, in the District of Colorado, and at West Point, where he commanded the Corps of Cadets. Throughout his career Upton clamored for a competent officer corps and advocated for the professionalization of the American military by adjusting tactics to new weapon technology, by awarding commissions by examination and promotions by merit, by disciplining its rank and file fairly, and by training its commanders at war colleges. In his influential theoretical writings on military science, most notably *A New System of Infantry Tactics* (1867) and *The Armies of Asia and Europe* (1878), Upton conceptualized, among other changes in the American military, the three-tiered system (the professional army, the reserves, and the National Guard) that came to comprise America's fighting force today. He also recommended the General Staff command structure headed by a chief of staff that became law when congress passed the General Staff Act in 1903. Upton's reforms in military organization, policy, tactics, and training, according to Hedtke, contributed significantly to the long-term development of the modern US Army.

In "Ulrich Bonnell Phillips and World War I: Finding '*pax plantation*' at Camp Gordon, Georgia," John David Smith examines Phillips (1877–1934), who emerged as the leading historian of the South during the Progressive Era. During the First World War, Phillips served as a nonmilitary volunteer staff officer for the Young Men's Christian Association at a boot camp in DeKalb County, Georgia, that hosted more than nine thousand African American draftees. Phillips, whose influential writings transformed him into America's most influential historian of slavery between the two world wars, took leave from the University of Michigan to finish what became his landmark book, *American Negro Slavery* (1918), a work that remained influential among historians until after World War II. While so engaged he found his diverse responsibilities at Camp Gordon exhilarating—teaching English and French, organizing social events for the recruits, supervising construction, procuring postage stamps, and, he proclaimed, many "*et ceteras.*" To a certain extent, Phillips's war work brings to mind conservative white northern white missionaries who flocked to the South during the Civil War and Reconstruction to teach and "civilize" the newly freedpeople. Smith, however, maintains that Phillips's service with black recruits at Camp Gordon contributed to his understanding of white-run, regimented organizations and confirmed his understanding of the benefits of slavery, plantation paternalism, and the management of subject peoples for both races. It also underscored Phillips's obsession with racial control and order—in short, the maintenance of the first New South's racial status quo, itself a byproduct of post–Civil War racial accommodations by northern Republicans and their capitalist supporters.

The final contributions to *The Long Civil War* connect the mid-nineteenth-century conflict to larger twentieth-century controversies, debates, and questions about historical memory, some of which continue to reverberate in American popular culture in the twenty-first century. These essays address changing attitudes toward Abraham Lincoln by African Americans, Confederate and Neo-Confederate commemorations, President Dwight D. Eisenhower's gradual metamorphosis from a racial conservative to an integrationist, and historical memory, including interpretations of the Civil War and Reconstruction in Walt Disney's twentieth-century films and television series.

In "The Man and the Martyr: Abraham Lincoln in African American History and Memory," James Oliver Horton and Lois E. Horton sketch the evolving evaluations of the sixteenth president by such diverse black persons as H. Ford Douglas, Frederick Douglass, John Rock, Harriet Tubman, Sojourner Truth, Elizabeth Keckley, Booker T. Washington, W.E.B. Du Bois, Martin Luther King Jr., and Lerone Bennett. Prior to issuing his final Emancipation Proclamation, men and women of color generally judged Lincoln "a conservative antislavery man" who favored gradually emancipating the South's slaves, repatriating them abroad, and compensating their owners. As white northerners and southerners engaged in a bloody internecine war, African Americans, most notably Douglass, chided the president for hesitating to embrace abolition fully, or to provide succor for escaped slaves who reached Federal lines, or to mobilize black troops. Determined to redirect the course of the war both militarily and politically, on January 1, 1863, Lincoln issued his final emancipation edict, which "changed the war" as "the war itself was changing Lincoln." While generations of African Americans chastised the president's toleration of slavery, his racial intolerance, his inconsistency (Du Bois dubbed Lincoln "a big, inconsistent, brave man"), and his unconcern for black suffering, many black persons nonetheless revered him. His assassination apotheosized Lincoln into "a white martyr for black freedom, an image that remained strong among African Americans through the rest of the nineteenth and most of the twentieth century."

Drawing on a broad range of sources—including film, historiography, iconography, literature, television, and built memorials—Stephen J. Whitfield's essay "'If at First You Don't Secede': War and Remembrance" assesses why the Civil War continues to be a historical leitmotif for white southerners—a lens through which they continue to define themselves and their place in the American experience. For them the internecine mid-nineteenth-century war remains inescapable; it lingers in "the sheer tenacity of Southern white consciousness." Whitfield considers the "Southern white mentality" premised on the inferiority of persons of African descent. It emerged decades before the Civil War, erupted into secession in 1860–1861, continued during and after Reconstruction, experienced a resurgence as die-hard segregationists reacted to the civil rights movement of the 1950s and 1960s, and remains alive today. In his opinion, white southerners' "regionally-inflected [race] consciousness combines truculence with grievance, tenacity with defensiveness." "No wonder then," Whitfield argues, "that, as late as the twenty-first century, controversy over the display of Confederate flags and the monuments to Confederate generals have remained an irrepressible conflict, a recurring debate over the meaning of secession." The war resulted from slavery, what Vice President Alexander H. Stephens in 1861 proclaimed to be "the cornerstone of the Confederacy."

Michael J. Birkner's "Dwight Eisenhower and Civil War Legacies" examines how history generally, and Civil War history in particular, shaped Ike's "historical mindedness and public policy." Eisenhower read history, especially Greek and Roman military history. During his presidency, portraits of George Washington, Benjamin Franklin, Abraham Lincoln, and Robert E. Lee adorned his office walls. Eisenhower studied the Civil War and revered both Lee and Lincoln. Opposed to extremism, and committed to limited federal government, he admired Lee's character, leadership, and nobility. Lincoln, Ike maintained, successfully kept the Union intact. Birkner explains that while Eisenhower sympathized with longstanding white southerners' understandings of states' rights, in 1957 he considered it his constitutional duty to mobilize the Arkansas National Guard during the desegregation crisis at Little Rock's Central High School. Convinced that during the Civil War "good men on both sides died for causes in which they believed," throughout his presidency Eisenhower struggled with the disconnect between militant segregationists and advisors who promoted civil rights legislation. While he eventually "got right with Lincoln" and admonished Americans to "subordinate self to the country's good," Eisenhower continued to struggle with the Civil War questions of race and region.

In "Playing with History: Walt Disney's Historical Films, 1946–1966," Raymond Arsenault traces the pioneer animator's historical filmmaking from the 1940s until the 1960s, a period when he became one of "the world's most powerful culture brokers." Committed to advocacy, not to constructing historically accurate, contextualized narratives, Disney disseminated and reinforced nostalgic images and traditional values popular in Cold War America. In what Arsenault terms "a Disneyfied version of American history," the filmmaker scrupulously avoided controversial questions pertaining to class, poverty, race, or sectionalism. He also generally shunned consulting the extant professional historical scholarship as sources for his work. Instead, Disney favored quasi-fictional, moralistic, uplifting stories about heroes such as Daniel Boone, Davy Crockett, Francis Marion, and James J. Andrews, the hero of the 1956 Civil War thriller *The Great Locomotive Chase.* Disney often dealt with important historical themes—westward expansion, civil wars, frontier violence, and conflicts between white settlers and Native Americans. But he did so as "a purveyor of fantasy and commercialized popular culture," and not as a balanced, nuanced, truth-telling interpreter of the past.

The essays in this collection thus expand the geographic, temporal, and thematic focus of what previous generations of historians judged to be mid-nineteenth-century history. Rather, they suggest, as Warren asserted in 1961, that the Civil War itself "draws us to the glory of the human effort to win meaning from the complex and confused motives of men and the blind ruck of event."[24] The conflict continues to have an enduringly firm grip on the American imagination broadly conceived and articulated. As Alice Fahs and Joan Waugh have explained, "From 1865 to the present each new generation has actively reinterpreted the Civil War to support its own ideological agendas," often breaking sharply with past interpretations.[25]

The contributions to *The Long Civil War* present case studies treating complex questions pertaining to slavery and race, abolition and the military, historical memory, and film and culture, underscoring what Warren decades ago explained were "how individual men, despite failings, blindness, and vice, may affirm for us the possibility of the dignity of life." Disagreements, past or present, provide dialectics that in resolution often lead to strength and clarification of "confused issues, shadowy chances and brutal ambivalences" that, with luck, "may rub off on us." Writing during the early civil rights era, Warren reminded readers that slavery and race lay at the heart of the causes of the Civil War, despite the "proxy struggles over the tariff, states' rights, constitutional interpretation, and internal improvements and economic development" that his fellow white southerners across time had used to justify secession.[26]

In 1961 Warren, who possessed "a dark awareness of how the past haunted and weighed on the present," made clear that in his opinion Americans had fallen woefully short of learning the many lessons that the Civil War had proffered. "Perhaps we continue to contemplate the story of the Civil War because we yearn for that," he concluded.[27] Here Warren documented "his constant disappointment and disenchantment with the world that emerged from the Civil War and modernity more generally."[28] More recently, Edward L. Ayers, viewing Reconstruction with both a microscope and a telescope, observed: "We were the agents of revolution and its opponents, its beneficiaries and its victims. Reconstruction, looked at in the full light of history, offers one of our best opportunities to see ourselves more clearly."[29]

As Warren accomplished so brilliantly in *The Legacy of the Civil War: Meditations on the Centennial* (1961), we have assembled essays that suggest that long after the Confederate defeat, the Civil War as analogy, idea, memory, metaphor, and symbol continued to capture the attention of Americans, North and South. As a broad cultural and intellectual touchstone, the war helped to define how Americans understood and defined themselves—how they interpreted their past and their present, their diversity—their "Americanness."

The essays in this collection expand the boundaries of contemporary American historical scholarship. They suggest how—whether examining antebellum, late nineteenth- or twentieth-century topics—the Civil War and its wide-ranging consequences and implications remain a yardstick that can be used to measure the American experience. The essays illustrate how historians can accommodate and integrate ambiguity, selective memory, and the power of myths and symbols in their assessments of the war's geographic, temporal, and thematic importance.

The individual contributors to *The Long Civil War* employ a number of methodological approaches to researching and writing this history, collectively drawing upon a wide range of sources, including autobiographies, documentary editions, historical fiction, federal records, film, historical markers, literature, manuscript collections, newspapers, presidential papers, popular magazines, proceedings, scrapbooks, and sermons. Such diversity is necessary when the subject at hand is as challenging and complex as the Civil War, with its multilayered elements of personal and generational experience embedded in racial, regional, and national myths about the nature and meaning of the war.

Twenty years ago David W. Blight examined the nation's collective postwar memory in his classic study *Race and Reunion: The Civil War in American Memory* (2001), a work that takes the "history and memory" theme up to 1915, fifty years after Lee's surrender at Appomattox. But we are now entering the third decade of the twenty-first century, more than a century after the close of Blight's postwar material, still grappling with the meaning and consequences of a war that continues to bear relevance to our national life. It is the war that simply will not go away, the one that still generates engaged scholarship among hundreds, and perhaps even thousands, of historians. As Paul Christopher Anderson observed recently, "The lastingness of the American Civil War, its ongoingness," remains "in the union of two peoples—no longer merely 'Northern' or 'Southern': but a people of defeat, and a people of victory—joined in their epic, at the weakest points of both."[30]

The essays in *The Long Civil War* demonstrate that this almost obsessive fascination with the war—from its origins to its aftermath and legacies—can be attributed in part to the mythic structures that surround it, several of which have animated and sustained the politics of regional and racial identity across a century and a half of history. But as the essays make clear, much more than myth is involved in this long legacy. As Warren explained, "Many clear and objective facts about America are best understood by reference to the Civil War."[31] In our current age of allusions to "fake news" and "alternate facts," a Civil War volume stressing factual accuracy and the cold, hard realities of slavery, secession, and civil war might prove useful to a society still struggling to live up to the ideals of freedom, and of liberty and justice for all.

Notes

1. Mark Twain, *The Gilded Age: A Tale of To-Day* (1873; Hartford: American Publishing Company, 1874), 168.

2. Patrick Rael, *Eighty-Eight Years: The Long Death of Slavery in the United States, 1777–1865* (Athens: Univ. of Georgia Press, 2015).

3. Thomas J. Brown, "Civil War Remembrance as Reconstruction," in *Reconstructions: New Perspectives on the Postbellum United States,* ed. Thomas J. Brown (New York: Oxford Univ. Press, 2006), 207; Thomas J. Brown, "The Undead War," in *Remixing the Civil War: Meditations on the Sesquicentennial,* ed. Thomas J. Brown (Baltimore: Johns Hopkins Univ. Press, 2011), 1–16.

4. See, most influentially, John W. Burgess, *The Middle Period, 1817–1858* (New York: Charles Scribner's Sons, 1907). Writing at the *fin de siècle,* Burgess remarked that when examining the years before the Civil War, "We find ourselves in the midst of the ideas, the motives, and the occurrences which, and of the men who, have, in large degree, produced the animosities, the friendships, and the relations between parties and sections which prevail *to-day.*" See page vii (emphasis added).

5. Joseph Fronczac, "Hobsbawm's Long Century," *Jacobin,* June 9, 2017, https://www.jacobinmag.com/2017/06/eric-hobsbawm-historian-marxism-communist-party-third-reich-stalingrad (accessed July 18, 2019). "Hobsbawm," according to Anette Schlimm, "was surely not . . . [the Long Nineteenth Century's] only inventor, but he was instrumental in popularizing this temporal division." Anette Schlimm, "The Guerrilla Historian: Eric J. Hobsbawm and the Long Nineteenth Century," *German Historical Institute London Bulletin* 41 (November 2019): 99.

6. Eric J. Hobsbawm, *The Age of Capital, 1848–1875* (New York: Charles Scribner's Sons, 1975), 155.

7. Kevin Gannon, "Historical Periodization and the Long Civil War," *The Tattooed Professor: History, Teaching, and Technology with a Custom Paint Job,* September 19, 2016, https://www.thetattooedprof.com/2016/09/19/historical-periodization-and-the-long-civil-war/ (accessed July 8, 2019).

8. Cody Marrs, "Against 1865: Reperiodizing the Nineteenth Century," *J19: The Journal of Nineteenth-Century Americanists* 1 (fall 2013): 259–61, 279–80; Cody Marrs, *Nineteenth-Century American Literature and the Long Civil War* (New York: Cambridge Univ. Press, 2015), 3.

9. Cody Marrs, "Three Theses on Reconstruction," *American Literary History* 30 (fall 2018): 407.

10. Aaron Sheehan-Dean, "The Long Civil War: A Historiography of the Consequences of the Civil War," *Virginia Magazine of History and Biography* 119, no. 2 (2011): 107–8. Having said this, Sheehan-Dean suggests that "Civil War scholars should press forward in time rather than back."

11. J. Hector St. John de Crèvecoeur, *Letters from an American Farmer: Describing Certain Provincial Situations, Manners, and Customs Not Generally Known; and*

Conveying Some Idea of the Late and Present Interior Circumstances of the British Colonies in North America, 2nd ed. (1782; London: Printed for T. Davies, 1783), 51.

12. Robert Penn Warren, *The Legacy of the Civil War: Meditations on the Centennial* (1961; New York: Vintage, 1964), 78. For an excellent analysis of Warren's reflections on the Civil War, see David W. Blight, *American Oracle: The Civil War in the Civil Rights Era* (Cambridge, Mass.: Belknap Press of Harvard Univ. Press, 2011), 31–79. On various aspects of the continuing lure of the Civil War and its ongoing meaning for Americans, see, for example, Tony Horwitz, "Battle Acts," *New Yorker* 74 (February 16, 1989), 58–67; Tony Horwitz, *Confederates in the Attic: Dispatches from the Unfinished Civil War* (New York: Random House, 1998); David Goldfield, *Still Fighting the Civil War: The American South and Southern History* (2002; Baton Rouge: Louisiana State Univ. Press, 2004); William A. Blair, "Finding the Ending of America's Civil War," *American Historical Review* 120 (December 2015): 1753–66; David Goldfield, "How Americans Can Stop Fighting the Civil War," October 30, 2017, https://www.whatitmeanstobeamerican.org/identities/how-americans-can-stop-fighting-the-civil-war/ (accessed July 8, 2019); Tony Horwitz, *Spying on the South: An Odyssey Across the American Divide* (New York: Penguin Press, 2019); Susan-Mary Grant, Keisha N. Blain, Tim Stanley, Erin Stuart Mauldin, "What Are the Enduring Legacies of the American Civil War?" *History Today* 69 (August 2019): 8–10; and Heather Cox Richardson, *How the South Won the Civil War* (New York: Oxford Univ. Press, 2020).

13. Gregory P. Downs, Eric Foner, and Kate Masur, "Remembering Reconstruction," *New York Times,* December 14, 2016, A27.

14. Victoria E. Bynum, *The Long Shadow of the Civil War: Southern Dissent and Its Legacies* (Chapel Hill: Univ. of North Carolina Press, 2010), xi.

15. Nina Silber, *This War Ain't Over: Fighting the Civil War in New Deal America* (Chapel Hill: Univ. of North Carolina Press, 2018).

16. Melvyn Stokes, "*Gone with the Wind* (1939) and the Lost Cause: A Critical View," in *The New Film History: Sources, Methods, Approaches,* ed. James Chapman, H. Mark Glancy, and Sue Harper (New York: Palgrave Macmillan, 2007), 13.

17. Goldfield, *Still Fighting the Civil War,* 1, 29, 41, 298.

18. David Goldfield, *Southern Histories: Public, Personal, and Sacred Histories* (Athens: Univ. of Georgia Press, 2003), 20.

19. Bruce Baker, "Are We Still Fighting the Civil War?" H-Net Reviews, H-South (June 2002), https://networks.h-net.org/node/512/reviews/656/baker-goldfield-still-fighting-civil-war-american-south-and-southern (accessed July 24, 2019).

20. Robert Penn Warren, "A Mark Deep On: 'The Great Single Event of Our History,'" *Life* 50, no. 11 (March 17, 1961): 82 (emphasis in original). Portions of this essay appeared later in Warren's *The Legacy of the Civil War.*

21. Adam Gopnik, "The Takeback," *New Yorker* 95 (April 8, 2019): 76.

22. Gregory P. Downs and Kate Masur, eds., *The World the Civil War Made* (Chapel Hill: Univ. of North Carolina Press, 2015), 3. Other studies of the

so-called Long Reconstruction include Brown, *Reconstructions*; Heather Cox Richardson, *West from Appomattox: The Reconstruction of America after the Civil War* (New Haven: Yale Univ. Press, 2007); and Orville Vernon Burton, Jerald Podair, and Jennifer L. Weber, eds., *The Struggle for Equality: Essays on Sectional Conflict, the Civil War, and the Long Reconstruction* (Charlottesville: Univ. of Virginia Press, 2011).

23. See for example, most recently, Lester D. Langley, *The Long American Revolution and Its Legacy* (Athens: Univ. of Georgia Press, 2019), and Angie Maxwell and Todd Shields, *The Long Southern Strategy: How Chasing White Voters in the South Changed American Politics* (New York: Oxford Univ. Press, 2019).

24. Warren, *The Legacy of the Civil War,* 108.

25. Alice Fahs and Joan Waugh, eds., "Introduction," *The Memory of the Civil War in American Culture* (Chapel Hill: Univ. of North Carolina Press, 2004), 4. For example, in 1941 the journalist W. J. Cash wrote acerbically that "The Civil War and Reconstruction represent in their primary aspect an attempt on the part of the Yankee to achieve by force what he had failed to achieve by political means: first, a free hand in the nation for the thievish aims of the tariff gang, and secondly, and far more fundamentally, the satisfaction of the instinctive urge of men in the mass to put down whatever differs from themselves—the will to make over the South in the prevailing American image and to sweep it into the main current of the nation." Cash, *The Mind of the South* (1941; New York: Vintage, 1991), 103.

26. John Burt, "Robert Penn Warren's Civil War," in *A History of American Civil War Literature,* ed. Coleman Hutchison (New York: Cambridge Univ. Press, 2016), 304.

27. Horwitz, *Spying on the South,* 132; Warren, "A Mark Deep On," 88.

28. Burt, "Robert Penn Warren's Civil War," 303.

29. Edward L. Ayers, "Exporting Reconstruction," in *What Caused the Civil War? Reflections on the South and Southern History* (New York: Norton, 2005), 166.

30. Paul Christopher Anderson, *A Short History of the American Civil War* (New York: Bloomsbury Academic, 2020), 242.

31. Warren, *The Legacy of the Civil War,* 4.

1

West African Missions, Colonies, and Imperial Anxieties in the United States, 1834–1865

Daniel Kilbride

This is the story of two southern-born American missionaries to Africa in the mid-nineteenth century. It is also a story about Americans' ambivalent embrace of imperial ways of thinking in the decades before the Civil War. J. Leighton Wilson, the privileged son of a coastal Georgia slave-owning family, toiled with his wife, Jane Bayard Wilson, for almost twenty years in West Africa as a missionary for the American Board of Commissioners for Foreign Missions (ABCFM) before retiring to the United States in 1853. At that very time, another Georgian, Thomas Jefferson Bowen, was serving in Yorubaland, in present-day Nigeria, under the auspices of the Southern Baptist Convention. He would return to America in 1856 after a seven-year stint in Africa. Like most Protestant missionaries to Africa in Britain and the United States, both Wilson and Bowen had ambitious plans for bringing the whole continent to Christ and integrating it into the "civilized world." But they had very different plans for how that ought to be done, and those differences broadly conformed to divisions in American public opinion over the wisdom and propriety of imperial expansion—especially overseas expansion. The Wilsons reached maturity in the era of Cherokee removal, an event they viewed as an act of grave injustice and naked aggression. They would come to view the treatment of African peoples at the hands of African American settlers in Liberia through the lens of Indian removal under Jackson and Van Buren.[1]

Bowen's youthful experiences could not have been more different. Just a few years younger than Leighton Wilson, Bowen had joined armed companies of white Georgians committed to expelling the Cherokee from the state. He fought with such skill and enthusiasm that his company elected him captain in 1836. Cherokee removal did not signal the end of Bowen's career as an agent of Anglo-Saxon expansion, however. From Georgia he trekked to Texas, eager to help white, slave-owning settlers seize control of the territory from Mexico. He arrived too late to participate in the decisive battle of San Jacinto, but he did join in border patrols and Indian pacification efforts. An experienced proponent of American imperial expansion, Bowen would apply the lessons he learned in Georgia and Texas to developing a scheme for the conversion and civilization of Africa. Crucially, Wilson was uninterested, when not actively opposed, to the project of civilizing Africa—to linking or facilitating its Christian redemption with the introduction of western European culture and commercial development. Although Wilson softened his position somewhat after his return to the United States, he never wavered in his conviction that civilization and commerce would not only subvert the primary goal of conversion, but would lead to the oppression and even the extermination of native peoples.[2]

In the 1830s, Wilson and likeminded missionaries in Liberia emerged as effective spokespersons against the American Colonization Society (ACS) and its state auxiliaries, especially the Maryland State Colonization Society (MSCS), which he saw as the leading wedge of an American imperial presence in sub-Saharan Africa. Coming on the heels of Indian removal—an event that progressive Protestants like Wilson viewed as a shameful moral travesty—the campaign Wilson led against the MSCS struck a nerve among many Americans who had seen colonization as a practical means to gradually end slavery in the United States, rid the country of what they saw as a troublesome population of free people of color, and use that population to civilize and Christianize Africa. By the time Bowen became an active, much-sought-out proponent of an American-sponsored empire in western Africa led by freed American slaves, attitudes toward imperial expansion had shifted in the United States. Vast territories wrested from Mexico, the peaceful acquisition of lands in the Pacific Northwest, and filibustering adventures in the Caribbean and Central America whetted the appetites of some Americans for further expansion.[3]

The association of schemes of African development with the eminently respectful and conservative colonization movement lent those plans a progressive aura that other expansionist movements lacked. Indeed, in the 1850s even some African American leaders, long implacable critics of colonization, began to consider emigration to Africa, so hopeless did the prospects seem for people of color in the United States in the decade marked by the Fugitive Slave Act and the Dred Scott decision. Other developments also promoted Americans to consider Africa as a promising venue for imperial adventures. A growing consensus that the conversion of Africa had to be accompanied by commercial development and westernization, Liberia's emergence as an independent republic, and a flood of books and articles on African exploration also led to that assessment. Of course, Bowen's plan, and other programs for African expansionism, came to nothing. For all the interest they attracted, these plans were far too ambitious to garner the necessary private capital and crucial government support they required. They also lacked the support of the most ambitious expansionists in the United States—slaveholders. These women and men had little reason to back a plan that proposed to develop African sources of cotton as a morally attractive alternative to the slave-grown American supply. Nevertheless, the widespread attention that Bowen's plan for an American empire in West Africa received testifies to the blossoming of an imperial mindset in the mid-nineteenth-century United States.

From a modern perspective, the American colonization movement seems like a fantastical scheme. In one respect, however, it was as idealistic as the most rabid supporter of William Lloyd Garrison. Colonizationists argued that the repatriation of people of color to their African homeland would result in the introduction of western civilization and Christianity to so-called benighted Africa. Some even suggested that slavery should be understood as part of God's plan to redeem that continent. According to the Reverend Henry Ward Beecher, "[w]hat men meant for evil, God meant for good; and the accomplishment of his comprehensive plan will at last cause the wrath of man to praise him in the civilization and Christianization of Africa." In His inscrutable way, the injustices visited upon generations of enslaved people in the Americas would be the occasion for Africa's salvation.[4]

Not everyone agreed that Christianization and civilization would work together in Africa, however. Many missionaries believed it was their brief only to bring the gospel to Africans, unaided by either secular culture or commerce. As Leighton Wilson argued, commerce and civilization were more likely to harm than help Africans. If "unattended by Christianity,"

Wilson warned, commerce "goes to curse and not to bless. Abundant proofs of this are not now wanting on the coast of Africa." He insisted that only "the preaching of the Gospel—that simple, but powerful and divinely appointed instrumentality"—would "affect [the] great object" of Africa's conversion. Wilson's allusion to coastal Africans appeared frequently in the writings of those who considered themselves the friends of Africa. Most of what Americans and Europeans thought they knew about Africa they learned from coastal peoples. That impression confirmed their worst prejudices—that Africans were indolent, violent, and unscrupulous. Wilson and others who spent time in Africa strained to show not merely that coastal peoples were far from representative of Africans generally, but that their vices stemmed from corruption by trade with westerners, not innate depravity. David Livingstone's best-selling *Missionary Travels and Researches in South Africa* (1857), a reader observed, proved that the "slave-trade has corrupted the habits and hearts of the people" on the west coast. In the interior, Livingstone "found a standard of practical morality which needed very little palliation."[5]

The debate about the proper relationship between preaching, trade, and civilization had implications beyond the narrow question of how best to bring Africans to Christ. It implicated the colonization movement, which represented itself not only as the means for solving America's racial dilemma, but as the vehicle for Africa's modernization. Beecher was hardly alone in envisioning the "emancipation of Africa" as colonization's "great and primary object," with the "emancipation of the colored race at home" merely "an incidental result." The idea that colonization would be the opening wedge for western civilization in Africa proved to be enormously attractive to Christians active in the benevolent empire, so colonizationists repeated it constantly. Because disease had rendered Africa off-limits to white men, they reasoned, only African Americans could redeem it. Under the influence of colonies, one advocate claimed, "heathenism must come to an end, the horrid slave trade must cease, cruelty and despotism cannot live, and the millions of Africa may be redeemed." Colonization was "the only scheme which even promises . . . to open a door by which the enslaved may go free, and to civilize and Christianize Africa." Despite these lofty principles, the colonies established by various American organizations did not coexist peacefully with the Africans living in their vicinity. News of violent conflict between settlers and Africans undermined the colonization message in the United States. It also sparked a debate about the relationship between means and ends in the opening of Africa to the West, a goal that nearly all Americans—even white southerners—supported. Should the West lead with the Bible alone? Or must evangelization be assisted by commerce and secular culture? And, as some individuals began to propose in the 1850s, should Americans assist in establishing an African American empire across the sea to promote the great object of Africa's redemption?[6]

In the 1830s and 1840s, missionaries emerged as especially credible critics of colonization. They were among the loudest advocates for engagement with Africa, not only to spread the gospel but to suppress the slave trade. Their advocacy for native peoples, however, forced them to confront the discrepancy between what colonization promised and what it delivered to African peoples. The colonies' imperial footprint in Africa seemed to work to the detriment of African societies. The Wilsons were among the best-known African missionaries of the mid-nineteenth century. They were antislavery, which was nothing out of the ordinary for missionaries, but they were also both slaveowners, which certainly was unusual. As they planned to remove to Africa, they made plans to wash their hands of slaveholding. The couple assigned to Jane's half-brother Nicholas Bayard their power of attorney, stipulating that upon their notice he was to free their slaves and send those willing to go to West Africa. There they would have a bright future, the Wilsons believed—that is, until they saw Liberia for themselves. What they witnessed completely changed their minds about colonization.[7]

Leighton and another missionary, John Wynkoop, had reconnoitered Cape Palmas in the new colony of Maryland in Liberia in 1833 to assess its suitability as a mission station. Their confidential report expressed reservations about locating the mission within the colony. Not only did he doubt that Liberia helped Africans; he believed "that in some respects it has had a very injurious tendency" upon them. He concluded, "the more remote mission operations generally are from these settlements, the better." Nevertheless, Wilson and the board accepted the conventional wisdom that colonies provided material aid and security to missionaries, so they swallowed their misgivings. In 1834 Leighton and Jane established their mission, Fair Hope, outside of Harper at Cape Palmas, Liberia.[8]

Relations between the missionaries and the colony deteriorated after John Russwurm became Maryland in Liberia's governor in 1836. Wilson had difficulty accepting the authority of a black man, and Russwurm chafed at the presence of slave-owning southerners. They also came into conflict over substantive issues regarding the legal jurisdiction of the colonial government over the mission. What positively infuriated Wilson and other missionaries, however, was what they saw as the hostility of the settlers toward the natives, which he was convinced would eventually lead to the latter's annihilation. In a six-part letter to the ABCFM in 1838, Wilson charged that colonization was "productive of innumerable evils of which [Americans] had not the most distant apprehensions." Far from improving the moral condition of the natives, the colony's influence had been harmful. Wilson cited the work of Reverend John Philip of the London Missionary Society, who had indicted British imperialism at the Cape Colony. Philip's work led to the establishment of the Select Committee on Aborigines in 1835, which concluded that "the intercourse of Europeans in general . . . has been, unless when attended by missionary exertions, a source of many calamities to uncivilized nations." Why, wondered Wilson, should anybody be surprised? After all, had not the settlement of the Americas been "a long detail of wrongs and injuries inflicted upon the native inhabitants?" Whenever civilized people settled among savages, the latter had been exterminated. "On what ground then can the abettors of colonization to Western Africa expect to form an exception to this almost universal rule?" Wilson wondered.[9]

Matters had not improved by 1842. In that year, six missionaries from three denominations addressed a joint statement to their boards. They "disclaim[ed] all wish or intention to assail the scheme of American Colonization," but the statement was in fact an indictment. Every point focused on the colonists' oppression of the natives. Well-meaning Americans who thought that migrants would identify with native Africans and work for their improvement were being misled. Colonization was imperialism, and imperialism meant the inevitable destruction of less-developed peoples. The petitioners requested confidentiality, not wishing to entangle their boards in a public spat over colonization. Inevitably, though, rumors about these communications leaked. The missionaries had repeated these charges in private letters and to audiences during home visits. The MSCS learned of Wilson's feelings from a letter he sent to Nicholas Bayard. Despite Wilson's having asked that the letter be given "no needless publicity," Bayard forwarded it to the MSCS home agent. Wilson held back nothing in what he thought was a private note between friends. Colonization was "little else than a system of iniquity & oppression." Either the Grebo would rise up and annihilate the colony, or the colonists would enslave the Grebo. In

America, Wilson had thought that "any thing was better than unconditional slavery," but he had come to believe that "any thing is better than colonization." Bayard naively assumed that the MSCS was ignorant of these abuses and would "promptly & effectually . . . suppress" them. Instead, the colonization societies circled the wagons.[10]

They did so because they understood their very existence would be imperiled if the association between colonization and imperialism became widespread—and that is very nearly what happened. Accusations of imperial behavior discredited the movement just when it was reeling from abolitionist attacks and financial reverses stemming from the Panic of 1837. Many donors supported the movement to advance the glorious cause of extending Christianity to Africa. One of them told Benjamin Latrobe that his friends supported colonization "principally because they believed that the colonists were exerting a good influence upon the natives." Wilson's statements, and reports from Episcopal missionary Thomas Savage stating that "the colonists instead of doing good to the natives, were exerting a demoralizing influence," gave the lie to that belief. This charge was "a more potent objection than any yet encountered" to the colonization scheme because the missionaries had enormous credibility. "I have been accustomed to suppose those men who could forsake home & every thing we hold dear in civilized society to go among pagan and savage nations . . . were always to be credited and this is the general opinion of others." The missionaries' charges threatened to expose colonization's ambition to redeem Africa as a sham. R. R. Gurley, secretary of the American Colonization Society, explained that the movement was already losing support in the North because of "the impression made by missionaries against the moral & religious nature of the colonists." The future of colonization was at stake. "If the influence of all the missionary boards be thrown against colonization it will be difficult to sustain it," he concluded.[11]

The friends of colonization waged an all-out assault on the missionaries' credibility. Methodist minister Samuel McGill charged that at issue was an "extreme aversion on the part of the white missionary to be subject to the authority of a coloured man." He dismissed Wilson's characterization of the settlers. To the contrary, they "consider themselves a great mission family, labouring for the good of their benighted brethren." But, paradoxically, colonizationists also insisted that a hard line toward Africans was necessary because of their savagery. Joseph Tracy of the Massachusetts Colonization Society asked, were not African societies rife with human sacrifice, cannibalism, lawlessness, devil worship, and slave trading? And had not colonies been the only means for the elimination of these evils? Tracy acknowledged that there had been violence between the settlers and the colonies. But the Americans had the right to defend themselves. People in the United States had been misled by the missionaries' misrepresentations, Tracy said. The true "character of the natives" was "vicious and contaminating in the last degree." As if that appeal to the worst "dark Africa" tropes was not enough, Tracy attacked the missionaries. He suggested that these women and men—many of whom had sacrificed their lives or constitutions to the cause of converting Africa—had been embittered by sickness and failure.[12]

This very public spat forced the ABCFM to investigate. Its commission came down on the side of the missionaries. The "attempt to coerce military duty from colored persons in the employ of the mission" contradicted the spirit of the missionary endeavor, which relied "upon the strong arm of Jehovah instead of the sword . . . in their attempts to carry the gospel of peace to the dark and benighted heathen world." The core problem was that the settlers pursued their "temporal interests" and not, their protestations to the contrary, the welfare of the natives. The inevitable result of the settlers' pursuit of material wealth was hostility "both to the native inhabitants of the coast and to the missionaries who are laboring for the[ir] spiritual welfare." Abolitionists, inveterate critics of colonization, seized on the annual report of the ABCFM, which warned that the fate of the Grebo might become "that of the native tribes of South Africa and of our own country." The ABCFM was to be credited with finally "dissipating forever the idea of [colonies] lending aid to the introduction of the gospel to benighted Africa."[13]

The missionaries' charges set back the colonization movement for years. Their effect, wrote the Maryland Society, was "to cripple the Society in its operations—to sow distrust among its friends of all religious denominations—[and] to comfort and succor the enemy, the abolitionists." The charge that colonization was an imperialist movement, not the harbinger of civilization and Christianity, severely damaged its credibility in the North. Yet this estrangement proved to be short lived. The resurgent racism of the 1850s, providing no sign that whites were ready to lift their collective foot off the necks of black Americans, gave new life to colonization and emigration movements.[14] They also received a boost from the popularity of African travel accounts—especially David Livingstone's bestselling *Missionary Travels and Researches in South Africa,* but also a popular book by Thomas Jefferson Bowen. The colonization press lavished attention on these books.

The "wonderful discoveries" of Bowen, Livingstone, and others would stimulate "labor for Africa's redemption." The world would see "mission stations and Christian settlements greatly multiplied there within the next ten years," one author predicted. In 1856, Wilson published *Western Africa: Its History, Conditions, and Prospects.* In a bold act of appropriation, colonizationists claimed Wilson as one of their own. All three authors, they claimed, showed that sub-Saharan Africa was ready to be brought into the bosom of civilization. Colonization would be the instrument for Africa's deliverance.[15]

Bowen developed a distinctive vision for Africa's conversion that foregrounded colonization of the Niger Valley under American authority. After seven years of service among the Yoruba, Bowen returned to the United States in 1856 with definite ideas about how to bring the gospel to the African interior. He agreed wholeheartedly with Livingstone that preaching alone would never establish Christianity. His remark that "It has, indeed, an appearance of simple energetic faith, to affirm that the Gospel alone is sufficient to evangelize the barbarous nations" echoed Livingstone and may have been a rebuke to Wilson. Without the supporting apparatus of schools, western goods, and a Christian community, he was convinced that converts would lapse back into barbarism. The Baptist divine Francis Wayland insisted that missionaries had no charge to civilize, but only to convert. "[C]ivilizing the heathen" was not a command "found in the Gospel of Jesus Christ," he maintained. But Bowen and other missionaries found that separating the two was easier said than done; it was hard to secure conversion without a secular scaffolding. As he explained after a sustained period of preaching around Ogbomosho in 1855, "The seed is sown but the crop cannot be reaped tomorrow. The people are fettered by a thousand conventional bonds, which will require accumulated force to break asunder." Bowen came to believe that trade in commodities like cotton, palm oil, and ivory was the abrasive most likely to break those bonds. Trade would create a demand for education, useful knowledge, and industry, the last "indispensable to the existence of virtue." Commerce laid the foundation without which Christianity would atrophy. It would destroy the slave trade by providing a more lucrative alternative. Finally, by introducing consumer goods that would provide a means to display social distinctions, it would undermine the chief obstacle to Christianity—polygamy.[16]

In one very important respect, Bowen took issue with Livingstone and Wilson. Wilson had little faith that enough talented African American preachers could be produced to minister to Africa, so he demanded that white Christians shoulder the burden. Livingstone assumed that the establishment of commerce would necessitate a British colonial administration. Bowen insisted that African Christianity must be spread by Africans, who would adapt the faith to conform to the genius of their people. "It is not wise," Bowen maintained, "to commit the too common mistake of supposing that our form of civilization is the exemplar for the whole earth. It is not the best form for ourselves, and is not adapted to Africa at all. The climate and the moral and mental constitution of the people are unanimous in demanding an African civilization for Africa . . . which only needs to be developed on its own basis, in conjunction with pure Christianity." Howard Temperley has observed that "[c]ultural relativism was not a viewpoint that commended itself to the minds of Victorians." Yet, their experiences in Africa sometimes provided Bowen and other westerners with some perspective on their culture's crude sense of universalism.[17]

Bowen became a popular advocate for mass colonization as the most likely means for the conversion of Africa. He rejected the abolitionist charge that colonization was imperialist aggression or a proslavery scheme to rid the country of free people of color. The "single object and motive" of colonialism was "to plant a great negro nation in Africa, which shall be a means of diffusing civilization and Christianity throughout the whole continent." That "great nation" would not be Liberia. Rather, it would be in the interior, along the banks of the Niger. Bowen identified the Yoruba as the African people most likely to adopt western civilization. "The influence of a Christian colony would be far greater in Yoruba and other parts of Sudan than it has been in Liberia," he argued, "because the Sudanese generally are almost prepared to receive civilization and the gospel." The Niger, which Bowen supposed to be navigable for hundreds of miles into the interior, would become the "highway for a vast commerce." Like other missionaries and explorers, he insisted that Central Africa was healthier than the coast and far emptier of population; both conditions would prove attractive to African Americans when they finally gave up on the United States, which he was sure would be soon. Colonization societies, in short, were doing their part to fulfill God's plan for humanity. History was "tending always to the same point, the conversion and the civilization of the whole world." God had decreed Africa to be next, and had made colonization His instrument.[18]

Bowen knew that a benevolent organization did not have the means for realizing his epic vision. Only a government had the necessary resources. In

1857, Bowen urged a House of Representatives committee to sponsor an expedition to the Niger. Explorers under the protection of the Stars and Stripes would purchase land, which would over time expand into an American colony. To envision central Africa, Bowen invited Congress to call to mind the "mesquite prairies in western Texas." The land was healthy and flat. It was moderately populated by a people ready to receive the blessings of civilization. "In some respects the Sudanese are considerably advanced from mere barbarism," he reported. It was especially significant to proper Victorians, who measured a society's level of civilization by the status of women, that "[t]he women do not labor on the farms."[19] The land produced an abundance of crops, including cotton and sugar, and was "admirably adapted to coffee and other tropical productions of great value to the civilized world." Bowen appealed to Congress's benevolence and self-interest. Not only would trade with the region "add to the civilization of the country and to the development of its resources," but it "would be worth millions of dollars per annum." In 1857 the US Senate approved funding for this expedition in a naval appropriations bill, but the House rejected it. It never resurfaced.[20]

Bowen's plan was not entirely fantastic. In 1850, the House Naval Affairs Committee had proposed establishing a steamship line for the promotion of African colonies. Settlements would, it was thought, more effectively suppress slave trading than the African Squadron. Also, millions of African American migrants would carry the gospel and civilization to Africa. As "a missionary enterprise," an American colony in West Africa "deserves, and no doubt will receive, the countenance and support of the whole Christian world." It would also benefit the United States economically. Besides, the British would surely step into a void unfilled by the United States. "The belief is now confidently entertained in Great Britain, that an immense commerce may be opened up with that continent, by putting an end to the slave trade, and stimulating the natives to the arts of peace," the report explained. Although it claimed that the federal government had full authority to establish and maintain colonies of its own, this proposal merely sought to support colonies set up by benevolent societies. Settlements in Africa, populated by millions of freed American slaves and supported by the US government, would benefit the United States, Africans, and African Americans. Like Bowen's 1857 plan, this one went nowhere.[21]

Their failure notwithstanding, these were imperial visions. Bowen proposed the establishment of US authority on foreign soil, which could be established without conflict because the Sudanese would welcome African

American immigrants "with open arms and give them lands on easy terms." And then they "would unite with the colonists from America, and thus lead the natives to do the same." Thus would spring forth a new nationality, an Americanized, Christianized African people. Bowen acknowledged that US authority would be necessary until the colony found its feet. The first settlements ought to be considered an "American trading post, and thus come under the protection of our flag." This would be imperialism, albeit a new kind, one that Wilson would have found hopelessly naive: it was "*founding a great English-speaking Empire*—not by fire and sword, like the conquerors of the earth, but by the peaceable powers of commerce, science, art, and Christianity." Bowen's vision inspired some Americans to aspire to Britain's example, to become an imperial power. The United States, enthused the *African Repository,* the organ of the American Colonization Society, "will be aroused to emulate Great Britain—never slow to avail herself of advantages laid open to her commercial enterprize, by those who have explored Africa or other unfrequented regions of the globe." Bowen and his colonization allies argued that the 1850s was the time, and Africa the place, for the United States to assume its place as a great power.[22]

Although Congress showed little interest in this scheme, some Americans were positively enthusiastic. Among them numbered advocates for colonization and emigration, both of which enjoyed a resurgence in the 1850s, an unpromising decade for African Americans. Repelled from colonization by its racist foundations, emigrationists like Martin Delany and Henry Highland Garnet found voluntary resettlement to Africa to be people of color's best hope for realizing the American dream. Livingstone and others had made Africa seem like an accessible alternative to the United States. Quaker Benjamin Coates, a leading emigrationist, thought that Bowen's and Livingstone's books had for the first time shown Americans "what Africa actually is." Together he hoped they would "do a great deal of good" to break down opposition to emigration.[23]

The leaders of this movement touted central Africa's health and economic potential. Cultivating cotton promised to provide a steady market as well as a way to undermine American slavery—a way to serve both God and mammon. Coates cited Bowen as an authority on central Africa's cotton-growing potential. Likewise, Delany identified Bowen and Livingstone as his inspirations for exploring the Niger region. Theirs, too, was an imperialist program. They assumed the cultural superiority of western civilization over indigenous African cultures. Bowen asserted that treaties for the cession of African land would be made—and enforced—by American might. Delany argued that disease-festering African lands could be made safe and productive by development. Swamps drained, forests felled, and farmland cultivated would eliminate the miasmas that proved so deadly to migrants. Making Africa safe for American-born blacks would also make it safe for economic development, cultural penetration, and self-rule. Bowen and other Christians had laid out "the importance of colonial possession," one observer enthused. Central Africa would become the hub of a glorious American empire, the tip of the spear for the millennium in Africa.[24]

Most activists in the benevolent empire supposed that Africa's redemption would come about through Anglo-American cooperation. David Livingstone gave voice to this sentiment when he wrote "[i]t is on the Anglo-American race that the hopes of the world for liberty and progress rest" at the conclusion of *Missionary Travels.* However, that sentiment coexisted alongside a strain of Anglophobia that impeded collaboration. Bowen dismissed Britain's contributions to the civilization of Africa. Instead, he marshaled spread-eagled nationalism to inspire Americans to answer the call. To the United States, "the appointed arbiter of the earth," Bowen maintained, "God has brought the barbarous negro race, and from this country he is leading them back, civilized and Christianized, to Africa."[25] Advocates of empire ignored the significant differences between Wilson, Livingstone, Bowen, and other explorers, representing them all as proponents of colonization. "The remarkable discoveries of Livingstone, Bowen, and [Heinrich] Barth, and the interesting accounts by Wilson and [George] Thompson, have opened a new field of Christian enterprise, as well as commercial activity," one colonizationist enthused. The colonization press was especially opportunistic in exploiting explorers' celebrity. "The friends of African colonization have every reason for substantial encouragement in the great work in which they are engaged," ran a typical article in the *African Repository.* These men had revealed to the world "stalwart races, noble chiefs, in lands of singular fertility and abundant resources." Colonizationists seem to have taken special glee in appropriating their old antagonist, J. Leighton Wilson. His discoveries were "full of promise for the future of Liberia," the *Repository* enthused. Livingstone had been drafted as an advocate of the slave trade by proslavery ideologues, and Wilson had been appropriated as a friend to colonization.[26]

Empire's advocates placed special emphasis on Africa's commercial potential. Some missionaries, but especially Bowen and Livingstone, emerged as authorities on that capacity. Both argued that conversion could not succeed without the introduction of western goods, which would help break down indigenous cultures. Both also emphasized the cotton-growing potential of central and southern Africa. In 1858 Bowen delivered a series of lectures in which he portrayed Africa's promise in characteristically "glowing colors." Besides cotton, Bowen told of central Africa's mineral wealth, including "great quantities" of gold, as well as palm oil, silk, ivory, and skins. Whichever nation sent "out the necessary force, with steamers . . . will be repaid in a marvelous manner," he reported. A writer in the *Richmond Daily Dispatch* wrote that the United States needed to match Britain's imperial energies. The missionaries' discoveries "ought to arrest the attention and stimulate the enterprise of the commercial men of this country." Americans "should be prompt to avail themselves of the observations and discoveries of scientific travelers, in a part of the world which may possibly contain the materials of a commerce as rich as that which India yields to British hands."[27]

For all the enthusiasm generated by Bowen and others, their efforts came to naught. Congress proved singularly uninterested in foreign adventures, whether in Lajos Kossuth's Hungary or Bowen's Africa. British ministries refused to be swayed by the arguments of abolitionists like Thomas Fowell Buxton that slave trade suppression required territorial expansion.[28] The United States was not likely to venture where the British refused to go. The Civil War quashed colonizationist and emigrationist sentiment for decades, as the victorious Union committed itself to abolishing slavery and granting citizenship to the freedpeople. The Reconstruction-era debate over annexation of Santo Domingo also suggests why Americans would be reluctant to launch into Africa. Samuel Gridley Howe, President Ulysses S. Grant, and Frederick Douglass hoped that Santo Domingo's statehood would expose the hollowness of racial essentialism. But other progressives, notably Charles Sumner, were certain that a tropical region like Santo Domingo could never be part of a white nation like the United States. Under those circumstances, it was unlikely that Americans would marshal the courage to wade into the more contentious waters of African colonization.[29] Also, the missionary-explorers who seemed like such heroic figures in the 1850s diminished in stature. The disastrous Zambesi expedition tarnished Livingstone's image. Leighton Wilson withdrew from public celebrity, taking a position with the Presbyterian Board of Foreign Missions in New York and then with the Presbyterian Church of the Confederacy. Bowen likewise never returned to Africa. His health wrecked like that of so many other African missionaries, he preached in the South before embarking for Brazil. His weakened constitution, compounded by the return of the mental illness that had plagued him in Africa, compelled his return to the United States in 1861. Soon after, he made the first of several stays at the Georgia Lunatic Asylum. He died in obscurity in 1875.[30]

In the end, colonization's friends failed to convince Americans to embark on an imperial venture in central Africa, but that they had tried—and received a generally positive hearing—testifies to the changing fortunes of both colonization and empire from the 1830s through the 1850s. An association between colonization and imperialism had badly damaged the prospects of the former in the 1830s and 1840s; a decade later, colonizationists touted that connection. In fact, even colonization's inveterate critics like Wilson and George Thompson, head of the American Missionary Association's Mendi mission, came around to embrace it. For Wilson, the events of the early 1850s reinforced his conviction that people of color could never live freely in the United States. His fears about Liberia were also assuaged by B.V.R. James, with whom Jane and Leighton had become warm friends while in Africa. James had shared Wilson's apprehensions about the settlers' treatment of native Africans when they lived at Cape Palmas together. Before their departure for the United States in 1852 he hosted the Wilsons at his home in Monrovia, where he had become a Liberian patriot. Under James's influence and in view of the bleak prospects for African Americans in the United States, Wilson had come to see colonization as the lesser of two evils. He had become a reluctant imperialist. Many of his compatriots were not reluctant at all; many more later in the century would embrace the imperial way of seeing the world as the newly reunited United States put the traumas of the Civil War and Reconstruction behind it.[31]

Notes

1. Erskine Clarke, *By the Rivers of Water: A Nineteenth-Century Atlantic Odyssey* (New York: Basic Books, 2013).

2. David Carson Davis, "Thomas Jefferson Bowen and His Plans for the Redemption of Africa" (Master's thesis, Baylor University, 1978).

3. Carroll Smith-Rosenberg, *This Violent Empire: The Birth of an American National Identity* (Chapel Hill: Univ. of North Carolina Press, 2010); Julian Go, *Patterns of Empire: The British and American Empires, 1688 to the Present* (New York: Cambridge Univ. Press, 2011); Peter Onuf, *Jefferson's Empire: The Language of American Nationhood* (Charlottesville: Univ. of Virginia Press, 2001); Andy

Doolen, *Fugitive Empire: Locating Early American Imperialism* (Minneapolis: Univ. of Minnesota Press, 2005); Amy S. Greenberg, *Manifest Manhood and the Antebellum American Empire* (New York: Cambridge Univ. Press, 2005).

4. "Dr. Beecher's Address," *African Repository and Colonial Journal* [hereafter *ARCJ*] 10 (November 1834): 280.

5. Reverend John Leighton Wilson, "The Moral Condition of Western Africa," *Southern Presbyterian Review* 4 (March 1848): 96; "Recent Researches in Africa," *North American Review* 86 (April 1858): 556.

6. "Dr. Becher's Address," 281; "A Review of the Past, Throws Light upon the Future," *ARCJ* 22 (January 1846): 5–7. On trade's relationship to conversion, see Brian Stanley, "'Commerce and Christianity': Providence Theory, the Missionary Movement, and the Imperialism of Free Trade, 1842–1860," *Historical Journal* 26 (March 1983): 71–94; Andrew Porter, "'Commerce and Christianity': The Rise and Fall of a Nineteenth-Century Missionary Slogan," *Historical Journal* 28 (September 1985): 597–621.

7. Clarke, *By the Rivers of Water*, 66–67, 92–93.

8. "Report on the State of the Colony of Lib[eria], March 24, 1834," 21, 15, 19, reel 149, microfilm edition of the American Board of Commissioners for Foreign Missions Archives, 1810–1961 [ABC 1–91], 15.1, Houghton Library, Harvard University [hereafter ABCFM]. See Emily Conroy-Krutz, *Christian Imperialism: Converting the World in the Early American Republic* (Ithaca: Cornell Univ. Press, 2015), 25–30, on the assumed dependence on missions to imperial authorities.

9. Wilson to Rufus Anderson, March 13, 1838 (ABCFM); *Report of the Parliamentary Select Committee on Aboriginal Tribes* [British Settlements] (London: William Ball, Aldine Chambers, Paternoster Row, and Hatchard and Son, 1837), 3. On Philip, see Alan Lester, "Humanitarians and White Settlers in the Nineteenth Century," in *Missions and Empire: Oxford History of the British Empire*, ed. Norman Eterington, Companion Series (Oxford: Oxford Univ. Press, 2005), 64–71; Nigel Penn, "The British and the 'Bushmen': The Massacre of the Cape San, 1795 to 1828," *Journal of Genocide Research* 15 (June 2013): 183–200; Robert Moss, "Missions, Respectability, and Civil Rights: The Cape Colony, 1828–1854," *Journal of Southern African Studies* 23 (September 1999): 333–45; Andrew Bank, "The Politics of Mythology: The Genealogy of the Philip Myth," *Journal of Southern African Studies* 25 (September 1999): 461–77.

10. J. Leighton Wilson to N. J. Bayard, April 26, 1838, enclosed with Bayard to Ira Easter, July 10, 1838, reel 3, Maryland State Historical Society Papers [hereafter MSCS], Maryland Historical Society, Baltimore, Maryland [microfilm edition]). On efforts to access the letters, see R. R. Gurley to James Hall, August 13, 1842, reel 4, MSCS.

11. Samuel Cornelius to John H. Latrobe, November 20, 1843; R. R. Gurley to James Hall, December 9, 1843, August 13, 1842, reel 5, MSCS.

12. Joseph Tracy, *Colonization and Missions. A Historical Examination of the State of Society in Western Africa, as formed by Paganism and Muhammedanism,*

Slavery, the Slave Trade and Piracy, and of the Remedial Influence of Colonization and Missions, 4th ed. (Boston: Press of T. R., Marvin, 1845), 22.

13. "Connection of the Mission at Cape Palmas with the Maryland Colony," *Missionary Herald* 38 (November 1842): 426–27; "The American Board and the African Colonies," *Liberator,* October 14, 1842.

14. Joseph Campbell, *Middle Passages: African American Journeys to Africa, 1787–2005* (New York: Penguin Press, 2006), 68–76; David Brion Davis, *The Problem of Slavery in the Age of Emancipation* (New York: Knopf, 2014), 121–25.

15. "African Civilization," *ARCJ* 34 (September 1858): 268–69; David Livingstone, *Missionary Travels and Researches in South Africa; Including a Sketch of Sixteen Years' Residence in the Interior of Africa . . .* (New York: Harper and Brothers, 1858); Thomas Jefferson Bowen, *Central Africa: Adventures and Missionary Labors in Several Countries in the Interior of Africa, from 1849 to 1856* (Charleston, S.C.: Southern Baptist Publication Society, 1857); J. Leighton Wilson, *Western Africa: Its History, Condition, and Prospects* (New York: Harper and Brothers, 1856).

16. Bowen, *Central Africa,* 323 ("energetic"); 338 (industry); Francis Wayland, "The Apostolic Ministry: A Sermon," in *The Principles and Practices of Baptist Churches,* ed. John Howard Hinton (London: J. Heaton and Son, 1861), 281; Bowen to James Taylor, October 1, 1855, Thomas Jefferson Bowen Papers, Southern Baptist Historical Library and Archives, Nashville, Tennessee (microfilm edition). On Bowen, see Jim Hardwicke, "An Examination of the Life and Work of Forgotten Missionary Pioneer T.J. Bowen" (Ph.D. diss., Southeastern Baptist Theological Seminary, 2010). On the practical difficulties of separating conversion and civilization, see Conroy-Krutz, *Christian Imperialism,* 24–30 and 218n9.

17. Howard Temperley, *White Dreams, Black Africa: The Antislavery Expedition to the River Niger, 1841–1842* (New Haven: Yale Univ. Press, 1991), 105, 81–82. On African exploration and cultural relativism, see Dane Kennedy, *The Highly Civilized Man: Richard Burton and the Victorian World* (Cambridge, Mass.: Harvard Univ. Press, 2005), esp. 159–63, 202–5.

18. Bowen, *Central Africa,* 57, 343 ("auxiliary"); "Letter from Rev. T.J. Bowen on the Commerce, Civilization, and Colonization of Yoruba," *ARCJ* 33 (September 1857): 280; "Annual Meeting of the American Colonization Society," *ARCJ* 33 (April 1857): 43, 40. Bowen's choice reinforces Emily Conroy-Krutz's argument about the "hierarchies of heathenism." See Conroy-Krutz, *Christian Imperialism,* 19–50, and Lysle E. Meyer, "T.J. Bowen and Central Africa: A Nineteenth-Century Missionary Delusion," *International Journal of African Historical Studies* 15, no. 2 (1982): 252–54.

19. Bronwen Everill notes that Liberian settlers tried to strike a middle-class pose to the outside world. See Bronwen Everill, "Destiny seems to point me to that country: Early nineteenth-century African American migration, emigration, and expansion," *Journal of Global History* 7 (2012): 68.

20. *The Congressional Globe: Containing the Debates, Proceedings, Laws, Etc., of the Third Session, Thirty-Fourth Congress* (Washington, D.C.: John C. Rives, 1857),

714, 990; "Africa Opening to Civilization and Christianity: Central Africa, by Rev. T.J. Bowen," *ARCJ* 33 (April 1857): 99; *Miscellaneous Documents of the Senate of the United States, for the Third Session of the Thirty-Fourth Congress, 1856–'57; also of the Special Session, 1857* (Washington, D.C.: A.O.P. Nicholson, 1857), 1–5.

21. *Report of the Naval Committee to the House of Representatives, August 1850, in Favor of the Establishment of a Line of Mail Steamships to the Western Coast of Africa . . .* (Washington, D.C.: Gideon and Co., 1850), 14, 18–19.

22. "Letter from Rev. T.J. Bowen," 280; "Annual Meeting of the American Colonization Society," 42; "Africa Opening to Civilization and Christianity," 109.

23. Coates to R. R. Gurley, May 28, 1858, in Emma J. Lapansky-Werner and Margaret Hope Bacon et al., *Back to Africa: Benjamin Coates and the Colonization Movement in America, 1848–1880* (University Park: Pennsylvania State Univ. Press, 2005), 109.

24. Benjamin Coates, *Cotton Cultivation in Africa: Suggestions on the Importance of the Cultivation of Cotton in Africa . . .* (Philadelphia: C. Sherman and Son, 1858), 3, 49; Martin Delany, *Report of the Niger Valley Exploring Party* (New York: Thomas Hamilton, 1861), 10, 13; *Alexandria (Va.) Daily Gazette,* January 26, 1858. On Delany, see Campbell, *Middle Passages,* 77–90, and R.J.M. Blackett, *Building an Antislavery Wall: Black Americans in the Atlantic Abolitionist Movement, 1830–1860* (Baton Rouge: Louisiana State Univ. Press, 1983), 175. The swashbuckling English explorer Richard F. Burton disliked missionaries for their wish to transform African societies, but he had a special aversion to Bowen. See Burton, *Abeokuta and the Camaroons Mountains, An Exploration,* 2 vols. (London: Tinsley Brothers, 1863), 1:90–95; Kennedy, *The Highly Civilized Man,* 156–57.

25. Livingstone, *Missionary Travels,* 724; Bowen, *Central Africa,* 65.

26. "African Civilization Society," *Middlebury (Vt.) Register,* September 11, 1850 ("remarkable"); "The Future of Africa," *ARCJ* 34 (January 1858): 187; "Union Meetings," *ARCJ* 33 (July 1857): 220 ("friends"); "The Future of Africa," *ARCJ* 34 (June 1858): 187 ("stalwart"). For the misuse of Livingstone to support reopening the slave trade, see L. W. Spratt, "Report on the Slave Trade, the Southern Convention," *De Bow's Review* 26 (May 1859): 480.

27. "Commercial Aspect of Central Africa," *Hunt's Merchants' Magazine and Commercial Review* 39 (December 1858): 771–72; *Richmond (Va.) Daily Dispatch,* November 24, 1857.

28. Seymour Drescher, "Emperors of the World: British Abolitionism and Imperialism," in *Abolitionism and Imperialism in Britain, Africa, and the Atlantic,* ed. Derek R. Peterson (Athens: Ohio Univ. Press, 2010), 129–49.

29. Nicholas Guyatt, "America's Conservatory: Race, Reconstruction, and the Santo Domingo Debate," *Journal of American History* 97 (March 2011): 974–1000.

30. Many African missionaries and explorers struggled with mental disability. See Tim Jeal, *Livingstone,* rev. ed. (New Haven: Yale Univ. Press, 2013), 226–27, 263–64; Clarke, *By the Rivers of Water,* 338–73; Hardwicke, "An Examination of the Life and Work of Forgotten Missionary Pioneer T. J. Bowen," 131–94; Dane

Kennedy, "The Perils of the Midday Sun: Climatic Anxieties in the Colonial Tropics," in *Imperialism and the Natural World,* ed. John M. MacKenzie (Manchester, UK: Manchester Univ. Press, 1990), 118–40; Warwick Anderson, "The Trespass Speaks: White Masculinity and Colonial Breakdown," *American Historical Review* 102 (December 1997): 1343–59; and especially Johannes Fabian, *Out of Our Minds: Reason and Madness in the Exploration of Central Africa* (Berkeley: Univ. of California Press, 2000).

31. On James, see Clarke, *By the Rivers of Water,* 195, 306–7; on George Thompson, see his *The Palm Land; or, West Africa, Illustrated . . . ,* 3rd ed. (Cincinnati: Moore, Wilstach, Keys, and Co., 1859), 402–6.

2

The Abolition Lobby

Its Development, Successes, and Disintegration, 1836–1845

Stanley Harrold

Joshua Leavitt was a Congregational minister and abolitionist who edited the *Emancipator* newspaper (first in New York and later in Boston). During the early to mid-1840s, he traveled frequently to Washington, D.C., where he reported on Congress and helped organize what became known as the *abolition lobby.* It consisted of abolitionists who sought to push a small group of congressmen toward aggressive antislavery action in the House of Representatives. These congressmen belonged to the northern wing of the Whig Party and tended to oppose the existence of slavery in the District of Columbia, slavery expansion into western territories, and the proposal to annex the huge slaveholding Republic of Texas to the United States. But they were also tied to their southern Whig colleagues.

During these years, most northerners hoped Congress would settle North-South disagreements through negotiation. Even such antislavery congressmen as John Quincy Adams, Joshua R. Giddings, and William Slade believed the existing party system could handle it. Many church-oriented abolitionists, who often aligned politically with the Whig Party, agreed. So did William Lloyd Garrison of Massachusetts and his immediate abolitionist associates, despite their demand by 1842 for disunion as the best means of ending northern support for slavery. In contrast, Leavitt and some other church-oriented abolitionists had come to believe they had to change the party system by forming the Liberty Party.

A half-dozen historians, most notably James M. McPherson and most recently Corey M. Brooks, have investigated the abolition lobby, with Brooks explicitly linking it to the Liberty Party.[1] This essay differs in approach from McPherson, Brooks, and the others. They place the beginning of the lobby in 1839. This essay traces its earlier development. It delves more deeply than they do into the ties between abolitionist lobbyists and the antislavery Whig congressmen. It describes a more complicated relationship between the lobby and the Liberty Party. It questions the role of the lobby in the repeal of the Gag Rule against antislavery petitions, investigates proslavery congressmen's counter tactics, and describes the termination of the lobby. The result is a more complicated view of the lobby.

A petitioning campaign, which began during the late 1820s and called for ending slavery in the District of Columbia, led to the election of congressmen, such as Adams, with whom abolitionists might cooperate. Such cooperation became more feasible with the completion in 1835 of a Baltimore & Ohio Railroad branch that connected the Northeast to Washington. The likelihood that such cooperation would elicit inflammatory statements by southern politicians that could be used to spread antislavery sentiment encouraged abolitionist leaders to make the journey.[2]

Historian Gilbert H. Barnes describes the abolition lobby as "one of the strangest . . . in history," because congressmen joined it. In fact, the relationship between antislavery congressmen and abolitionists did not amount to a united lobbying effort. Rather there existed a congressional antislavery *caucus,* which Giddings called a "select committee on slavery," and a *separate* abolition lobby. The caucus began in November 1833 when Whig congressmen John Dickson and William Slade visited Adams to discuss partisan political issues as well as abolitionist petitions.[3] Later abolitionists initiated the lobby as they approached caucus members, delivered antislavery petitions, provided information, and helped organize legislative opposition to slavery.

Gradual abolitionist Benjamin Lundy took the first steps in forming the lobby. In December 1836 he traveled from Philadelphia to Washington to meet with Adams regarding Texas's annexation. During the following year the American Anti-Slavery Society (AASS) sought to employ evangelical abolitionist Theodore Weld to facilitate presentation of antislavery petitions in Congress. Weld could not accept the mission. But, during September 1837, Whiggish abolition journalist Richard Hildreth of Boston traveled to Washington to report on a special session of Congress and stayed "for a large part of the regular [1837–1838] session." Several other northeastern abolitionists joined Hildreth. Among them were Henry B. Stanton of New

York and Garrison's associate J. Miller McKim of Pennsylvania. Stanton came to Washington "to look after the imperiled right of petition" and met with Adams. McKim spoke "in the lobbies of the Capitol . . . and in a few instances with proslavery members of Congress."[4]

During Congress's 1838–1839 session, abolitionists did not visit Washington. By then the AASS had begun to split into factions. Most members of the Garrisonian faction concentrated on influencing northern popular opinion. Others focused on organizing the Liberty Party as an independent abolitionist political force. As a result, support for petitioning Congress and lobbying members of it temporarily declined.[5]

But that December a way for more effective abolitionist cooperation with antislavery Whigs in the House of Representatives opened as the 1839–1840 congressional session began. Giddings, Slade, and their new associate Seth M. Gates, who represented western New York, rented rooms at Ann Sprigg's boarding house, located within two blocks of the Capitol. Gates, Giddings, and Slade formed the nucleus of an expanded antislavery caucus on which an abolitionist lobby might focus.[6]

The emergence of the Liberty Party had some negative effects on abolitionist relations with antislavery Whig congressmen. Liberty partisans criticized members of the antislavery caucus for supporting proslavery Whig candidates for office. They disliked the emphasis caucus members placed on Whig economic programs. When in December 1839 Gates, Giddings, and Slade (but not Adams) joined a North-South alliance that elected slaveholding Virginia Whig Robert M. T. Hunter as Speaker of the House, Leavitt chastised them. He used Gates, Giddings, and Slade's Whig Party loyalty to encourage abolitionists to "rally under our own banner" to "put men in Congress who do not care a straw for other questions in comparison with that of slavery."[7]

Nevertheless, Leavitt and other abolitionists believed they could influence the antislavery congressmen. Slade encouraged this belief when, during a speech he delivered in the House on January 18 and 20, 1840, he endorsed general emancipation. He declared that abolitionists represented "the best feelings of the human heart."[8] Yet, like Adams and other antislavery politicians, Slade maintained his allegiance to the Whig Party, which included slaveholders among its leaders and favored compromise on sectional issues. Later in 1840 Slade supported Whig presidential candidate William Henry Harrison, despite Harrison's ambiguous views concerning slavery.[9]

A week after Slade's January 1840 speech, Waddy Thompson Jr., a South Carolina Whig, and William Cost Johnson, a Maryland Whig, led the House to pass the Johnson Gag, designed to ban permanently the introduction of antislavery petitions in the House of Representatives. That same day John G. Whittier and two other Quaker abolitionists arrived in Washington from Philadelphia. The three men came mainly to visit slave-trading establishments and talk with slaves and traders. But they also lobbied, and Whittier suggested to Adams that the Johnson Gag "might perhaps be the best thing that could have been done to promote the cause of abolition." The Gag also encouraged organization of an expanded abolition lobby that would work with the antislavery caucus.[10]

Two other developments had roles in the abolitionist lobby's formation. They included Democratic control of the 1840–1841 winter session of Congress and the poor showing of Liberty nominee James G. Birney in the 1840 presidential election. These events, along with the Johnson Gag, led to more intense abolitionist concentration on Congress. In mid-January 1841 the *Emancipator* sent Leavitt to Washington, where he moved into Sprigg's boarding house and engaged the antislavery Whig congressmen who lived there.[11]

Leavitt spent his days in the House, listening to Adams and Giddings speak and taking notes for *Emancipator* articles. Adams talked about the right of petition and Giddings addressed the US government's war to remove Seminoles from Florida Territory and its efforts there to recapture escaped slaves. In early March, Leavitt (a former lawyer) spent a day helping Adams prepare a brief for the Supreme Court on behalf of Africans who had in 1839 violently freed themselves on board the Spanish slaver *Amistad.* This vessel had been captured by an American ship off the coast of Long Island, and the Africans imprisoned in Connecticut.[12]

Leavitt hoped that by working with antislavery congressmen on such volatile questions he would draw them into the Liberty Party. Instead the relationship between the pious and dogmatic Leavitt and the righteous and sensitive Whig politicians grew more contentious. Leavitt upbraided the congressmen when they, in his opinion, placed loyalty to the Whig Party above antislavery principle. When, during April and early May 1841, Leavitt temporarily left Washington for New York City, Slade charged him with publishing "constant" criticism of those who did not support the Liberty Party.[13]

Leavitt further exasperated the congressmen during a special session of Congress (called to produce a bankruptcy bill) that began during late

May. At that time Adams, Gates, Giddings, Slade, and a few other northern Whigs refused to vote for John D. White, a slaveholding Kentucky Whig who became Speaker of the House. Gates observed, "Mr. Slade, Giddin[g]s and myself, did all we could in caucus to get a Speaker from a free state nominated. . . . Went and saw father Adams and got him to go with us." Yet Leavitt, who was still in New York City, accused Gates, Giddings, and Slade, who voted with other Whigs to ban petitions during the special session so as to concentrate on their party's bankruptcy bill, of having bowed "to the dark spirit of slavery."[14]

Leavitt returned to Washington in mid-June to resume what he called his "seat" in the House. Shortly after he arrived, he met with the three Whigs and momentarily relented in his criticism of them. In a letter published in the *Emancipator* on July 1, he wrote that the three "firmly resisted the gag at great risk to their party objects." Yet, even as Leavitt asserted that he hoped to cooperate with the congressmen in the future, he soon returned to denouncing their support for the Whig short-term petition ban. He claimed that the antislavery congressmen used their disagreement with him "as a reason why they should abandon their principles."[15]

The antislavery congressmen responded predictably. Slade asked Leavitt, "Must I be driven to the conclusion that you are predisposed to censure me and my abolition friends in Congress?" Giddings wondered if Leavitt sought "to diminish the influence of the few individuals who are now placed between you and the common enemy." He charged that Leavitt, as a result of Liberty Party zeal, "often . . . assailed" members of the antislavery caucus. Giddings and the other antislavery congressmen continued to resist the third party in part because they believed its 1840 campaign had taken away enough votes to defeat some antislavery Whig candidates and thereby hurt (in Gates's words) "the cause of the slave."[16] Rather than ally with the Liberty Party, Giddings, Gates, and their associates had an alternate strategy to achieve their goals: They planned to use their relationship with Adams and slave unrest in and about Washington to influence the nation.

Meanwhile, abolitionists acted to keep the lobby going and strengthen the petition campaign. First, in September, the recently formed American and Foreign Anti-Slavery Society (AFASS), led by Lewis Tappan of New York, encouraged prominent abolitionists to go to Washington "for two or three weeks at the beginning of the [December 1841–March 1842] session." Second, in October, the Massachusetts State Liberty Party Convention pledged $200 to return Leavitt to the capital. Later that month Leavitt, who was about to move the *Emancipator* from New York City to Boston, charged in a letter to Giddings that the congressman, rather than advocate immediate emancipation, preferred to "aim first at specific points of politics, which [he] deem[ed] beneficial to free labor—or rather to the North—as in bank, tariff &c." Leavitt contended that this amounted to "continued toleration of slavery." He advised Giddings that only opposition to slavery itself could unite the North. Nevertheless, Leavitt helped shape Giddings's and other antislavery congressmen's antislavery actions.[17]

Early that December Leavitt once again became Gates, Giddings, and Slade's messmate at Sprigg's. By then three additional antislavery Whig congressmen had joined the antislavery caucus. Two of them were abolitionists. Sherlock J. Andrews of Ohio had in 1833 helped lead the Cleveland Anti-Slavery Society. Nathaniel Briggs Borden of Fall River, Massachusetts, had in 1834 formed a local antislavery society and from then through the 1850s assisted escaping slaves. The third, John Mattocks of Vermont, described himself as abolitionist, but his connection to the movement is less clear than Andrews's and Briggs's.[18]

As soon as Leavitt arrived in Washington he joined with the AFASS in urging other abolitionists, who could "afford" it, to come to the capital for "a few days or weeks." Charles T. Torrey and Weld responded. Torrey, a Massachusetts native living in Albany, New York, had, like Leavitt, served as a Congregational minister, journalist, and founder of the Liberty Party. In Congress Torrey worked with Slade, Borden, and Giddings. Torrey asserted, "The subject of abolition cannot be kept out of Congress. We shall get it in, in a multitude of forms, before the session closes."[19]

In contrast to Leavitt, Torrey, and others who came to Washington on behalf of abolitionist publications and organizations, Weld came solely in response to Leavitt and the antislavery congressmen's invitations. In Weld's words, they wanted him to help them "carry the war in upon the enemy . . . and attack slavery at every point." They proposed "a series of speeches" dealing with slavery in the District of Columbia and Florida, the domestic slave trade, black rights, Texas, Haiti, and attempts to send free African Americans to Africa. The congressmen paid for Weld's travel to Washington and his expenses during his stay. His duties, they suggested, would keep him in the Library of Congress "gathering and arranging materials" for antislavery speeches. Weld had two objectives for such speeches. First, he believed they could contribute to changing northern popular opinion. Second, (in contrast to Leavitt and Torrey) Weld hoped the speeches would help reorient immediatists "intoxicated" with the Liberty Party toward effective political action through the Whig Party.[20]

Weld arrived at Sprigg's on December 30, 1841. The next day he became more than a researcher as he, Giddings, and Leavitt attended Adams's New Year "saloon," where the former president revealed his admiration for Weld's abolitionist writings. According to Weld, Adams initiated a conversation about the recent slave revolt on the American brig *Creole,* in which the slaves took control of the ship as it went south from Virginia and sailed it to freedom in the British Bahamas. On January 8, Weld again met with Adams, this time at what Weld called "a genuine abolition gathering."[21]

Because of Weld's, Torrey's, and Leavitt's interactions with the antislavery caucus, the abolition lobby's influence peaked during the early months of 1842. In January, Weld helped members of the caucus prepare to present petitions and to address Congress. That same month Torrey, at caucus members' urging, traveled to Annapolis, where a slaveholders' convention seeking a means to end slave escapes had convened. Torrey's note-taking at the convention led municipal authorities to imprison him on several charges, including exciting "discontent among the colored people." Giddings and the Massachusetts congressional delegation then sent a team of lawyers to represent Torrey. A local judge dismissed the charges, and Torrey returned to Washington on January 17.[22]

In the House of Representatives on Thursday, January 20, with Weld's and Leavitt's assistance and with Torrey looking on, the antislavery Whig representatives along with several allies began a verbal onslaught. Gates presented a petition opposed to the admission of slaveholding Florida to the Union. Slade introduced antislavery resolutions from Vermont's legislature. And Massachusetts congressman William B. Calhoun submitted a petition from the town of Springfield calling for American recognition of the black Republic of Haiti. Adams took the floor on Friday, January 21. Before he spoke he told Weld he would "present some petitions that would set them [slaveholders] in a blaze."[23]

First Adams introduced a petition in favor of granting citizenship to "colored" immigrants. Upon Virginia congressmen Henry A. Wise's objection, the House tabled the petition by a 115–68 vote. When Adams regained the floor he criticized slave trading and slave-breeding. Then he presented a petition from Haverhill, Massachusetts, calling for the dissolution of the Union. As Adams, other antislavery congressmen, and abolition lobbyists anticipated, slaveholders in the House overreacted, with Virginia representative Thomas W. Gilmer moving to censure Adams. During the next two weeks, slaveholders attempted to intimidate Adams by browbeating him and physically surrounding him. Adams, assisted by Leavitt, coached by Weld, and supported by the other antislavery congressmen, used this outrageous conduct to draw other northern Whig congressmen and northern popular opinion to his side. In his "defense" against censure, Adams presented over two hundred more petitions. And, as Weld expected, on Monday, February 7, the House tabled the censure motion by a 106 to 93 vote.[24]

Some antislavery Whigs and abolitionists portrayed Adams's victory as one for the abolition lobby and a turning point in sectional politics. Giddings wrote, "I entertain not the least doubt that a moral revolution in this nation will take its date from this session of Congress." Weld declared, "Triumph is complete. . . . This is the first victory over the slaveholders *in a body* ever yet achieved since the foundation of the *government,* and from this time their downfall *takes its date.*" Historians agree. Weld biographer Benjamin P. Thomas asserts, "Slavery could not stand against free speech." McPherson claims Adams inflicted a "crippling blow" to the "conspiracy of silence" in Congress regarding slavery. Russell B. Nye concludes that "from such blows [as Adams struck] the 'gag rules' never recovered."[25]

Yet, a few days after the attempt to censure Adams failed, Weld realized the abolitionist effort in the House had achieved less than he had thought. Referring to slavery's defenders, Weld commented, "Satan never retreats without a death struggle. . . . Slavery has begun to fall," but "woe to abolitionists if they dream that their work is well nigh done." And an Adams victory did not necessarily mean an abolitionist victory. Weld had influenced Adams, as had other abolition lobbyists and abolitionists generally. Still, Adams advocated only "ultimate emancipation." And, following his "triumph" over the Gag, Adams had no success in derailing slavery's westward expansion or slaveholders' political power.[26]

Earlier in 1842 Weld had investigated international legal aspects of the *Creole* case in order to help Giddings prepare *Creole* resolutions. The resolutions declared that slavery could not be legal under national jurisdiction or on the high seas. Because this suggested that slaves had a right to revolt on oceangoing vessels, Weld predicted that the resolutions would "produce a tremendous sensation among the slaveholders." This proved to be the case. When Giddings introduced his resolutions on March 22, John Minor Botts, a moderate Virginia Whig, asserted that Giddings had "justified" "mutiny and murder." Botts called on the House to condemn Giddings's "conduct," and the body complied by a vote of 125 to 69. In response, Giddings resigned his seat, returned home, easily gained reelection in late April, and came back to Congress in May.[27]

As they had in regard to Adams's victory over those who sought to censure him, abolitionists portrayed Giddings's forced resignation and reelection as a triumph of antislavery politics and the abolition lobby. Whiggish Garrisonian journalist David Lee Child reported to Gates from Massachusetts that "hundreds who never sympathized with the abolitionists come out now and declare themselves abolitionists to the death." Gates in turn predicted, "This will be another instance . . . where the wrath of men will be made to praise God."[28]

Historians go further. According to Barnes, Giddings's reelection "changed the whole aspect of the antislavery agitation in the House" and opened slavery "to direct attack" so that petitions were "no longer essential." McPherson asserts that the reelection presaged the 1852 breakup of the Whig Party, the end of the Second American Party System, and the election in 1860 of Abraham Lincoln to the presidency. Yet abolitionists in Washington judged Giddings's impact as circumspectly as Weld had Adams's. Torrey perceived in the Gidddings censure an escalation of a proslavery threat in Congress from one limited to the right of petition to one against freedom of speech.[29]

More important for the future of the abolition lobby, southern congressmen soon realized they had gone too far against Giddings and therefore had to change their tactics. During the rest of 1842, through 1843, and into 1844, slavery's defenders in Congress became less confrontational, more restrained in their pronouncements, less committed to the Gag. This change in strategy reduced drama that the abolitionist press could publicize. It contributed to disillusionment among abolition lobbyists. And it had a role in attrition among antislavery congressmen. All of these things, plus the resounding Democratic victory in the 1842 national elections, contributed to the decline of the abolition lobby.

Initially, however, the lobby's influence appeared to increase. In April 1842, as Leavitt returned to his reporter's desk in the House after a brief absence, Botts acknowledged the abolitionist journalist's influence by threatening to expel him. This threat improved antislavery congressmen's regard for Leavitt, and Giddings asked him to enhance the lobby.[30] Such enhancement seemed to be taking place the following December as the 1842–1843 congressional session began. David Lee Child, who reported on

Congress for the *Liberator* and the *National Anti-Slavery Standard,* stayed in Washington throughout the session. During January, Lewis Tappan lobbied in the Senate. Lucretia Mott of Philadelphia and Jacob Knapp of Baltimore worked in Washington outside Congress to encourage antislavery sentiment. As a result of Mott's and Knapp's activities, Weld declared, "Abolition is talked not only at our table but all over Washington." Leavitt added, "Things are evidently improving here in the Anti-Slavery line, since I first came here alone and uncertain of my reception, less than two years ago." To take advantage of the circumstances, Weld, Leavitt, and the antislavery congressmen they worked with planned to raise the issue of slavery in Florida Territory, present more petitions, advocate legislation to protect black sailors in southern ports, and call for black citizenship.[31]

Weld understood that slaveholders in Congress believed they had erred in their verbal and procedural assaults on Adams and Giddings during the previous session. On this basis Weld and Adams assumed proslavery congressmen would *not* "rally" during the 1842–1843 session. But the two men misinterpreted what changed proslavery tactics meant for antislavery.[32] If, as Whittier had observed in February 1840, a more strident proslavery stand aided abolitionists, less aggressive proslavery tactics worked against abolitionists. And the session failed to reproduce the sectional drama of a year earlier.

During mid-January 1843, Giddings and Adams (supported by Weld's research) addressed the Florida slavery issue. Representatives from the Lower South replied briefly and moderately. During February, Giddings spoke against a bill to compensate American slave traders for slaves freed by Britain following a shipwreck. Slavery's defenders again responded mildly. As a result Weld complained that questions he had prepared for did not come up, that there had been little "of interest" in Congress concerning opposition to slavery. Therefore he decided to leave Washington in mid-February (two or three weeks before the session ended). Leavitt too despaired, as he had come to believe the congressmen could not be extracted from the Whig Party. He described Weld's lobbying as mere "foundation work."[33]

Lack of antislavery progress and abolitionist frustration continued. During late February, Adams presented a gigantic petition on behalf of George Latimer, who, with his wife, had escaped from slavery in Virginia in October 1842 and had recently been arrested in Massachusetts. In response to Adams's petition, the proslavery House leadership avoided confrontation. Rather than invoke the Gag, Speaker White referred the petition to the

Judiciary Committee. Southern absences, rather than confrontation, prevented the committee from acting on the petition. Shortly thereafter Leavitt left Washington.[34]

Historian William Lee Miller best describes the confusing situation in the House of Representatives as the 28th Congress reconvened in December 1843. Whig president John Tyler's veto of much of the Whig financial program and a national economic rebound had helped Democrats retake control of Congress in the 1842 elections. Therefore, that December 142 Democrats confronted 82 Whigs in the House. Northern Whig representatives had always accounted for most votes against the Gag. Now their strength, and especially that of the antislavery caucus, had declined. Core members of the caucus, including Gates, Slade, Andrews, and Mattocks, had not returned. They had either not sought reelection in November 1842 or had lost in their reelection bids. As a result, among caucus members, only Adams and Giddings remained. Despite these circumstances, Adams's motion on December 4 to repeal the Gag lost by only four votes (95–91).[35]

The abolition lobby weakened along with the antislavery caucus. Leavitt, like Slade and Gates, had tired of Washington, and his plan to begin a daily edition of the *Emancipator* required that he be in Boston. Therefore Leavitt departed the city in late January, well before the session ended. For his part Torrey turned his focus away from Congress and toward helping slaves escape from the Chesapeake region. And Lewis Tappan's offer of financial support and Adams's increased momentum in his effort against the Gag failed to revive Weld's commitment to lobbying.[36]

Even so, Giddings perceived that slaveholders could not keep the Gag much longer. To take advantage of this, he wanted abolitionist support in an effort "to abolish slavery in this district before we adjourn." Invoking ideas Whittier, Tappan, and Leavitt had developed over the past eight years, Giddings in January 1844 begged Weld for "the time and labor of one dozen abolitionists." Giddings wrote, "We want help. We want men here to [go] among the people of the city, get up petitions, hold meetings, prepare the minds of the people here, both Blacks and Whites." Giddings also wanted "men who will visit members [of Congress] in their rooms and talk to them and lead them into the subject." So far, he lamented, "We have been unable to get any body to come here."[37]

Eleven months later, as the House convened in early December 1844, Adams's motion to end the Gag passed by a vote of 108 to 80. No abolition lobbyist helped prepare Adams for this apparent victory. No abolition journalist entered the House chamber that day. Leavitt did not arrive at the capital until two weeks after the Gag had been repealed.[38]

As Miller shows, factors other than the abolition lobby led to the repeal. The most active, and vocal, of the Gag's defenders (like most of its strongest opponents) had left Congress. Also, for various reasons, northern Democrats joined northern Whigs in voting against the Gag. Some of the Democrats had always believed the Gag threatened civil liberties. Others responded to constituent pressure. They all sought revenge against their southern colleagues who had at the 1844 Democratic national convention passed over former president Martin Van Buren of New York to give the party's presidential nomination to Tennessee slaveholder James K. Polk. Most important, as historian William W. Freehling puts it, "Slaveholders had at last learned . . . gag rules deployed too little tyranny to silence antislavery northerners and too much tyranny for antislavery Yankees to tolerate."[39]

Leavitt had come to regard the Gag controversy as a sideshow to the issue of slavery's continued existence in the South. "The right of petition is worth defending," he wrote in the *Emancipator,* "but so far as our three millions of enslaved countrymen is [*sic*] concerned, it has long ceased to be of any consequence." Northern Democrats, Leavitt reasoned, joined northern Whigs to end the Gag in order to deprive abolitionists of a means to raise the slavery issue in Congress. He contended that a majority of the Democrats had concluded that receiving a petition "and reporting against the prayer" was "the readiest way to kill abolitionism."[40] He asserted that only Liberty Party victories in congressional elections could help the enslaved.[41]

During early 1845, Leavitt sat in the House of Representatives gallery and concentrated on reporting debate as members turned to the issue of whether or not to annex the slaveholding Republic of Texas. Although the great majority of northern Democrats had turned against the Gag, most of them did not object to slavery expansion. By February 28, 1845, when Congress passed a joint resolution annexing Texas, Leavitt had already returned to Boston. He had hoped northern Democrats would join northern Whigs to vote against it. But he had not tried to persuade them—the abolition lobby had died. When a new Washington lobby against slavery organized in early 1847, under new leadership, it was *not* an abolition lobby. It had a broader political scope and a more nuanced commitment to ending slavery.[42]

Notes

1. James M. McPherson, "The Fight against the Gag Rule: Joshua Leavitt and the Antislavery Insurgency in the Whig Party 1839–1842," *Journal of Negro History* 48 (July 1963): 177–95; Corey M. Brooks, *Liberty Power: Antislavery Third Parties and the Transformation of American Politics* (Chicago: Univ. of Chicago Press, 2016), 47–72; Hugh Davis, *Joshua Leavitt: Evangelical Abolitionist* (Baton Rouge: Louisiana State Univ. Press, 1990), 164–97; William Lee Miller, *Arguing about Slavery: The Great Battle in the United States Congress* (New York: Knopf, 1988), passim; William W. Freehling, *The Road to Disunion,* 2 vols. (New York: Oxford Univ. Press, 1990–2007), 1:343–52.

2. See Brooks, *Liberty Power,* 47–48, 51.

3. Gilbert H. Barnes, *The Antislavery Impulse 1830–1834* (1933; reprint, Gloucester, Mass.: Peter Smith, 1973), 180; Miller, *Arguing about Slavery,* 404; Giddings to Laura Waters Giddings, February 18, 1842, in *The Letters of Theodore Weld, Angelina Grimké Weld, and Sarah Grimké,* ed. Gilbert H. Barnes and Dwight L. Dumond, 2 vols. (1934; reprint, New York: Da Capo, 1970), 2:883n (quotation); John Quincy Adams, *Memoirs of John Quincy Adams, Comprising Portions of His Diary from 1795 to 1848,* ed. Charles Francis Adams, 12 vols. (Philadelphia: Lippincott, 1874–1877), 9:39–40.

4. Barnes, *Antislavery Impulse,* 128, 177; Adams, *Memoirs,* 8:316; Brooks, *Liberty Power,* 51–52; Joshua Leavitt to Weld, [November 16, 1837], in Barnes and Dumond, *The Letters of Theodore Weld, Angelina Grimké Weld, and Sarah Grimké,* 1:478; McPherson, "Fight against the Gag Rule," 178–79; Donald E. Emerson, *Richard Hildreth* (Baltimore: Johns Hopkins Univ. Press, 1946), 57; Reinhard O. Johnson, *The Liberty Party, 1840–1848* (Baton Rouge: Louisiana State Univ. Press, 2009), 227, 348; Henry B. Stanton, *Random Recollections* (New York: Harper and Brothers, 1887), 60; CHA'S L***** to William Goodell, [n.d.], in *Friend of Man* (Utica, N.Y.), March 22, 1838; *Pennsylvania Freeman* (Philadelphia), March 11, 1838 (quotation).

5. Adams to Samuel May, January 7, 1838; Adams to Samuel Webb and William H. Scott, January 19, 1838; Adams to A. Bronson, July 30, 1838; Adams to Oliver Johnson, December 13, 1838; Adams to Samuel Webb, April 23, 1839; Adams to American Anti-Slavery Society Committee of Arrangements, July 11, 1839; Adams to Gerrit Smith, July 31, 1839, all in Adams Papers, Massachusetts Historical Society, Boston; Barnes, *Antislavery Impulse,* 148; Richard H. Sewell, *Ballots for Freedom: Antislavery Politics in the United States* (New York: Oxford Univ. Press, 1976), 37.

6. James Brewer Stewart, *Joshua R. Giddings and the Tactics of Radical Politics* (Cleveland: Press of Case Western Reserve Univ., 1970), 51; "Ann Sprigg," in "Bytes of History," http://bytesofhistory.com/Collections/UGRR/Sprigg_Ann/Sprigg_Ann-Biography.html; Weld to Angelina Grimké Weld, January 1, 1842, December 27, 1842, in Barnes and Dumond, *The Letters of Theodore Weld, Ange-*

lina Grimké Weld, and Sarah Grimké, 2:883, 947; Johnson, *Liberty Party,* 343; American Anti-Slavery Society, *Annual Report 1837–1838,* University of Buffalo Special Collections, http://library.buffalo.edu.

7. *Emancipator,* December 26, 1839 (3rd–4th quotations); Stewart, *Giddings,* 67–68; Michael F. Holt, *The Rise and Fall of the American Whig Party: Jacksonian Politics and the Onset of the Civil War* (New York: Oxford Univ. Press, 1999), 126; Davis, *Joshua Leavitt,* 155.

8. [William Slade], *Speech of Mr. Slade of Vermont on the Right of Petition; Power of Congress to Abolish Slavery and the Slave Trade in the District of Columbia, and the Principles, Purpose, and Prospects of Abolition* (Washington, D.C.: Gales and Seaton (printers), 1840), 21–22 (1st–6th quotations), 33–34 (7th–8th quotations). William Lee Miller calls Slade's speech the "most advanced antislavery speech made in the House so far." See Miller, *Arguing about Slavery,* 361–62.

9. Adams, *Memoirs* (January 20, 1840), 10:198; [Slade], *Speech of Mr. Slade of Vermont on the Right of Petition,* 40–41.

10. Whittier to *Essex Transcript,* October 30, 1843, in *The Letters of John Greenleaf Whittier,* ed. John B. Pickard, 3 vols. (Cambridge, Mass.: Harvard Univ. Press, 1975), 1:610–15; Adams, *Memoirs* (January 29, 1840), 10:206 (quotation); Albert Mordell, *Quaker Militant, John Greenleaf Whittier* (Port Washington, N.Y.: Kennikat Press, 1969), 108; Miller, *Arguing about Slavery,* 362–72; McPherson, "Fight against the Gag Rule," 180.

11. Samuel Flagg Bemis, *John Quincy Adams and the Union,* 2 vols. (New York: Knopf, 1956), 2:422; Barnes, *Antislavery Impulse,* 177–78; McPherson, "Fight against the Gag Rule," 180, 185; Davis, *Joshua Leavitt,* 176–80. In effect Leavitt sent himself.

12. McPherson, "Fight against the Gag Rule," 182–83; Miller, *Arguing about Slavery,* 381–82; Stewart, *Giddings,* 63–65 (quotation); Adams, *Memoirs,* 10:439–40.

13. Slade to [Leavitt], April 29, 1841, in *Emancipator,* May 6, 1841 (quotation); Gates to James G. Birney, June 7, 1841, in *Letters of James Gillespie Birney, 1831–1857,* ed. Dwight L. Dumond, 2 vols. (New York: Appleton-Century, 1938), 2:630–31.

14. Gates to Birney, June 7, 1841, in Dumond, ed., *Letters of James Gillespie Birney,* 2:630–31 (1st–2nd quotations); McPherson, "Fight against the Gag Rule," 184–86; *Emancipator,* June 24, 1841 (3rd quotation).

15. Leavitt to Piercy and Reed, June 26, 1841, in *Emancipator,* July 1, 1841 (1st–2nd quotations); *Emancipator,* July 15, 1841 (3rd quotation). Leavitt had again returned to New York City when he made these comments.

16. Slade to [Leavitt], July 10, 1841, in *Emancipator,* July 15, 1841 (1st quotation); Giddings to [Leavitt], July, 10, 1841], in *Emancipator,* July 15, 1841; Gates to James G. Birney, December 11,1841, in Dumond, ed., *Letters of James Gillespie Birney,* 2:642–43 (2nd quotation).

17. *Emancipator,* September 16, 1841 (1st quotation); Leavitt to Giddings, October 29, 1841, Giddings Papers, Ohio Historical Society (2nd–3rd quotations).

18. Davis, *Joshua Leavitt,* 187–88; Gates to James G. Birney, December 11, 1841, in Dumond, ed., *Letters of James Gillespie Birney,* 2:642–43; Weld to Lewis Tappan, December 14, 1841; Weld to Angelina G. Weld, January 1, 1842, both in Barnes and Dumond, *The Letters of Theodore Weld, Angelina Grimké Weld, and Sarah Grimké,* 2:879–81, 883; "Cleveland's Freedmen's Aid Society," http://drbronsontours.com/bronsonclevelandfreedy; William Cheek and Aimee Lee Cheek, *John Mercer Langston and the Fight for Black Freedom* (Urbana: Univ. of Illinois Press, 1989), 132; Ken Champlin, correspondent, *Standard-Times* (Fall River, Mass.), February 12, 1998; "Nathaniel Briggs Borden," in *Memorial Biographies of the New England Historic Genealogical Society,* ed. [J. Gardner White], 9 vols. (Boston: New England Genealogical Society, 1880–1908), 6:94–95; Kathryn Grover, *Fugitive's Gibraltar: Escaping Slaves and Abolitionism in New Bedford, Massachusetts* (Amherst: Univ. of Massachusetts Press, 2001),140; Brooks, *Liberty Power,* 86.

19. Leavitt to Readers, December 4, 1841, in *Emancipator,* December 10, 1841 (1st–3rd quotations); [Torrey] to Mary, December 13, 1841, in Joseph P. Lovejoy, *Memoir of Rev. Charles T. Torrey Who Died in the Penitentiary of Maryland Where He Was Confined for Showing Mercy to the Poor* (Boston: John P. Jewett and Co., 1847), 88 (4th quotation); Weld to Angelina Grimké Weld, January 18, 1842, in Barnes and Dumond, *The Letters of Theodore Weld, Angelina Grimké Weld, and Sarah Grimké,* 2:895–96.

20. Weld to Lewis Tappan, December 14, 1841; Weld to Angelina Grimké Weld, January 2, 1842, both in Barnes and Dumond, *The Letters of Theodore Weld, Angelina Grimké Weld, and Sarah Grimké,* 2:879–82 (1st quotation), 879–80, (2nd–3rd quotations), 886. See Davis, *Joshua Leavitt,* 188.

21. Weld to Angelia Grimké Weld, January 1, 1842, January 2, 1842, January 9, [18]42, in Barnes and Dumond, *The Letters of Theodore Weld, Angelina Grimké Weld, and Sarah Grimké,* 2: 882–83, 285–86, 889 (1st–2nd quotations); Barnes, *Anti-Slavery Impulse,* 181–84; McPherson, "Fight against the Gag Rule," 188.

22. Stanley Harrold, *Subversives: Antislavery Community in Washington, D.C., 1828–1865* (Baton Rouge: Louisiana State Univ. Press, 2003), 71–72 (quotation); Weld to Angelina Grimké Weld, January 18, 1842, in Barnes and Dumond, *The Letters of Theodore Weld, Angelina Grimké Weld, and Sarah Grimké,* 2:895–97; Lovejoy, *Memoir of Rev. Charles T. Torrey,* 97, 100.

23. Seth M. Gates to James G. Birney, January 24, 1842, in Dumond, ed., *Letters of James Gillespie Birney,* 2:667; McPherson, "Fight against the Gag Rule," 188–91; Editorial Correspondence, January 28, 1842, in *Emancipator,* February 4, 1842; Weld to Angelina Grimké Weld, January [23], 1842, in Barnes and Dumond, eds., *The Letters of Theodore Weld, Angelina Grimké Weld, and Sarah Grimké,* 2:899 (quotation).

24. Editorial Correspondence, January 28, 1842, in *Emancipator,* February 4, 1842 (1st quotation); Weld to Angelina Grimké Weld, January [23], 1842, January 25, 18[42], January 30, 18[42], February 6, 1842, in Barnes and Dumond, *The Letters of Theodore Weld, Angelina Grimké Weld, and Sarah Grimké,* 2:897–906

(2nd quotation), 911–13; Bemis, *Adams and the Union,* 2:425–39; *Congressional Globe,* 27th Cong., 2nd sess. (January 25, 1842), 168–70, 202–7, (February 7, 1842), 215; McPherson, "Fight against the Gag Rule," 190–91; *Emancipator,* March 31, 1842.

25. Giddings to [Laura Giddings], February 2, 1842, in George W. Julian, *The Life of Joshua R. Giddings* (Chicago: A. C. McClurg, 1892), 111 (1st quotation); Weld to Weld, February [7], 1842, in Barnes and Dumond, *The Letters of Theodore Weld, Angelina Grimké Weld, and Sarah Grimké,* 2:913 (2nd quotation); Brooks, *Liberty Power,* 66–67; Benjamin Platt Thomas, *Theodore Weld: Crusader for Freedom* (New Brunswick: Rutgers Univ. Press, 1950), 208–12 (3rd quotation); McPherson, "Fight against the Gag Rule," 191–92 (4th–5th quotations); Russell B. Nye, *Fettered Freedom: Civil Liberties and the Slavery Controversy* (East Lansing: Michigan State College Press, 1949), 53 (6th quotation). Thomas notes limits to Weld's optimism, but contends Weld "helped to bring slavery's demise."

26. Weld to Angelina Grimké Weld, February 17, 1842, Barnes and Dumond, *The Letters of Theodore Weld, Angelina Grimké Weld, and Sarah Grimké,* 2:923–24 (1st–2nd quotations); Bemis, *Adams and the Union,* 443 (3rd–4th quotations—Bemis quoted).

27. Weld to Angelia Grimké Weld, January 2 (4), 1842, January 9, 1842, January 15 [?], 1842, January 25, [1842], February 9, 20, 1842, in Barnes and Dumond, *The Letters of Theodore Weld, Angelina Grimké Weld, and Sarah Grimké,* 2:887, 889, 893 (1st quotation), 901, 903–4, 906, 915, 922–28; Barnes, *Antislavery Impulse,* 183–84, 289n; Bemis, *Adams and the Union,* 2:425; Stewart, *Giddings,* 70–71; William M. Wiecek, *The Sources of Antislavery Constitutionalism in America, 1760–1841* (Ithaca, N.Y.: Cornell Univ. Press, 1977), 39, 213–19; Eric Foner, *Free Soil, Free Labor, Free Men: The Ideology of the Republican Party before the Civil War* (New York: Oxford Univ. Press, 1970), 73–102; *Journal of the House of Representatives,* 28th Cong., 2nd sess. (March 22, 1842), 567–80 (2nd–4th quotations); *Congressional Globe,* 27th Cong., 2nd sess. (March 22, 1842), 344–46; McPherson, "Fight against the Gag Rule," 192–93; Stewart, *Giddings,* 73–76. Bemis and Stewart give Weld credit for drafting Giddings's *Creole* resolutions. Wiecek suggests otherwise.

28. Gates to James G. Birney, April 4, 1842, in Dumond, ed., *Letters of James Gillespie Birney,* 2:687–88 (1st–2nd quotations).

29. Barnes, *Antislavery Impulse,* 188–90 (1st–3rd quotations); McPherson, "Fight against the Gag Rule," 194–95; Thomas, *Theodore Weld,* 211; Seth M. Gates to Gerrit Smith, March 14, 1842, Gerrit Smith Papers, Special Collections Research Center, Syracuse University Libraries, Syracuse, New York; Gates to James G. Birney, March 23, 1842, in Dumond, ed., *Letters of James Gillespie Birney,* 2:684–85; *Emancipator,* March 31, 1842; Torrey to Alden, March 19, 1842, in *Emancipator,* March 31, 1842; Torrey to *Emancipator,* n.d., in *Spirit of Liberty* (Pittsburgh), April 16, 1842 (4th quotation).

30. *Congressional Globe,* 27th Cong., 2nd sess. (April 22, 1842), 439; [Leavitt to *Emancipator*], April 28, 30, May 12, 1842, in *Emancipator,* May 5, 12, 19, 1842;

Adams, diary entry, July 20, 1842, quoted in Davis, *Joshua Leavitt,* 192 (quotation); Leavitt to Giddings, August 7, 1842, Giddings Papers, Ohio Historical Society.

31. *Liberator,* December 16, 1842; Barnes, *Antislavery Impulse,* 193–94; Weld to Angelina Grimke Weld, December 27, 1842, January 1, 4, 16, 1843, February 1, 1843, in Barnes and Dumond, *The Letters of Theodore Weld, Angelina Grimké Weld, and Sarah Grimké,* 2:947, 953–56 (3rd quotation), 964, 973 (1st–2nd quotations); *Emancipator,* January 5, 1843 (4th quotation).

32. Weld to Angelina Grimké Weld, December 27, 1842, January 1, 1843, in Barnes and Dumond, *The Letters of Theodore Weld, Angelina Grimké Weld, and Sarah Grimké,* 2:948–49, 953 (quote). Adams thought he could still "battle for liberty" even as slaveholders lay low. Historians have similarly misjudged the impact of "dispirited" southern congressmen on the effectiveness of the abolition lobby. See McPherson, "Fight against the Gag Rule," 194, and Davis, *Joshua Leavitt,* 194. See also Seth M. Gates to James G. Birney, March 24, 1842, in *Birney Letters,* 2:686. McPherson points out that the Whig Party adopted a policy of not confronting Giddings after his return to Congress in May 1842. But McPherson does not link this to a decline of the lobby/caucus.

33. Weld to Angelina Grimké Weld, January 9, 12, 14, 22, 1843, February 1, 3, 1843; Weld to Lewis Tappan, January 23, 1843, February 3, 1843; Leavitt to Angelina Grimké Weld, February 7, 1843, all in Barnes and Dumond, *The Letters of Theodore Weld, Angelina Grimké Weld, and Sarah Grimké,* 2:959, 962–65 (3rd quotation), 971, 973–75 (4th, 1st, 5th, and 6th quotations); *Congressional Globe,* 27th Cong., 3rd sess. (January 14, 19, 1843), 161, 176. D.L. C[hild] to [*Liberator*], March 14, 1843, in *Liberator,* March 17, 1843 (2nd quotation); Joshua R. Giddings, *Speeches in Congress* (1853; reprint, New York: Negro Universities Press, 1968), 32–51; Barnes, *Antislavery Impulse,* 194; Leavitt to James G. Birney, February 10, 1843, Dumond, ed., *Letters of James Gillespie Birney,* 2:715–16. In his letter to Birney, Leavitt also charged that Gates, Giddings, and Slade "risked everything" for "the Whig Party, with a bigotry and devotion worthy of monkdom."

34. Giddings to Weld, February 21, 1843, in Barnes and Dumond, eds. *The Letters of Theodore Weld, Angelina Grimké Weld, and Sarah Grimké,* 2:975–76; D.L. C[hild] to [*Liberator*], March 13,1842, in *Liberator,* March 17, 1842; [Leavitt to *Emancipator*], February 21, [1843], in *Emancipator,* March 9, 1843.

35. Weld to Angelina Grimké Weld, December 27, 1842, in Barnes and Dumond, *The Letters of Theodore Weld, Angelina Grimké Weld, and Sarah Grimké,* 2:947–48; Barnes, *Antislavery Impulse,* 193; Davis, *Joshua Leavitt,* 211; Gates to James G. Birney, December 11, 1841, in Dumond, ed., *Letters of James Gillespie Birney,* 2:642–43; Gates to Gerrit Smith, March 14, 1842, Smith Papers; Miller, *Arguing about Slavery,* 471–75; Davis, *Joshua Leavitt,* 211; *Congressional Globe,* 28th Cong., 1st sess., 335. See also *Emancipator,* January 11, 18, 25, 1844.

36. Leavitt to Giddings, April 22, 1842, Giddings Papers, Ohio Historical Society; Editorial Correspondence, January 4, 1844, in *Emancipator,* January 11,

1844; Editorial Correspondence, January 15, 1844, in *Emancipator,* January 25, 1844; Davis, *Joshua Leavitt,* 211–12; Weld to Tappan, [January 11, 1844], in Barnes and Dumond, *The Letters of Theodore Weld, Angelina Grimké Weld, and Sarah Grimké,* 2:990 (3rd quotation); Harrold, *Subversives,* 81–84; Thomas, *Theodore Weld,* 217.

37. Giddings to Weld, January 28, 1844, in Barnes and Dumond, *The Letters of Theodore Weld, Angelina Grimké Weld, and Sarah Grimké,* 2:990–91.

38. Harrold, *Subversives,* 84–85; Davis, *Joshua Leavitt,* 221–22; Freehling, *Road to Disunion,* 1:351.

39. Miller, *Arguing about Slavery,* 476–85; Freehling, *Road to Disunion,* 1:351.

40. *Emancipator,* December 11, 1844.

41. Ibid. (quotations); Leavitt to James G. Birney, December 18, 1844, in Dumond, ed., *Letters of James Gillespie Birney,* 2:890.

42. Davis, *Joshua Leavitt,* 223–24. Brooks mistakenly portrays the lobby Gamaliel Bailey began in 1847 as "a permanent abolitionist congressional lobby." It was in fact a nonabolitionist Liberty Party/nonabolitionist Free Soil Party lobby. See Brooks, *Liberty Power,* 72.

3

Officers of the US Army Veteran Reserve Corps

Motivation and Expectations of Veteran Soldiers during the Civil War and Reconstruction

Paul A. Cimbala

Erastus W. Everson fought long and hard for the Union cause. Enlisting in 1861 as a sergeant, he rose from the ranks to a lieutenancy in the 18th Massachusetts Volunteer Infantry, received two battlefield wounds, and earned two brevets for his trouble. Campaigning eventually put him in the hospital and his wounds, including a gunshot wound to the testicles that would have an "irritable influence upon his mental faculties," continued to trouble him. Nevertheless, he had no desire to leave the army; Everson apparently had grown used to the military life. "Being in sound health, always my wounds excepted," he explained as he recuperated in a hospital ward in October 1863, "I had rather die from exposure in the field than to leave the service, now that I have been in it since this war began." Furthermore, he continued to feel the need to be useful even though by any standard he had already done his part. "I find it extremely difficult to keep easy in hospital," he wrote, stressing that "My record is good & I do not desire to leave it unfinished." Thus, instead of seeking a discharge, he secured a commission in the army's Invalid Corps. Even after his transfer to the Corps, Everson requested a physical to prove himself capable of active duty at the front. Failing to convince the physicians, he had to settle for spending the rest of the war with the Invalids. With the coming of peace, Everson had no desire to leave the army. When it became apparent that the Veteran Reserve Corps—as the Invalid Corps became officially known in March

1864—would be consolidated and the need for commissioned officers greatly reduced, he secured an appointment in the Bureau of Refugees, Freedmen, and Abandoned Lands. It was in this organization in South Carolina that he served until his muster out on January 1, 1868.[1]

Everson's wish to stay in the service of the Union cause long after he had proven himself a true patriot was a desire shared by hundreds of veteran officers of the Civil War–era US Army. Not all were honorable men. There were enough scamps, drunks, thieves, Lotharios, and scoundrels looking for an easy berth behind the lines to diminish the Veteran Reserve Corps' reputation among civilians and soldiers alike. But many more officers wished to remain useful and to see the fight for the Union through to a successful conclusion. Probably most of them were seriously concerned about how they would adjust to civilian life, knowing that their wounds or dysentery-plagued bowels had rendered them unfit for their antebellum civilian professions, thus making them incapable of supporting themselves and their families. Many of them most likely envisioned that everyday life in a world that demanded a degree of physical competence would prove challenging, especially in a society that had yet to develop modern notions of state-sponsored philanthropy. Consequently, many of them expected a grateful nation to show some consideration for their past service and continued discomfort. They did not expect charity; rather, these wounded and camp-sick veterans expected the government to allow them to continue to serve during and after the war in a military organization that appeared to be suited for men of their record and abilities.[2]

The establishment of the Invalid Corps, authorized on April 28, 1863, by the secretary of war, was one means by which the US Army attempted to solve its insatiable need for men. Through this organization, the army expected to make use of veteran soldiers who were in some way disabled but were still fit for rear echelon duty. Enlisted men, who previously might have expected to spend time loitering around hospital wards or who would have received their discharge papers, now found themselves fair game for more service. Most enlisted invalids probably accepted their transfer to the new organization as an obligation, a duty that they had to fulfill at least until their terms of enlistment were up. Some disabled soldiers actually welcomed the opportunity to continue the fight. Others grumbled, complained, and wrote letters to the president, all the while assuming that their physical condition exempted them from further service. Understandably, the fact that the men of the Invalid Corps were the butts of humor, ridiculed by other soldiers who easily spotted them in their sky-blue uniform jackets, did not help matters. Nor did it speed the efforts of officers who tried to recruit eligible honorably discharged men into the Corps. The organization's heavy reliance on transfers to fill its ranks gives some indication of the enlisted man's enthusiasm for service in the Corps. Of the approximately 57,000 enlisted men that served in the Corps from its inception into the fall of 1865, only 5,275 had enlisted directly into the Corps, while 3,493 on duty with the Corps had reenlisted. The other soldiers received transfers into the organization, primarily from hospital wards. After the war, when these men had the opportunity to stay in the service or accept their discharges, the great majority of them chose the latter course of action.[3]

The officers who commanded these men, however, were another matter. Disabled officers eagerly sought places in the Corps, where they would hold their ranks on par with their counterparts in the Regular Army. Any shortage of officers in the organization was the consequence of the carefulness of the Corps' examining boards and the bureaucratic delays of the War Department rather than lack of interest on the part of veteran soldiers. By July 1863, the commanders could no longer simply transfer officers into the Corps; rather, Provost Marshal General James B. Fry, under whose jurisdiction the Corps fell, required that disabled officers make special application for an appointment.[4] Furthermore, receiving a commission was more complicated than simply asking for one. Intent on turning the organization into a Corps of Honor, Colonel Fry stressed the need to review with great care all applications for those commissions.[5] Applicants for commissions had to prove their good character, intelligence, sobriety, and courage; starting January 1, 1864, they had to appear before a review board and pass rigorous examinations before they were allowed to hold VRC commissions.[6] By early September 1863, there were over nine hundred applications on hand for commissions in the Invalid Corps; by the end of the month there were almost fourteen hundred.[7] By the end of October, the provost marshal general's office had reviewed a sufficient number of those applications to issue 501 commissions to invalids, of which 491 actually went on to serve in the Corps.[8] By the fall of 1865, the army had appointed a total of 1,036 officers to the Veteran Reserve Corps. Only fifteen declined their commissions, and only about 18 percent (181) resigned for various reasons at some point after accepting appointments.[9] The commissions were desirable. Veteran officers, as well as some enlisted men and noncommissioned officers, vied for them. And once they had them, they wished to hold on to them.

As the war came to a close, job prospects appeared to be limited for veterans who sought work outside of the military, thus making a commission in the VRC all the more valuable. In May 1865, Erastus Everson learned there was no work to be had in Massachusetts, which certainly contributed to his desire to find a position in the Freedmen's Bureau. In his hometown of Dedham, Massachusetts, editorialists urged businesses to do their duty by hiring veterans. Few individuals who had benefited from the veterans' "hardships and sufferings" would challenge the notion that faithful soldiers deserved "every consideration." But "these thoughts," his correspondent noted, "are seldom, made use of in practice."[10] In March 1866, Lieutenant Adolph Glackmeyer, who had some trouble walking because of a gunshot wound, also encountered poor employment prospects as he waited at home in New York City to hear from the War Department about his military future. "I have as yet been unable to procure something that would warrant me to make a change of Masters and by the looks of things generally it looks very dubious whether I shall be able to do so shortly," he wrote, "for that reason I unite my wish with your's [*sic*] that our present position may remain so indefinitely."[11]

Even if the prospects had been better, for many disabled veteran officers the Corps was an opportunity—perhaps the only opportunity—to replace an antebellum profession now rendered inaccessible because of wounds suffered in battle or illnesses contracted in camp. Disabled in some way while trying to preserve the Union, these men expected the government to take an interest in their future and offer them an alternative to unrewarding or unfulfilling civilian lives. When George Wagner applied for a commission, he explained that he "had been unable to work at my regular business." Wagner soon thereafter received a commission as a first lieutenant with the Corps in June 1863.[12]

Before the establishment of the Invalid Corps, Emil Munch, who eventually received an appointment in that organization, wrote to President Abraham Lincoln about his expectations of the government. Munch, who had first enlisted in October 1861, apologized for intruding on the president's time. Nevertheless, he was now compelled "to apply for a position at the gift of the Government, for the support of which I had freely offered my life at several occasions and lost my health in her service." Munch wanted no charity. Unable to return to lumbering after a wound and exposure rendered him unfit for active service, he was "unwilling to accept any Gift from the Government (in the way of Pensions), except for Services actually rendered, and Knowing, that it is the just intention of the Government, in making appointments, to regard the interests and claims of disabled soldiers, if otherwise they are qualified, I would most respectfully apply to be appointed to some position, either civil or military, that would render me the necessary subsistence of life."[13]

Indeed, that some sort of an invalid organization should provide deserving heroes with useful positions was part of the rationale for establishing the Corps, a notion not lost on the men who sought its commissions. In November 1863, for example, Colonel Richard Rush, an assistant to the provost marshal general in charge of matters pertaining to the Corps, explained that the Corps could provide "honorable employment, suited to their physical capacities" while sparing them "the necessity of becoming pensioners" and shielding them "from the undoubted evils of a life of idleness."[14] Officers such as Colonel John Speidel agreed with Rush. Speidel joined the army in April 1861, lost the use of his right arm because of a battlefield fracture, commanded the depot camp at Hartford, Connecticut, and served as the colonel of the 3rd Regiment VRC. In July 1864, he petitioned the provost marshal general's office for his retention in the VRC. Speidel reminded his superiors of the debt the nation owed to him. "Having now been so long connected with the military service of the United States," he explained, and "having given up all my business" to join the army, losing his commission in the VRC would deprive him and his family of their sole support.[15]

Other officers shared Speidel's expectations of the government. In August 1865, after learning of the War Department's plan to reduce and consolidate the Corps, Lieutenant J. Arnold Yeckley of the 21st Regiment VRC made a case for his retention by reminding his superiors that he had placed the Union above all selfish concerns. "In 1862, I left a college course nearly completed, a pleasant and comfortable house, against the affectionate regards of my parents, (being an only son) and fair civil prospects to serve my imperilled country as a private soldier, impelled by a sense of duty solely," he explained. Wounded at Gettysburg, suffering from blindness in one eye, he entered the VRC in May 1865. He wished to stay in the army, placing what he considered a reasonable and just claim on his nation. "In an hour of need I served my country without reward or hope of reward" but now "my former prospects in life have been blasted by the wound I have rec'd, and in consideration of the sacrifices I have made in the cause, I respectfully request to be retained on the service with my company."[16]

Receiving a commission or being retained in the service for men such as Yeckley was nothing less than "proof of the appreciation of my government for my humble services in a just and holy cause," as Lieutenant William A. MacNulty, a sergeant who had received his commission in the Corps in May 1864, later reflected.[17]

In the end, the army accommodated the expectations of only a minority of the veteran officers who sought to extend their military careers in the Corps. If a grateful nation conferred a place for a wounded officer, for some disappointed veteran officers it was an ungrateful one—or at least its ungrateful representatives—that withheld their commissions. In August 1863, Lieutenant James T. Bicknell received a second lieutenant's commission in the Corps, but during the consolidation process was ordered home in December 1865 and eventually mustered out of the service. The lieutenant based his claim for continuing his commission on his long service—he had joined the army in August 1861—and the hardship incurred during that service. He had suffered a wound and the loss of an arm, the consequence of the poor Confederate medical attention he received while he was a prisoner of war. A bitter Bicknell found it interesting how the army was able to leave him in suspense for several months, apparently ignoring his application for continuance, but promptly respond when he requested his papers be returned to him after he had concluded that his situation was hopeless. He blamed an "ungrateful" Ulysses S. Grant for pushing the disbanding of the Corps and considered himself misused by the officials who "slighted" his application to remain in the service.[18]

Financial security loomed large in the minds of handicapped officers when they sought out VRC appointments, but there were other reasons for veteran soldiers to request commissions and then fight to keep them. Some veterans found military life to be agreeable, while allowing them not only the opportunity to replace civilian vocations, but also to rise beyond their former civilian status. When Lieutenant William G. Vance wrote to his congressman in August 1865 for assistance in retaining his place, he did not linger on missed wartime opportunities, but stressed that he had high expectations for advancing in the military. "I had bright anticipations for the future," he explained, "for my past life I must say has not been bright but I have had to struggle hard to rise to a higher sphere." He wished to remain in the VRC "because I am fond of Military life."[19]

For such men, the Corps was the one place in the army that provided them with an outlet for their ambitions. Lieutenant Jacob Sheets, who had been an enlisted man in the antebellum army, claimed to be able to draw a greater salary as a civilian bookkeeper but wished to remain in the Corps because "it is my highest ambition to *excel as a soldier.*"[20] And Lieutenant Jacob F. Chur viewed the VRC as an avenue for advancement. When he heard a rumor that only wounded officers and not those who had become ill while in the active service would be kept in the Corps, he protested. "To be candid with you I will first remark that my present duty is no sinecure," he explained. "[F]rom early morning until midnight I am busily engaged, and in my present physical condition am seldom far from pain in consequence, but all would I cheerfully bear were I confident that promotion which is coveted by all in the service was open to me. I feel and have always felt a deep interest in the service and would much prefer remaining in it."[21]

VRC officers, therefore, commonly had selfish motives for desiring to remain in the army and believed that their sacrifices for the cause gave them a claim on the nation. Such motives and expectations, however, are understandable given the circumstances in which veteran officers developed them. Furthermore, they did not necessarily exclude the consideration of more noble motives. The need to be useful, to do something constructive especially in the service of the nation, was an important factor for many of them in seeking their commissions, even as they worried about supporting their families. And if one were to judge these men by their words, at least some of the VRC officers had sought continued service because they were indeed patriots.

In October 1863, a meeting of Invalid Corps officers stationed at Burnside Barracks near Indianapolis, including First Lieutenant George Wagner, commended the government for establishing the Corps. Their resolutions acknowledged that wounded and diseased men remained "anxious, to render such assistance as in their powers, to aid in maintaining the Union and defending their Flag and Country, in this the hour of the Nation's peril."[22] Erastus Everson confirmed the assumptions of these fellow officers when he pleaded for a place in the Corps to have an opportunity to finish the job he had started, while Emil Munch successfully requested a VRC commission because, along with his desire to be useful, he wished "to serve the cause as far as capable."[23] And S. S. Stevens, who had been a captain in the Corps, petitioned for reappointment, explaining, "My whole time has been devoted to the best of this great and good Government and I trust that you will favor me if deserving and that what assistance I can feebly add until the Rebellion is crushed will be cheerfully given."[24] It was this theme of self-sacrificing patriotism that permeated the VRC officers' lobbying campaign of August 1865.

During the summer of 1865, the officers of the VRC learned that the War Department was preparing to consolidate their organization, reducing the number of regiments from twenty-four to possibly six. Fewer regiments meant fewer places for officers, so most of them, they realized, would be sent home. The veteran officers launched an extraordinary lobbying effort in the hopes that Congress would give them and their Corps a reprieve. In August 1865 and again in October, VRC officers met in Philadelphia to discuss their best strategy for at least delaying the War Department's actions until Congress could meet to consider their corps' fate.[25] A committee collected assessments from the Corps' officers to finance their efforts and continued to function into 1866.[26] Intent on remaining in the service, Erastus Everson sent along his contribution, as did other officers, including those of the 16th Regiment VRC, who forwarded a total of $124 for the campaign.[27]

VRC officers asked their brother officers, congressmen, senators, and governors to intercede with Secretary of War Edwin Stanton.[28] Groups of regimental officers violated the chain of command and sent petitions directly to Stanton, pleading for a stay in the organization's consolidation. "A large proportion of us were engaged in the active pursuits of civil life, which we abandoned, and took up arms against traitors and rebels when they inaugurated war and fired upon our flag, the emblem of our nationality," the commonly used standard petition explained. "We were prompted in this course by the spirit of patriotism and loyalty to our common country, and the principles of Government under which we live." The petitioners noted that many of them had suffered wounds in the line of duty and now only wished to continue to serve their country by remaining in the army.[29]

Petitioning for the government's favor claiming consideration for patriotic service might have appeared opportunistic to cynics. But many veteran officers already had provided proof of their honorable motives by their political allegiance, actions, sacrifices, and good service that indeed had contributed to the Union war effort. One of Everson's comrades, a Maryland native who had been wounded, continued his service in the Corps even though his service in the Union cause had "estranged him from his parents & friends who were of secession tendencies." Everson believed that his comrade's personal distress had led him to drink.[30]

John J. Knox had been a Democrat before the war and had lived in Alabama, until secession drove him out of the state and back to his Michigan home. Fighting with the 5th Michigan Infantry, he received a serious neck wound on May 31, 1862, at Fair Oaks, recovered sufficiently to campaign with the Army of Virginia, and was wounded again. He suffered the rest of his life from the effects of the neck wound, which limited the use of his right arm and impaired his breathing. Yet when he had the opportunity to enter the Corps in June 1863, he did, taking a reduction in rank from captain to first lieutenant, a common practice for officers wishing to join the VRC. He became a firm supporter of the Lincoln administration and actively campaigned for the Republicans among his relatives and friends during the 1864 election, despite the animosity his party change generated among former political allies. He continued his service with the Freedmen's Bureau in Mississippi and in Georgia until his discharge in late December 1868.[31] One would imagine that Knox believed he had a stake in seeing the Union cause brought to a successful conclusion.

Charles F. Johnson, like Knox, appeared to be committed to the Union cause, if one were to judge from the sacrifices he made to stay in the VRC. He endured four battlefield wounds, including a testicular wound that made it difficult for him to remain on a horse. He also suffered from recurring discomfort caused by an illness that produced a painful rash on parts of his body. He frequently confessed to missing his wife and family, yet he also expressed his love for the Union and his hatred of the rebels, "the arch-fiends who are creating all this disaster for our country."[32] After learning of the depredations of guerrillas while stationed in St. Louis, Missouri, he declared that "if I was only able to stand the constant use of the saddle and had a few good men, how I would cut down the sons of bitches."[33] Johnson longed for another opportunity to meet the enemy in battle and, after continuous service in rigorous field assignments, had his wish granted. In June 1864, he participated in a fight with rebel raiders at White House Landing, Virginia. Johnson died in 1867 while on duty with the Freedmen's Bureau in Kentucky.[34]

Judging by their actions, other officers shared Knox's and Johnson's commitment to the cause by risking their lives in the line of duty. In December 1863, Captain P. Devyer of the 5th Regiment Invalid Corps, stepped into danger after a group of "rowdies" had beaten a local policeman. He and a guard from his company arrested the perpetrators.[35] A year later in December 1864, Captain John W. Southworth of the 16th Regiment VRC led a detachment of men through the snowy mountains of Clearfield County, Pennsylvania, and engaged in a gunfight with a gang of deserters before capturing his quarry.[36] Southworth's commanding officer, Major Frederick A. H. Gaebel, recommended him for a brevet for his personal bravery in the action.[37] Farther west, about the same time that Southworth was performing his duties in Pennsylvania, Captain C. L. Clark and his company of men from the 6th Regiment VRC engaged in a "hazardous and arduous" campaign of night patrols through densely forested countryside populated by inhabitants of a "beligerant [*sic*] character" to track down deserters. On one occasion, a detachment of his company tracked down men who had ambushed some of their fellow invalids in Auglaize County in western Ohio. Clark did not need to engage in a gunfight when he arrested them, but given his company's past experience, the risk was real. In the earlier ambush the attackers had wounded two of his men. Despite the danger, Clark was determined to remain in western Ohio to deal with any future disloyalty and ultimately arrested almost one hundred deserters.[38]

Such men made the patriotic protestations of the petitioners ring true and no doubt contributed to the generally favorable reaction to the VRC lobbying effort. A significant record of service that included maintaining order in various northern towns and tangling with Copperheads, rebel raiders, draft dodgers, and deserters while keeping volunteers and conscripts in line as they passed to and from the front provided a foundation of good will that led many politicians and editorialists to support their cause before Stanton.[39] To be sure, the VRC certainly had its civilian and military wartime critics who considered its men deadbeats, a view that led at least one Congressman to speak out against the Corps after the war.[40] But the support for at least delaying the War Department's plan for consolidating the VRC until Congress gave it careful consideration was impressive. Apparently, many northerners agreed that the nation owed the VRC men something for their service and suffering. In writing about the consolidation efforts of the War Department in August 1865, the editor of the *Indianapolis Daily Journal* was quite blunt in his sentiments in favor of keeping the VRC, reminding his readers that "These men deserve the sympathy and cordial support of every patriot and friend of humanity in this country."[41]

Some politicians contributed to the letter-writing campaign by offering practical reasons for retaining the VRC or at least delaying a decision until Congress was in session.[42] But others reminded the nation of its obligation to its men. For New Hampshire governor Fred K. Smith, these were "brave, but unfortunate men" whose "sufferings and service in the cause of their country certainly entitle them to unusual consideration."[43] Meanwhile, Congressman

Daniel Morris of New York argued that "These veterans have a high claim upon their country," and Conrad Baker, the lieutenant governor of Indiana, reminded the secretary of war that "no branch of the army deserves more at the hands of the government."[44]

Public recognition of the claims that VRC officers placed on their government indicated at least some appreciation for what they had contributed to the war effort, but by this time the War Department had set a course that would be too difficult to reverse. The efforts of the VRC officers did little to stop the movement to a smaller, less expensive army. By the end of 1865, officers of the VRC were receiving orders "to go to their respective homes, and . . . to await the disposition which may be made of them."[45] Once home, many of the officers would hear no word concerning their future for months to come. No wonder VRC men became "somewhat anxious for the fate of that corps."[46] In the end, Congress failed to offer them much consolation. In December 1865, the House passed a resolution in favor of delaying the mustering out of the VRC until Congress could give the matter its full consideration, but in July 1866 the Senate finally postponed indefinitely its consideration of the House resolution.[47] If VRC men wished to remain in government service after the end of the war and especially after April 1866 when the reduction of their ranks was no longer avoidable, they most likely would need an appointment in the Freedmen's Bureau.

Veteran Reserve Corps officers generally claimed appointments in the Freedmen's Bureau using the same lines of argument that had won them their VRC commissions.[48] The patriotic Erastus Everson, for example, may have been influenced by the dearth of employment opportunities back home in Dedham, Massachusetts, to seek a place in the bureau. Lieutenant M. M. Kistler, who still carried a ball in his lungs from a near-mortal wound suffered at Antietam, informed Bureau Commissioner Oliver Otis Howard that he was "totally disabled for hard labor" and that he had "a wife and four children totally dependent on my earnings." Of Stanton, he asked if his past service "intitled [*sic*] the favour of the government for to remain in the service."[49] Second Lieutenant George Barton, who had first entered the service in April 1861, explained to Howard that he was "unable to follow my legitimate business on account of disability caused by the loss of my right leg at the Battle of Fredericksburg."[50] And Charles E. Campbell, a former captain in the 23rd Regiment VRC, also suggested to Howard that he believed his "services while in the U. S. Army for a period of over four years in the late war, entitle me to a consideration in the matter" of a bureau appointment.[51]

Many of the VRC men who made application for bureau appointments in 1866 were already at their homes living in a military limbo. They were still attached to the army on inactive duty, they still craved to be useful, but they were well aware that new orders would probably mean the severing of their ties with the military. The Freedmen's Bureau provided them with the opportunity to "be able to return some service to the Country in return for my pay," as Second Lieutenant James Walker explained as he whiled away the time at his Langley, Virginia, residence.[52] First Lieutenant Henry Wallace was in a similar situation when he asked Howard for a job, noting that "I have been at my home for the last four months" and "have had nothing to do." He hoped that he "could be of service" to the commissioner.[53]

Since Congress empowered the Freedmen's Bureau in its March 1865 legislation to supervise all affairs concerning the freedpeople of the South, one might expect that the War Department agency would attract officers who were concerned about the plight of the former slaves.[54] In fact, few applicants expressed such concern. First Lieutenant J. S. Taylor, however, was one of those men who felt a need to help the ex-slaves. He explained to General Howard that he held a "deep sympathy in the progress, elevation, and wellfare [*sic*] of the unfortunate people whose especial care your Bureau has been provided." Perhaps knowing Howard's reputation for being a religious man, Taylor further noted that he believed bureau service was "a noble field for a Christian soldier."[55] Captain James A. Bates also explained, "my sympathies for & interest in the Freedmen lead me to ask assignment to your Bureau." But his motives also included practical concerns. "I have been in service since April 19, 1861 and have lost my right leg above the knee, which incapacitates me for duty in my former civil profession."[56]

The Freedmen's Bureau, a part of the War Department, provided invalid officers with continued military employment, but serving with the agency was by no means any less taxing than wartime service with the Veteran Reserve Corps. Veteran officers on duty with the bureau took on yet another job that strained their physical abilities and tested their commitment to the cause for which they had already sacrificed much. If they failed to express great concern for the freedpeople when applying for transfers to Howard's agency, they did not ignore the ex-slaves' needs. Indeed, many proved to be staunch friends of the freedpeople or at least sympathetic to their plight. Lieutenant Yeckley, perhaps giving credence to his earlier claims of selfless dedication to the cause, reported that he was "almost heartsick at the present state of affairs" in his Virginia bureau district because "outrages on the freedmen are alarmingly on the increase." Frustrated by his inability to see justice done through the civil courts, he warned his superiors, "Unless I have power given to give these people protection, self respect will compel me to resign."[57]

If other veteran officers were not exactly staunch friends of the freedpeople, they were certainly committed to a just Reconstruction that in the end could only benefit the ex-slaves. Consequently, they understood that their presence in the South made a difference. As First Lieutenant F. J. Massey of the 5th Regiment VRC realized while stationed with the agency in Virginia, "Were it not for the controlling hand of the Bureau and the Military Authorities, I am satisfied the whites would treat them [the freedpeople] in a most *unfair* and *unjust* manner." At the same time, he made it clear that the bureau's presence was necessary for training the freedpeople in the ways of free labor and self-reliance. As far as Massey was concerned, his bureau was there to give the freed slave the opportunity "to place himself in a position, where he will be able to maintain himself, after the Bureau shall cease to exist."[58]

The VRC men who assumed roles in Reconstruction acted as if they understood that the war would not be over until they had secured the fruits of victory. If they had not expressed their patriotism in their letters to Howard, once in the South they acted as if they understood the significance of their work for the nation's future. In December 1867, Erastus Everson learned that he would soon be mustered out of the service and that he had an opportunity to remain in the Freedmen's Bureau as a civilian. He informed his superiors that he had no desire to remain on duty with the agency in such a capacity. However, "if my service would be of value to the country," he continued to explain, "in perfecting the plans, and forwarding the objects for which the Bureau was established, and for which the officers who have had the charge of the advancement & betterment of the condition of the freedpeople have so earnestly labored, I would be glad to stay." Everson also realized there remained a connection between his duties in the bureau and his earlier wartime efforts. He would stay, "that I might as far as possible be an instrument of perpetuating the principles which caused me to leave my home in 1861 & which in part have been my guide and support under the trials & hardships since endured."[59]

Bureau jobs were not sinecures; they required an effort that could only come from a commitment to something more than a paycheck, and they were critical for making sure the Union victory endured. Furthermore, they could be lonely and dangerous. Captain Samuel A. Craig, of the 17th Regiment VRC, for example, served with the bureau in Brenham, Texas, during 1866. He found himself "utterly tabooed in social ways." Craig brought this situation upon himself not by being a special or ardent friend of the freedpeople. Indeed, he found them to be "ignorant." However, he attempted to interpose himself between the freedpeople and violent ex-masters who still treated them as slaves. Consequently, Texans ostracized him: "[A]t church no one would come into the seat with me; even at entertainments they avoided the place where I sat, in the Court House the same, my uniform seemed to be sufficient notice." His only friend was the postmaster, who had survived the war as an ardent Union man. Of greater concern than his social life was keeping himself alive in such a hostile environment. After Craig had some threatening encounters with the locals, his superior officer, the assistant commissioner of Texas, Joseph B. Kiddoo, transferred him because he feared for Craig's life.[60]

There is no indication that Major John J. Knox pleaded any special concern for the freedpeople when he asked for his appointment with the bureau; however, he became a great defender of the freedpeople's cause, especially while stationed in Georgia.[61] As a bureau officer, Knox became a vocal critic of President Andrew Johnson's Reconstruction policies. He was also an ardent supporter of the continuation of the agency, once arguing that he would be saddened to learn that Congress would leave the freedpeople of the South "to the tender mercies of a wicked rebellious people who get glory in their shame."[62] On one occasion, Captain Craig had been prepared to use his weapons in the face of an ugly crowd; Knox actually had to defend himself with his pistols because he made decisions that were contrary to the wishes of white southerners. His experience in the bureau may have been unusual only in that he participated in two such gunfights—one in Meridian, Mississippi, and another in Athens, Georgia—and lived to return to his home in Michigan.[63] A handful of officers were not so fortunate. Such was the sad case of VRC officer Lieutenant Jabez Blanding.

Lieutenant Blanding, who entered the war at the commencement of the rebellion as a private and had been wounded twice, received a position in the bureau in the early spring of 1866 while other VRC officers waited at their homes for orders.[64] He was assigned to Grenada, Mississippi, on March 23, 1866, as an assistant subassistant commissioner of the Freedmen's Bureau and in little over a month was dead.[65] In the short time that he was on duty there, he strove "to obtain the good will and co-operation of those with whom" he came into contact. His associate, Captain Silas May, the subassistant commissioner of the Grenada district, had presumed that they were succeeding in doing so.[66] But on April 30, in the evening hours, a white Mississippian shot Blanding in the back and head while the officer was walking on the street. Blanding died the next day.[67] Any VRC officer serving with the bureau risked finding himself in any of these situations if he tried to do his job. The white South was far from pacified during the late 1860s, and veteran officers were well aware of the situation in which they found themselves. More than a salary of $1,000 to $1,200 per annum kept these men on duty in the face of the dangers and hardships they encountered.

The Freedmen's Bureau provided only a short-term solution for those veteran officers who wished to remain in the service. Experience, patriotism, usefulness, and sentiment were insufficient bulwarks in the face of the retrenchment that came with peace. Even the guerrilla warfare that VRC veterans serving in the bureau encountered was insufficient for convincing the government otherwise. After a rapid reduction of the ranks, in 1866 the VRC found itself reduced to four Veteran Reserve regiments within the regular army. Most officers serving in the bureau lost that hold on a military career by the end of 1868, when the agency began to reduce its presence in the Reconstruction South. Eventually, in March 1869, regular army regiments absorbed any remaining Veteran Reserve men who could perform active duty; the rest received honorable discharges.[68]

The officers of the VRC had given up antebellum careers, trades, or businesses and had left behind their families to defend the Constitution. Many of them, if not most, had rallied to the flag in the earliest days of the war and willingly placed themselves in harm's way for the cause. Men such as Lieutenant Benjamin Cook, who had been a joiner before the war, lost his right arm because of a wound received at Gettysburg, and continued to suffer abscessing and the discharging of pieces of bone from the stump months after the war had ended,[69] or Colonel John Ely, whose leg wound from the Battle of Fair Oaks continued to trouble him long after May 31, 1862,[70] assumed that their sacrifices deserved some consideration from the government. They were not unique because of these aspects of their personal histories. Rather, what made them different from most other Union officers was that they suffered from wounds or illnesses sufficiently serious to render them unfit for active duty and they continued to serve. Instead of seeking pensions, they asked for work. Worried about making a living, desirous of having something productive to do, and eager to see the war to a successful conclusion, they considered serving with the Veteran Reserve Corps as the best way to address their concerns. When the government planned to deprive them of their place in the army by reducing and consolidating their Corps, many of them loudly protested. When their protests failed to change the course set by the War Department, many of them sought positions with Oliver Otis Howard's Freedmen's Bureau. But even as they worried about supporting their families, they placed themselves in circumstances that forced them to forego the comforts of home as well as the safety of civilian life, while delaying the hero's place in their communities that they could have claimed. In the end, they contributed much to winning the war and they also worked hard to secure the peace. If these veteran officers expected some consideration from their nation, it was because they deserved it.

Notes

A longer version of this essay appeared as "Lining Up to Serve: Wounded and Sick Union Officers Join the Veteran Reserve Corps during the Civil War, Reconstruction," *Prologue: Quarterly of the National Archives and Records Administration* 35 (spring 2003): 1–12.

1. E. W. Everson to Colonel J. B. Fry, October 8, 1863, Letters Rec'd, Veteran Reserve Corps, Records of the Provost Marshal General's Office, Record Group 110, National Archives Building, Washington, D.C. (hereinafter cited as VRC, RG 110); Captain J. M. Walsh to Major A. G. Brady, January 31, 1864, Regimental Papers, 20th Veteran Reserve Corps (VRC), Records of the Adjutant General's Office, Record Group 94, National Archives Building, Washington, D.C. (hereinafter cited as AGO, RG 94); and Erastus W. Everson, Pension File, Civil War and Later Pension Files, Records of the Veterans Administration, Record Group 15, National Archives Building, Washington, D.C. (hereinafter cited as Civil War Pensions, RG 15).

2. For nineteenth-century ideas about philanthropy, see Robert H. Bremner, *The Public Good: Philanthropy and Welfare in the Civil War Era* (New York: Knopf, 1980). For background information on the Veteran Reserve Corps, see Paul A. Cimbala, "Union Corps of Honor," *Columbiad* 3 (winter 2000): 59–91; Paul A. Cimbala, "Soldiering on the Home Front: The Veteran Reserve Corps and the Northern People," in *Union Soldiers and the Northern Home Front: Wartime Experiences, Postwar Adjustments,* ed. Paul A. Cimbala and Randall M. Miller (New York: Fordham Univ. Press, 2002), and Paul A. Cimbala, *Soldiering Behind the Lines: The United States Army Veteran Reserve Corps and the Preservation of the*

Union, 1863–1869 (Athens: Univ. of Georgia Press, forthcoming). For a brief overview of the work of the Freedmen's Bureau, see Paul A. Cimbala, *The Freedmen's Bureau: Reconstructing the American South after the Civil War* (Malabar, Fla.: Krieger, 2005). For veterans after the Civil War, see Paul A. Cimbala, *Veterans North and South: The Transition from Soldier to Civilian after the American Civil War* (Santa Barbara, Calif.: Praeger, 2015).

3. Colonel Richard H. Rush to Colonel James B. Fry, November 6, 1863; [Colonel M. N. Wisewell] to Brigadier General James B. Fry, October 24, 1864, Annual Reports of Operations, VRC, RG 110; Captain J. W. De Forest to Brigadier General J. B. Fry, November 30, 1865, in US War Department, *The War of the Rebellion: A Compilation of the Official Records of the Union and Confederate Armies,* 128 vols. (Washington, D.C.: Government Printing Office, 1880–1901) (hereinafter cited as *Official Records*), series 3, vol. 5, p. 544; and Edwin M. Stanton to Andrew Johnson, November 22, 1865, *Official Records,* series 3, vol. 5, p. 510.

4. Commanding officers were able to transfer subordinate officers to the Invalid Corps until sometime in July 1863, when that procedure became no longer possible. No doubt, the provost marshal general feared that the Corps would become a dumping ground for incompetent officers. After the Corps stopped that practice, it required that officers, either discharged or still in the service, make application regardless of their circumstances. Colonel Richard H. Rush to Major W. H. Sidell, July 28, 1863, vol. 1, Letters Sent, VRC, RG 110.

5. Colonel R. H. Rush to Colonel C. M. Prevost, August 11, 1863, vol. 1, Letters Sent; Colonel R. H. Rush to Captain R. Touty, August 28, 1863, vol. 2, Letters Sent, VRC, RG 110.

6. Captain J. W. De Forest to Brigadier General J. B. Fry, November 30, 1865, in *Official Records,* series 3, vol. 5, 550–51; Circular, November 6, 1863, Provost Marshal General's Office, Regimental Papers, 13th VRC, AGO, RG 94.

7. Colonel R. H. Rush to Dr. Jesse R. Brown, September 3, 1863; Colonel R. H. Rush to W. Schouler, September 30, 1863, vol. 2, Letters Sent, VRC, RG 110.

8. Colonel R. H. Rush to Colonel J. B. Fry, November 6, 1865, Annual Reports of Operations, VRC, RG 110.

9. Captain J. W. De Forest to Brigadier General J. B. Fry, November 30, 1865, *Official Records,* series 3, vol. 5, p. 567.

10. F. D. Ely to E. W. Everson, May 8, 1865, Erastus W. Everson Papers, South Carolina Historical Society, Charleston.

11. Adolph Glackmeyer to John T. Durang, March 1, 1866, Durang Papers, Schoff Civil War Collection, William L. Clements Library, University of Michigan, Ann Arbor; Adolph Glackmeyer, Pension File, Civil War Pensions, RG 15.

12. George Wagner to Colonel J. B. Fry, May 27, 1863; Edwin M. Stanton to First Lieutenant George Wagner, June 15, 1863, Invalid Corps Papers, George Wagner Collection, Hargrett Rare Book and Manuscript Library, University of Georgia, Athens.

13. Emil Munch to Abraham Lincoln, February 26, 1863, Emil Munch Papers, Minnesota Historical Society, St. Paul.

14. Colonel R. H. Rush to Colonel J. B. Fry, November 6, 1863, Annual Reports of Operations, VRC, RG 110.

15. Colonel J. Speidel to Colonel M. N. Wisewell, July 2, 1864, Letters Received, VRC, RG 110.

16. Second Lieutenant J. Arnold Yeckley to General James B. Fry, August 15, 1865, Letters Received, VRC, RG 110.

17. First Lieutenant W. A. MacNulty, January 31, 1866, entry 238, 1st competition, Left Handed Writing Competition, William Oland Bourne Papers, reel 3, *A People at War: Civil War Manuscripts from the Holdings of the Library of Congress*, ed. John R. Sellers (Alexandria, Va.: Chadwyck-Healey, 1989–90).

18. James T. Bicknell, June 20, 1867, entry 56, 2nd competition, Left Handed Writing Competition, William Oland Bourne Papers, reel 10, *A People at War.*

19. Second Lieutenant William G. Vance to George S. Bantwell, August 22, 1865, Letters Received, VRC, RG 110.

20. First Lieutenant J. C. Sheets to Brigadier General J. B. Fry, July 23, 1864, Letters Received, VRC, RG 110.

21. Lieutenant Jacob F. Chur to Colonel M. N. Wisewell, February 8, 1864, Letters Received, VRC, RG 110.

22. Resolution dealing with the formation of an Invalid Corps, Officers of Burnside Barracks, near Indianapolis, Ind. 1863 [October 22, 1863?], George Wagner Collection.

23. Emil Munch to [—], June 23, 1863, and Colonel Richard H. Rush to Captain Emil Munch, August 19, 1863, Emil Munch Papers, Minnesota Historical Society, St. Paul.

24. S. S. Stevens to Abraham Lincoln, September 14, 1864, Letters Received, VRC, RG 110.

25. Colonel S. D. Oliphant to Captain J. D. De Forest, November 6, 1865, Letters Received, VRC, RG 110.

26. Colonel J. C. Strong and Major D. F. Foley to Brigadier General Fry, November 11, 1865, copy forwarded by Brevet Colonel R. E. Johnston, Letters Received, VRC, RG 110; Lieutenant Colonel F. E. Trotter to Captain J. T. Durang, January 12, 1866; Lieutenant Adolph Glackmeyer to J. T. Durang, February 17, March 4, 1866, Durang Papers.

27. Major A. G. Brady to Brigadier General J. B. Fry, November 14, 1865, Letters Received, VRC, RG 110; Lieutenant Colonel F. E. Trotter to E. W. Everson, January 13, 1866, Erastus W. Everson Papers, South Carolina Historical Society, Charleston; endorsement of Major F. A. H. Gaebel, November 10, 1865, on Captain J. D. De Forest to Commanding Officer, 16th Vet. Res. Corps, November 3, 1865, Letters Received, VRC, RG 110.

28. The provost marshal general's VRC files in RG 110 contain numerous examples of letters from politicians and others asking Stanton to delay action

concerning the consolidation of the Corps on behalf of their VRC constituents, some of which are cited below.

29. Colonel E. P. Fyffe et al. to E. M. Stanton [August 1865], Letters Received, VRC, RG 110, and numerous other petitions scattered throughout this collection. There was a printed form, probably provided by the committee, that the officers used or copied.

30. Undated endorsement of E. W. Everson on [E.] Gault to E. W. Everson, October 5, 1865, Erastus W. Everson Papers, South Carolina Historical Society, Charleston.

31. R. E. Trowbridge to E. M. Stanton, December 13, 1864, August 29, 1865, Letters Rec'd, VRC, RG 110; Station Books, vol. 1, 1867–1868, reel 35, Records of the Assistant Commissioner for the State of Georgia, Bureau of Refugees, Freedmen, and Abandoned Lands, National Archives Microfilm M798; John J. Knox, Pension File, Civil War Pensions, RG 15.

32. Charles F. Johnson to Mary Johnson, July 18, 1863, Archives, US Army Military History Institute, Carlisle, Pennsylvania (hereinafter cited as USAMHI).

33. Charles F. Johnson to Mary Johnson, August 27, 1863, USAMHI.

34. Johnson's career is documented in the voluminous collection of letters between him and his wife, Mary, in the Charles F. Johnson Papers, USAMHI. For a description of the White House Landing fight, see *Trenton (N.J.) Daily State Gazette,* June 30, 1864.

35. Captain P. Devyer to Captain A. J. Marsh, December 15, 1863, Regimental Papers, 11th VRC, AGO, RG 94.

36. Major F. A. H. Gaebel to Major R. T. Dodge, February 2, 1865, Letters Received, VRC, RG 110.

37. Major F. A. H. Gaebel to Major General Lorenzo Thomas, November 8, 1865, Letters Received, VRC, RG 110.

38. Captain C. L. Clark to Lieutenant Colonel Frederick S. Palmer, November 10, 1864, Miscellaneous Papers, VRC, AGO, RG 94; Captain Garrett Nagle to Captain J. W. De Forest, October 17, 1865, Letters Received, VRC, RG 110.

39. Cimbala, "Soldiering on the Home Front," 182–218.

40. *New York Times,* April 21, 1866.

41. *Indianapolis Daily Journal,* August 25, October 19, 1865.

42. M. Russell Thayer to E. M. Stanton, August 14, 1865; and T. A. Hendricks to E. M. Stanton, August 21, 1865, Letters Received, VRC, RG 110.

43. Governor F. K. Smith to E. M. Stanton, August 18, 1865, Letters Received, VRC, RG 110.

44. D. Morris to E. M. Stanton, August 2, 1865; and C. Baker to E. M. Stanton, August 19, 1865, Letters Received, VRC, RG 110.

45. *Indianapolis Daily Journal,* December 7, 1865. See Thomas M. Vincent to Chief Mustering Officers, November 30, 1865, Letters Received, VRC, RG 110; and General Orders, No. 165, November 24, 1865, AGO, Library, USAMHI.

46. A. Wheeler to Alexander H. Reis, April 17, 1866, reel 30, Registers and Letters Received by the Commissioner of the Bureau of Refugees, Freedmen, and Abandoned Lands, 1865–1872, National Archives Microfilm Publication M752 (hereafter cited as BRFAL, M752).

47. US Congress, *House Journal,* 39th Cong., 1st sess., December, 13, 1865, p. 38; US Congress, *Senate Journal,* 39th Cong., 2nd sess., July 18, 1866, p. 1050.

48. Second Lieutenant George Barton to O. O. Howard, May 19, 1865, reel 13; A. Wheeler to A. H. Rice, April 17, 1866, reel 30; Second Lieutenant S. W. McClure to G. S. Orth, May 1, 1866, reel 28; Second Lieutenant John J. Toffey to Ooh, May 12, 1866, reel 30; First Lieutenant A. W. Lomas to Brevet Brigadier General C. H. Howard, June 11, 1866, reel 31, BRFAL, M752; Second Lieutenant William A. MacNulty to O. O. Howard, September 5, 1865, Letters Received, VRC, RG 110.

49. First Lieutenant M. M. Kistler to Major General O. O. Howard, May 10, 1866, and enclosures; First Lieutenant M. M. Kistler to E. M. Stanton, May 11, 1866, reel 28, BRFAL, M752.

50. Second Lieutenant G. Barton to O. O. Howard, May 19, 1865, reel 13, BRFAL, M752.

51. C. E. Campbell to O. O. Howard, July 28, 1866, reel 31, BRFAL, M752.

52. Second Lieutenant James Walker to Major General O. O. Howard, May 12, 1866, reel 30, BRFAL, M752.

53. First Lieutenant Henry F. Wallace to Colonel Maxwell Woodhull, April 24, 1866, reel 30, BRFAL, M752.

54. For a general survey of the duties of the Bureau, see George R. Bentley, *A History of the Freedmen's Bureau* (Philadelphia: Univ. of Pennsylvania Press, 1954; reprint, New York: Octagon Books, 1974).

55. First Lieutenant J. S. Taylor to Major General O. O. Howard, April 22, 1866, reel 30, BRFAL, M752.

56. Captain James A. Bates to Colonel Haggert, August 24, 1865, reel 13, BRFAL, M752.

57. Lieutenant J. Arnold Yeckley to Captain James A. Bates, April 19, 1866, reel 30, BRFAL, M752.

58. First Lieutenant F. J. Massey to Brevet Brigadier General Orlando Brown, May 1, 1866, reel 32, BRFAL, M752.

59. E. W. Everson to Major E. L. Deane, December 9, 1867, reel 12, Records of the Assistant Commissioner for the State of South Carolina, National Archives Microfilm Publication M869.

60. Captain Samuel A. Craig, "Memoirs of Civil War and Reconstruction," 77–83, USAMHI. For the problematic climate in Reconstruction Texas, see Barry A. Crouch, *The Freedmen's Bureau and Black Texans* (Austin: Univ. of Texas Press, 1992).

61. Cimbala, *Under the Guardianship of the Nation,* 76–77, 128, 210.

62. Major J. J. Knox to T. D. Elliot, December 30, 1867, vol. 169, Letters Sent, Athens Subassistant Commissioner, Field Offices, State of Georgia, Bureau of

Refugees, Freedmen, and Abandoned Lands, Record Group 105, National Archives Building, Washington, D.C.

63. Major General T. J. Wood to Major General O. O. Howard, May 5, 1866, reel 28, BRFAL, M752; Paul A. Cimbala, "Reconstruction's Allies: The Relationship of the Freedmen's Bureau and the Georgia Freedmen," in *The Freedmen's Bureau and Reconstruction: Reconsiderations,* ed. Paul A. Cimbala and Randall M. Miller (New York: Fordham Univ. Press, 1999), 329–31.

64. W. B. Blanding to Henry R. Anthony, June 4, 1866, reel 28, BRFAL, M752.

65. Roster of Officers, State of Mississippi, Bureau of Refugees, Freedmen, and Abandoned Lands, March 1866; Major General Thomas J. Wood to Major General O. O. Howard, May 4, 1866, reel 28, BRFAL, M752.

66. Captain Silas May to Lieutenant Stuart Eldridge, May 3, 1866, reel 28, BRFAL, M752.

67. Jabez E. Blanding, Pension File, Civil War Pensions, RG 15.

68. General Orders, No. 116, June 17, 1865; General Orders, No. 155, October 26, 1865; General Orders, No. 165, November 24, 1865; General Orders, No. 56, August 1, 1866; General Orders, No. 92, November 23, 1866; and General Orders, No. 16, 1869, Adjutant General's Office, War Department, trace the consolidation of the VRC. The orders are bound and on file in the library of the US Army Military History Institute, Carlisle, Pennsylvania.

69. Benjamin C. Cook, Pension File, Civil War Pensions, RG 15.

70. John Ely, Pension File, Civil War Pensions, RG 15.

4

"Bent on Suicide"

The Political Rhetoric of Suicide in the Civil War–Era South

Diane Miller Sommerville

> A friend of mine once said, "You know what I learned in high school? I learned that the greatest days of the South were the heroic years from 1861 to '65 during which she was committing suicide."
>
> —James McBride Dabbs, 1962

As the nation throttled toward disunion and news of Confederate batteries unleashing on federal forces at Fort Sumter spread, Sarah Palmer, a northern woman teaching in Knoxville, Tennessee, encountered William "Parson" Brownlow, a native southerner and prominent preacher, editor, and politician, on a walk. She broached the alarming matter of secession with the well-known parson, who commiserated: "Ah, my dear Miss Palmer, it is bad, bad news for the whole country; but still worse for the South itself. It is suicide!"[1]

Brownlow was not alone in bathing the political crisis of secession and disunion in the language of self-destruction. In fact, the political rhetoric of suicide proliferated in northern and southern presses, speeches, and letters. Whether it was the *New York Herald* denouncing secession—"This is worse than folly. It is absolute suicide."[2]—or the *Charleston Mercury* placing the blame on northern actions—"How the Yankees have committed suicide!"[3]—the language and imagery of suicide appeared frequently in the political discourse during the secession crisis and then during the war.

Antebellum northerners and southerners deployed the rhetoric and imagery of suicide in the discourse of disunion for two reasons. One, it resonated widely with most Americans, regardless of region, class, ethnicity, or gender; and two, it aptly and effectively conveyed the severity of the political crisis in a way few other images could. Very simply, political discourse harnessing suicide imagery emphatically condemned the path to civil war, which was to be avoided at all costs. Nearly all Americans had been steeped in the religious and cultural taboo against suicide, so they well understood the implications: national suicide was self-inflicted, immoral, shameful, and unforgivable. Political suicide was lethal and permanent and helped to delegitimize opposing views and actions. This near universal association of suicide with exceedingly negative connotations before and during the war, however, eventually gave way to a competing version in the postwar South, one that painted suicide as heroic and courageous.[4]

This essay explores the changed meaning of suicide that grew out of civil war and defeat. Confederates, enveloped in extreme emotional, psychological, and material suffering during and after the Civil War, had become more familiar with incidents of suicide. Distraught soldiers, southern statesmen, and civilians turned to self-murder in order to exit personal misery, shame, loss, hopelessness, and war-related trauma and distress.[5] Consequently, the war hastened a reassessment of the taboo of suicide that came to engender greater sympathy toward its practitioners and an amelioration of its association with cowardice, sinfulness, and insanity, the attributes attached to the act of self-murder in antebellum America. The more sympathetic reception of suicide in the wartime South, including a greater willingness to consider self-destruction a reasonable response to defeat and devastation, appears in the evolving meaning of suicide as it was used in the political discourse about secession and civil war.

At the outset of war, the language of suicide was harnessed to extreme denunciations of actions deemed to be existential threats to the fundamental principles and values of northerners and southerners. But by war's end, when defeat of the Confederacy was all but certain, stunned white southerners reflected on the actions that had led to the demise of their short-lived nation and its way of life predicated on slavery. Had their vaunted efforts to secede and form a slaveholding republic, actions that in fact led to the death of slavery and, with it, the slaveholder's way of life, been suicidal after all? The imagery of suicide, in the wake of defeat and the nascent rise of the Lost Cause mentalité, began to take on new meaning, meaning that came to shed its most deplorable and sinful connotations while valorizing and romanticizing the act of self-murder in order to sanitize and reimagine the reasons for their treasonous, senseless, costly decision to take up arms against the United States. Rather than accept responsibility for the suicidal attempt at independence and its resultant scourge of death and destruction throughout the South, ex-Confederates instead refashioned suicide as laudable, heroic, and reasonable, and they appropriated new representations of self-destruction that they used effectively to launch the Lost Cause and with it a reimagining of the causes of secession and comportment of Confederates.

The infusion of political discourse with suicidal imagery was not new to antebellum America. The founding generation regularly invoked the language of suicide in discussions about the viability of the new nation. Alexander Hamilton alluded to suicide in his political writings as a point of emphasis. In advancing his program of debt relief, for example, Hamilton equated the government's failure to provide for the public debt with self-destruction: "It would have been an act of suicide in the Government at the very commencement of its existence."[6] Later, in making the case for a tough stance against France for its depredations against the United States, he cautioned, "The honor of a nation is its life. Deliberately to abandon it is to commit an act of political suicide."[7] Perhaps most famously, John Adams channeled a longstanding fear about republics collapsing from within. "There was never a democracy that did not commit suicide."[8] As Richard Bell has argued, early Americans, consumed by fears that the fragile republic would succumb to political and societal instability and disorder, regularly invoked the language of suicide, a reflection of their own deeply held anxieties and insecurities.[9]

The rhetorical device of invoking the language of suicide in early republican political discourse captured the gravity of political events and crises in a way that other allusions could not, which no doubt explains its embrace by those writing and talking about secession and civil war in the mid-nineteenth century. Shaping the disunion narrative around self-murder enabled writers and politicians to underscore the lethality of the act, something that distinguished it from all previous crises in the run up to the Civil War. Northern publications warned that allowing southern states to secede was akin to national suicide. "A surrender to secession is the suicide of government," opined the *Cincinnati Daily Commercial* in May 1861.[10]

Littell's Living Age reprinted a piece from early 1861 that suggested the threat of disunion presented an opportunity to "emancipate ourselves from moral servitude to a community of slave-owners." If not, "it will be national suicide."[11] Southern Unionists employed the rhetoric of suicide to try to dissuade their home states from leaving the Union. In likening secession to death by suicide, former Whig and president of the Virginia secession convention John Janney tried to convince others of the enormity of their vote for disunion.[12] Virginia countryman John D. Sharp likewise opposed secession, decrying it an act of political suicide that would "aggravate an hundred fold every grievance complained of, rather than remedy a single one."[13] Similarly, Robert Toombs of Georgia famously opposed Jefferson Davis's proposed attack on Fort Sumter, warning, "Mr. President, at this time it is suicide, murder, and will lose us every friend at the North. You will wantonly strike a hornet's nest which extends from mountains to ocean, and legions, now quiet, will swarm out and sting us to death. It is unnecessary; it puts us in the wrong; it is fatal."[14] Like Toombs, North Carolinian Jonathan Worth equated secession with self-murder. "I think the South is committing suicide." He nonetheless resigned to going down with the doomed ship. "My lot is cast with the South and being unable to manage the ship, I intend to face the breakers manfully and go down with my companions."[15] A year into the war, Worth, while steadfastly loyal to his new country, repeated his condemnation of the region's ruinous path: "The South, with one voice, seems bent on suicide."[16] Alexander Stephens, who would go on to become the Confederacy's vice president, castigated his Georgia brethren for their "unwise and ill-timed measure" and warned that posterity would hold them to "strict account for this suicidal act."[17]

Allusions to political suicide during the secession crisis were usually paired with extremely negative and disapproving language, couching denunciation of actions and decisions in the most emphatic, alarming way possible. An editorial in the Democratic-leaning *New York Herald,* for instance, denounced northern actions as "signs of a national suicide so atrocious, so wicked, that they have caused sober minded men everywhere to shrink with dismay from the prospect which is opening before them."[18] The *Herald* bemoaned the slide into civil war following bloodshed at Fort Sumter, referring to the crisis as a "hideous national suicide."[19] The abolitionist Wendell Phillips evoked ghastly imagery when he announced to a Boston audience in August 1861 that "The South has cut her own throat. . . . She has consummated her own suicide."[20] In condemning political suicide in such graphic, stark language, both northerners and southerners drew on longstanding cultural and religious attitudes that denounced suicide as sinful, injudicious, and even folly.[21]

Both supporters and opponents of secession weaponized the language of self-destruction and, in doing so, highlighted the illegitimacy of separation and warfare by conveying the criminality of suicide and, by extension, the criminality of political maneuvering that led to disunion. The *Carrollton Sun* of Louisiana blamed "Lincoln rulers" and the "ruinous consequences" of their actions for provoking southerners into embracing secession. "Suicide is no less a crime when committed by a nation than by an individual."[22] The *New York Journal of Commerce* condemned separation as unlawful, a "rash and dreadful crime of national suicide."[23] Suicide, long regarded a form of murder at law, remained "on the books" as a crime in most states, even if rarely enforced. So, in framing secession, or events leading to secession, as suicidal (and hence criminal), protagonists hoped to delegitimize the efforts of the opposition.[24]

Deploying the language of suicide in sectionalism discourse also tainted the offending act or acts with irrationality, further discrediting opponents' views on secession. Medical authorities as well as most laypeople believed that those who committed suicide were driven to do so by "insanity," a belief premised on the assumption that sane persons would never take their own lives.[25] In Victorian America, suicide was *prima facie* evidence of lack of reason among its practitioners; suicidal actors were, by definition, insane.[26] Political commentators, then, sought to discredit acts by individuals or governments by tainting them with suicidal references, suffusing those acts with hints of insanity or madness. Secessionists embraced the language of suicide and madness when they denounced US mobilization after Fort Sumter as crazy and foolish. "It is not the mere existence of the Government that the mad North is now testing. It is its capacities for mischief—its powers of self-destruction. The not infrequent end of a long career of folly, vice and phrensy, is suicide. It is upon this last act of madness and despair, that the North is rushing the Government."[27] Northerners likewise framed their critiques of secession as mad. The *Liberator,* upon learning that Virginia had followed the path of other slaveholding states and seceded, derided the decision, asserting, "she raves and rages like a suicide, and will destroy herself at least, if not restrained by those who can see her difficulty, and are strong enough to save her from destruction."[28] A correspondent with the *Washington National Intelligencer* speculated about the sanity of southerners who stood to lose their slave property in the wake of war. He marveled that slave "contraband," now under confiscation by federal military authorities, was costing southerners thousands of dollars in lost property. He asked rhetorically, "What has the

South done to herself?," then answered, "Destroyed her own cherished institution. How true '*Quem Deis,*'" a truncated reference to a Latin phrase meaning, "whom the gods would destroy, they first make mad."[29] Methodist minister Daniel Steele delivered a sermon in September 1861 in Massachusetts in which he, too, extensively deployed suicidal language that equated the slide into war with lunacy. He demanded to know what "wo[e]ful insanity" transformed brother into murderer. In a sermon entitled "The Cause, the Crime, and the Cure of our National Suicide," Steele pondered how a "large section of the nation" had become "so demented." Stoking the image of a mad South, Steele asked, "what baneful, malignant power has disordered her intellect, and fired her brain with wild delirium?"[30] Critics of political acts and principles who deployed suicidal rhetoric effectively maligned them as lunacy, thus depriving them of credibility.

Ministers like Steele wielded enormous influence through their denunciations of political events as suicidal. Northern clergy censured seceding southern states, analogizing their actions as suicidal while imbuing condemnations with sacred credibility and authority. As Steele preached, "Suicide has always been considered, by Christian moralists, the most culpable form of murder." A sinful act, self-murder rendered those who committed it unredeemable, making it "a crime against God."[31] Other ministers followed suit and framed their critiques of political developments in the religious condemnation of suicide. Reverend Egbert Smyth, on a day of fasting and prayer, warned against disunion by underscoring the sinfulness of suicide and preaching that "God has made us a nation; and, if we perish, we fall by a suicide as much more enormous in its wickedness than the self-destruction of an individual, as a nation is vaster and nobler than any of its members."[32] The Reverend B. Sadtler of Pennsylvania likewise equated disunion with self-destruction: "Secession is national suicide. . . . By the help of God, Secessionism shall succumb."[33] While not a minister, Unionist Joseph Holt of Kentucky invoked God when he advocated "a war of duty" against the South because "under our Christian civilization no nation can commit suicide without the perpetration of a cowardly and infamous crime; but morally at least, that nation does commit suicide, which surrenders up its life to an enemy from which courage and manhood could have saved it."[34] The Reverend Doctor Stephen H. Tyng of St. George's Episcopal Church in New York City and editor of the *Protestant Churchman* blamed southern states for the war but warned, "The people are ready to pour out copiously their best blood, and also uncounted material treasure, in arrest of national suicide."[35] Just as an individual's act of suicide was judged to be sinful and an affront to God, so too was a nation's suicide.

Southern ministers likewise fused suicidal imagery with their denunciations of the political crisis. The *Macon Telegraph* reprinted what appears to have been a summary of a sermon excerpt delivered by Episcopal bishop Stephen Elliott in response to Jefferson Davis's call for a fast day in August 1863. Elliott castigated the South for its displays of corruption and venality. Armies might destroy a "noble people," he conceded, but at least they are not "lost to themselves, to posterity, or to God." He continued: "But the wretched suicide by his own degrading and besotting vices, is alike loathed by himself and abhorred by all goodness."[36] Wartime southerners, by abandoning virtue, were choosing a path of loathsome self-murder.

In addition to violating religious precepts, political suicide constituted an assault on democracy and an affront to the nation's common heritage and history. Some speakers used suicidal rhetoric to cast disunion as anathema to the grand republican experiment and to the nation's glorious past. Senator Milton Latham of California denounced disunion and worried that "We shall be held to a terrible account by humanity, even for having blasted all hopes of the success of republican institutions; and by a monstrous national suicide, forever destroying the popular faith in self-government."[37] Senator Joseph Holt of Kentucky implied the shamefulness of political suicide by appealing to the shared heritage of sacrifice in the nation's war for independence. "Our fathers won independence by the blood and sacrifices of a seven years' war and we have maintained it against the assaults of the greatest power upon the earth; and the question is now whether we are to perish by our own hands and have the epitaph of the suicide written upon our tomb."[38] An indignant Reverend Daniel Steele played the exceptionalism card as well, demanding to know, "Can a nation with such a history and such a future, madly destroy herself?"[39] One northern publication judged the destruction of a nation "a thousand times worse than suicide" because it entailed the "destruction of posterity" as well.[40]

Framing disunion as suicide also allowed commentators to challenge the logic of those willing to commit political suicide, which, paradoxically, subverted their goals. An anonymous author questioned the reasoning of secessionists who sought to "dissolve the Union to escape the hostile opinion of the North." Their response, he asserted, constituted extreme overreaction. "This remedy is far worse than the disease; it is taking yellow fever to cure dyspepsia—voluntary suicide."[41] A prominent Presbyterian pastor from

Buffalo also pointed out the contradiction of secessionists choosing disunion and (presumably) defeat. In seceding, was not the South accomplishing the very thing that abolitionists had been trying to do in vain for thirty years? "Will a brave man commit suicide because his life is threatened by a ruffian hitherto baffled of his purpose?"[42] A Pennsylvania pamphleteer, in assessing his state's political situation in February 1861, embraced the same argument, but turned it against abolitionists of the North. He exposed the folly of accepting disunion and national dismemberment over the issue of slavery. "'But slavery!' you exclaim. 'We cannot abide it. It is an accursed thing!' Very well, we will not argue the point; suppose it is an accursed thing. Do you mean to commit political suicide, in order to get rid of it?"[43] Reports that the rebels were engaged in wholesale destruction of property, including levees, in order to impede the progress of federal armies prompted a correspondent for the *New York Herald* to remark on the self-harm southerners were inflicting on their region: "There never was a suicide committed by a people more complete than that the South is now perpetuating upon itself."[44] For some, national suicide exacted too high a price in the country's squabble over slavery and secession.

Robust use of suicide rhetoric can be discerned in the debate over whether secession was permitted under the US Constitution. Those who answered in the negative equated secession with revolution. James A. Hamilton, son of Founding Father Alexander Hamilton and a New York lawyer, explained that a rebellion was tantamount to political suicide. "When the people of a state . . . rise up in rebellion against the Government, and use the organs of their state to destroy the Government of the United States, they destroy the organism of their State Government, and thus accomplish the political suicide of their State Government. The Soul of the State remains, but its organs are destroyed."[45] Peter Cooper, a New York City industrialist, inventor, and philanthropist, insisted that neither the Constitution nor "events or circumstances" since its adoption sanctioned disunion. To illustrate the "peculiar process" of secession he borrowed from a speech delivered by the duke of Argyle on the American crisis. In making his point that it strained credulity to consider that any government in the world would concede the right of secession, the duke recounted the peculiar antics of a starfish native to Scotland. When brought to the surface, the creature "performs the most extraordinary and unaccountable acts of suicide and self-destruction." In the grasp of a perceived enemy, the starfish "throws off all of its arms" and nothing remains "but a thousand wriggling fragments." The beautiful creature, like the South, Cooper implied, destroyed itself rather than risk being destroyed by a predator.[46] In the end, it is destroyed either way. A letter published in the *Liberator* in February 1864 concurred that secession was incompatible with governance, denying that states could legally separate from the Union. "Secession in the United States has but one meaning—revolution, which is no more constitutional than suicide."[47] And a few months before the onset of hostilities, the *New York Herald* pointed out that the first law and necessity of government is self-preservation. "It will not commit suicide, and cannot permit its destruction at the hands of malcontents."[48]

Secessionists, sensitive to accusations of political suicide, were put on the defensive when pressed to justify their withdrawal from the Union, seemingly an act of national destruction. They shifted instead to a different position, one that insisted that the right of secession (national self-murder) existed in the US Constitution, but was to be invoked only as a last resort under extraordinary circumstances, a stance that allowed Confederates to continue to cling to the idea that political suicide was anathema—except when a people were as aggrieved and violated as southerners had been. A Raleigh newspaper, arguing that national suicide was warranted, introduced a discussion of the constitutional question of secession with two quotes about political suicide, the first attributed to an antisecession delegate to the Georgia secession convention—"Tis Liberty forging its own chain; happiness poisoning its own cup; prosperity committing suicide,"—the second to the "Paris presse": "For the American Union, separation is suicide; it is the murder of a great nation, and a great principle. France cannot lend a hand to this suicide and this murder." By conceding that the stakes of secession were serious—the deployment of suicide rhetoric formed an implicit acknowledgment that the issue had grave consequences—the author of the editorial aimed to imbue his position with credibility by allowing that only extraordinary and compelling circumstances could justify separation from the federal government. The compact that was the Constitution of the United States had been violated and southern states suffered an egregious wrong. The remedy, secession, might well constitute suicide, but slaveholding states were left with no alternative.[49]

As the tide turned against the Confederacy and defeat loomed, some stalwarts harnessed the language of suicide to admonish fellow southerners to avoid surrender at all costs, to spur a depleted, dejected people. Reverend William Hall in 1864 quoted Edmund Burke: nations "are never murdered; they commit suicide—never destroyed by external power, they sink under their own corruptions and cowardice. If, therefore, the Southern people are what they profess to be. . . . then is the subjugation of the South an absolute historical impossibility."[50] Confederate boosters, hoping to buoy a despairing people they feared might give up in the face of northern victory, attempted to shame southerners with the taint of contemptible suicide by equating capitulation with suicide and its long-established association with spiritual and moral weakness; giving up would signal degeneracy and cowardice, a perpetuation of longstanding negative connotations associated with self-murder. Weeks before Lee surrendered, the rebel Congress issued a call for perseverance and resolve. Also invoking the famous words of Burke—that "Nations never are murdered—they commit suicide"—the Congress implored, "Let us not be guilty of the folly and the crime of self-destruction. Let us show the fortitude, endurance and courage that belong to our race."[51] Surrender, then, was equated with suicide, submission a mark of dishonor. The *Richmond Examiner* went so far as to predict that the Confederacy would turn to "suicide" only as a last resort and after having been utterly exhausted. "Nothing but utter hopelessness will ever induce them to commit the suicide of a nation."[52] After Lee's surrender, southerner J. W. Yale wrote, "And now we are a subjugated People. . . . How did it befall us, that is [the] worst part. We conquered ourselves, committed Suicide—Such a people does not deserve independence."[53] Surrender, a form of self-destruction, could only be understood as the failure of a people's character. The repugnant view of suicide continued to hold considerable sway in the thinking of southerners.

As Confederates debated surrender, wondering whether capitulation was tantamount to self-destruction, Republicans in Congress latched onto suicide as a way to imagine the status of rebel states that had left the nation and to plan for their reentry into the Union. As federal troops made inroads into the South and occupied areas of the Confederacy, Congress and the president grappled with how to govern those regions and searched for a constitutional and theoretical basis for reintegrating those state entities back into the United States. Lincoln had regarded secession as illegal. The southern states, to his mind, never actually left the Union; their governments, though, comprised of rebels, were illegitimate. Lincoln theorized that all that would be needed to bring the errant states back into the fold would be to replace the rebel governments with new, loyal officials. But Lincoln's critics questioned his premise, that slaveholding states had in fact never left the Union. Radical Republican Thaddeus Stevens argued that by seceding the southern states had ceased to exist as legal entities and should be rightly regarded as conquered provinces. Enter Senator Charles Sumner, another Radical Republican, who embraced what he termed the "state suicide theory." To his mind, states that had seceded had committed political or state suicide. Through this lens, Radicals viewed secession as a treasonous act by which Confederate states "forfeited their rights as states and, so as to be civilly dead."[54]

As early as February 1862, Sumner had introduced to Congress a resolution declaring that seceded states had abdicated all their rights under the Constitution, thereby forfeiting the functions and powers of a state and reverting to the status of territories. Confederate states would become, "according to the language of the law, *felo-de-se*."[55] *Felo de se* is a Latin term used in English common law to define and classify suicide as a felony. In early modern England, a coroner's finding of *felo de se* signaled the suicide as completion of a deliberate, fatal, and punishable act, which permitted the state to seize the suicide's property. The suicide in this case, the Confederacy, was adjudged to have possessed full faculties and committed suicide in a rational state of mind, and so was undeserving of leniency. By contrast, a *non compos mentis* determination concluded that the decedent had not been of sound mind at the time of the self-destructive act, and thus could not be held accountable. Leniency, in this case, not punishment, should be extended. A *non compos mentis* verdict spared the suicide's family embarrassment and possible religious and state sanctions.[56]

Sumner's choice of words in invoking the suicide metaphor for southern secession, his labeling it *felo de se,* conveyed the same weighty connotations as the legal term: it was a deliberate, rational, and punishable act, meriting severe retribution, not leniency, which contrasted sharply with Presidential Reconstruction plans. Sumner elaborated on the lethality of the Confederacy's actions in an essay that appeared in the *Atlantic Monthly* over a year later. "It is sometimes said that the states themselves committed suicide, so that as States they ceased to exist, leaving their whole jurisdiction open to the occupation of the United States under the Constitution." The rebelling states had forfeited their rights "so as to be civilly dead" and thus had "abdicated their places in the Union." The willful act of self-destruction by the Confederate states mandated submission to the victorious Union and forced them to leave "their whole jurisdiction open to the occupation of the United States under the Constitution."[57]

But complete submission including forfeiture of rights proved difficult for former Confederates to swallow and they rejected Sumner's theory of state suicide. As Georgians considered the terms of reunion, they equated acceptance of the odious stipulations, especially the ratification of the Fourteenth Amendment, with suicide. They drew a distinction between acquiescing (suicide) and being forced to accept peace terms (murder), with the latter being preferable. "If Georgia is to be sacrificed and reduced to a mere dependency of a despotic central government, with all her liberties destroyed, she prefers to suffer this fate at the hands of others and not her own. If to die, she prefers murder to suicide."[58] The US government would have to impose its conditions for peace on a defeated people, who would have no hand in their own degradation. Confederates might well have no choice in the matter, but they would not be complicit in their own demise. Surrender, in peace as in war, was an abomination. Georgia's "death" would be effected by the enemy occupier; she herself would not take part in her own destruction. By refusing to capitulate to Union demands, Georgians believed themselves "innocent of suicide" and better able to "bear our fate with that proud fortitude."[59]

Even well after defeat, and as the US Congress debated the future of the former Confederate states, white southerners refused to concede they had committed political suicide. They distinguished between acts of self-injury and those imposed by outside forces, the latter being preferable to the former, a feat that also absolved southerners of agency. The *Macon Telegraph*, for example, expressed resignation in the face of harsh legislative measures sure to come. "Whatever may come now, will be imposed upon us by the strong arm of military power, and there is no dishonor in acquiescing in what we are powerless to prevent. It is a very different thing to voluntary self-abasement, no matter under what apprehension it is conceded. It is just the difference between murder and suicide."[60] Better to be a victim of murder than suicide. Jonathan Worth, governor of postwar North Carolina, said as much when considering that state's response to Congressional Reconstruction measures, including disfranchisement of southern white men and the suffrage of black men. "If we are to be utterly ruined, which now seems probable, the general feeling is that it is not justifiable to commit suicide even to avoid being hanged."[61] Civil and political death might well prove unavoidable in a newly configured, defeated South, but it should not be accomplished by its own hands. A Virginia newspaper, even before the war had ended, explained, "If such a calamity is to befall us we infinitely prefer that Lincoln shall be the instrument of our disaster and degradation, than ourselves should strike the cowardly and suicidal blow."[62]

Throughout the war and the earliest years of Reconstruction, southerners clung to the notion that suicide, political or otherwise, was abhorrent, cowardly, and unmanly. They doggedly denied they had committed suicide by seceding and executing civil war. But in the years after surrender, ex-Confederates, awash in desolation and despair, reflected on the high cost of their rebellion and began to wonder. The deaths of hundreds of thousands of its men and boys, the legions of disabled veterans, and pervasive financial calamity called into question the wisdom of secession and war. The institution of slavery, which the Confederacy fought to preserve, had ended. Had the short-lived southern independence movement been suicidal after all?

Ultimately, former Confederates and their descendants doubled down, denying what had been obvious to those who launched civil war, that slavery was its root cause, and insisting that secession had been a legitimate and legal response to the federal government's abrogation of their constitutional rights. But they also had to account for their self-inflicted demise and failure. In doing so, they crafted a new postwar narrative, one that reconceptualized secession and civil war as suicidal, but that purged the imagery of self-murder of its dishonorable attributes and instead lauded the ill-fated disunion attempt as virtuous and commendable.[63]

Southerners after the war pivoted to a different, more heroic understanding of suicide to avoid considering that their actions had been irrational, selfish, unmanly, and immoral, the traits closely identified with suicide before and during the war. Thus, the Civil War, as Richard Bell has conjectured in the conclusion to his fine study on suicide rhetoric in early America, "recast the relationship between suicide and citizenship."[64] Not only did postbellum southerners enthusiastically embrace with pride the political act of self-destruction, it became elevated as a cornerstone of Lost Cause canon. A reconfiguration and reassessment of the contemptible ideas about suicide emerged as white southerners crafted a (re)definition of political suicide that was heroic and honorable, and in the process jettisoned the negative connotations previously associated with self-destruction.

Southerners began to couch their submission to federal Reconstruction policies as martyrdom. The former Confederate general John B. Gordon, who vigorously resisted Radical Reconstruction, opposed calling a constitutional convention in Georgia to address mandated changes in state government, including black suffrage. "If perish we must, as Tennessee has perished, let us welcome rather the epitaph of the martyr rather than that of suicide."[65] While Gordon's distinction between martyrdom and suicide seems more rhetorical than real, the change in language signals a deliberate effort to recast self-destruction as honorable. Such changes can be detected in Lost Cause explanations for the South's committing national suicide. Whites in the postwar South, exercising herculean contortions of intellect and reason, increasingly embraced the suicide motif in reimagining Confederate political and military actions that led to war. Benjamin Hill, a former Confederate senator from Georgia, who had opposed secession, conceded that disunion had been imprudent. Reflecting fifteen years after the start of war, Hill, like so many other white southerners, pondered the meaning of the ill-fated independence effort. "Whatever else may be said of secession—and I conceded it was a madness—it was at least manly and direct. . . . It was unwise and suicidal, but still brave and manly."[66] By acknowledging that the Confederate experiment may have been a mistake, Hill nonetheless upheld the good and honorable intentions of the insurgents. Unwise? Yes. Mad? Yes. But now heroic—honorable, manly, brave.

Another illustration of southern efforts to reconceive the meaning of political suicide can be found in a story appearing in the pages of *Southern Magazine,* an influential publication devoted to the perpetuation of the Lost Cause. In January 1873, it featured a historical account of a failed exploit by the US Navy in the First Barbary War in which a ship, the *Intrepid,* packed with explosives, was to have sneaked into the Tripoli harbor and blow itself up, taking the enemy fleet with it. Instead, the *Intrepid* exploded prematurely, killing at least thirteen crew members including Lieutenant Richard Somers, who had volunteered to command the unconventional mission. While the author allowed that one might question the "morality" of an expedition that included a "provisional suicide," one could only admire Somers for his heroic sacrifice to country. Somers was heralded for being "exceedingly chivalrous."[67] Somers's death was not exactly a willful self-murder, but, the story suggests, the mission was so inherently risky that one could properly regard it as "provisionally" suicidal. Accordingly, the account praised Somers for his willingness to sacrifice himself for the cause.

Yet another example of the reconstituted definition of political suicide in the postwar South appears in a collection of wartime reminiscences published by the Missouri chapter of the United Daughters of the Confederacy (UDC) at the turn of the twentieth century.[68] The setting is an unidentified occupied southern town where a war widow engaged Union soldiers in a tense exchange about the recent president's assassination, proclaiming that Lincoln had "gotten his just desserts" by being murdered. The following day, Union soldiers, intent on retribution, visited the home of the "rebel sympathizer" and insisted that she deck the outside of her home in black drape out of respect for the dead president. When she refused, soldiers restrained her and searched her home, which yielded a long crape veil, part of the bereavement outfit she wore following the deaths of her husband at Antietam and her fifteen-year-old son, a drummer boy who had also perished in battle. Eventually the Confederate woman agreed to display the black veil as bunting on her veranda, but on the condition that she be left alone to do so. Onlookers gathered across the way where they watched intently as the widow emerged onto the veranda dressed in black mourning clothes, the crape veil cascading from her shoulder. She slowly mounted a chair and threw the veil, which had been wrapped around her neck, over fretwork above. Unexpectedly, the woman pushed the chair with her foot and, to the astonishment and horror of spectators, hanged herself and perished.[69]

It is not clear how much of this story is true, how much it is embellished, or whether it is entirely fabricated. The veracity of the account is less important than the political meaning attached to the Confederate woman's suicide, fictional or not. The widow, Mrs. Stuart, remained defiant to the end: she had refused to evacuate despite federal orders to do so, swearing she would only leave her house carried out "feet first." Death would come before acquiescing to the occupiers. She exhibited bravery in speaking her mind about the dreaded Yankees and made no effort to hide her glee at news of their president's death. A sympathetic figure, the Confederate woman had grieved for the husband and son she sacrificed for the cause and emerged as an object of pity who had been humiliated by soldier-thugs bent on forcing her into submission. She also carried herself with dignity. The act of self-murder was represented as a reasonable response by a sane woman being harassed by Yankee soldiers. Far from mad, she exhibited courage, not cowardice, by taking her own life. There was a fate worse than death, and that was living as a subjugated people under an occupying army that humiliated and taunted its most esteemed citizens. Suicide, under such circumstances, was not only understandable but commendable.[70]

The rhetoric of suicide was used extensively by both northerners and southerners in political discussions about secession, the war, and Reconstruction in no small measure because the repugnant act was universally and thoroughly associated with sinfulness, dishonor, cowardice, and lethality.

Few other analogies could have as effectively conveyed the highest levels of contempt and abhorrence than suicide. War's end, however, forced a defeated and demoralized people to reconstitute the meaning of suicide. White southerners rejected the loathsome association of suicide with weakness and insanity, cultural markers of self-destruction in the antebellum and wartime South, opting instead for a new construction of suicide as heroic self-sacrifice, one that advanced the ideological and nationalistic agenda of the New South.[71]

This cultural reformulation of the discourse on suicide would not have been possible without the catalyst of the Civil War, which played a significant role in destigmatizing suicide, in creating a space where news of a suicide provoked compassion, not ridicule. Reports of Confederate suicides after the war were frequently attributed to war-related loss and suffering and swathed in sympathy. Take for example the suicide of Elijah Hise of Kentucky, a respected diplomat and jurist, who was elected as a Democrat to Congress after the war. His published suicide note in May 1867 cited his inability to "aid in saving the country from the impending disaster and ruin in which despotic and unconstitutional rule has involved her." The newspaper explained that he harbored "gloomy feelings" regarding the nation under "radical rule."[72] Later that year another Kentuckian, Judge E. F. Buckner took his life. He began his suicide note, "I have no country." He mourned his wife, but also "the loss of the liberties of my country."[73] When a former South Carolina congressman, John D. Ashmore, killed himself in 1871 the news account explained how the sorry state of national affairs led to his death. "The condition of his people and state, and the losses to which he has been subjected by the Federal despotism, preyed upon his spirits till hope was lost."[74] Suicide, in the wake of civil war, defeat, emancipation, and subjugation, had come to be seen as a rational response to extraordinary conditions.

Southerners after the Civil War reconsidered their long held view of suicide as sinful, shameful, and cowardly, in part because of the "suicide mania" that was sweeping the devastated region, claiming lives of notables, neighbors, and relatives, warranting greater sympathy to victims' loved ones and their losses.[75] It would have been unusual for someone to have remained untouched by the impact of suicide in the postwar South, whether it had been someone close or a well-known official. Suicide also came to be seen as a rational choice to miserable circumstances and a hopeless future. Those suffering—and very few southerners were not—might not have entertained self-destruction as an escape for themselves, but they could at least understand those who did.

But southerners also grappled with the knowledge that their fledgling nation had committed suicide. Ex-Confederates either implicitly or explicitly connected postwar suicides of southerners to the suicidal impulse and the death of their failed nation state. Given that so many southerners chose suicide in the wake of personal losses and national defeat, and the recognition that the South had indeed committed suicide after spending years denying it, the question became: Had the Confederacy and its citizens behaved in ways that were shameful and cowardly? Was dying by one's own hand, whether by a state or an individual, really the immoral, sinful act nineteenth-century southerners believed it was as they headed into war? What followed in war's aftermath was a complete rehabilitation of the meaning of suicide that can be traced to both the self-inflicted deaths of hundreds of southerners as well as the suicide of the failed Confederacy.

The conflation of the suicide of fire-eater Edmund Ruffin with that of the Confederacy best demonstrates this war-driven ideological and intellectual shift. No Confederate suicide garnered more attention, inside the South and out, than that of Edmund Ruffin, ardent secessionist and wealthy Virginia planter. In June 1865, he plotted his demise and recorded an extensive explication of his decision that laid out historical and biblical justifications for his fateful act. Accounts of his death outside the South, clinging to the contemptible connotations of suicide, mocked Ruffin's suicide while some recognized the obvious irony: he shared the same fate as his beloved country. *Harper's Weekly* pontificated, "He that taketh the sword must perish by the sword, even though it be through madness and by his own act."[76] A Boston paper mocked Ruffin's defiant last act by reporting that he "blew out what little brains he possessed." It continued, "Pity there are not others to follow his example."[77] The *Davenport (Iowa) Daily Gazette* was even more strident in its contempt for Ruffin and his manner of death: "The miserable wretch who claimed the honor (?) of having fired the first gun on Fort Sumter—Edmund Ruffin, of Va., committed suicide. . . . Among his papers was found a memorandum stating that 'he could not live under the Government of the United States and that he preferred death to doing so.' He evidently preferred a *hotter* place, and has probably found it."[78] The parallels between Ruffin's demise and that of the Confederacy were not lost on a Philadelphia newspaper that used the obituary to chastise a "hot-headed, unsound and fanatical class" that fomented failed revolution. "The rebellion was an attempted suicide of the nation; he committed suicide when the rebellion was defeated. Both have gone out together, the cause and effect, and no more fitting act could have crowned Mr. Ruffin's life than his style of death."[79] The *Portland (Maine) Transcript* took issue with the reasons Ruffin gave for killing himself. "He didn't have the grace to commit the deed from feelings of remorse—he did it because he preferred death to living under the government of the United States. Well. Such a man wasn't fit to live under such a government.—and it is well that he knew it."[80] A more reserved journalistic treatment of Ruffin's death found in the *New York Times* concluded that "the collapse of the rebellion and the utter prostration of his schemes, drove him mad."[81]

Southern obituaries of Ruffin, unsurprisingly, signaled a very different tone when reporting his death. For one thing, southern newspapers had to account for such a rash act by a beacon of the cause. Why would someone so revered kill himself? The *Richmond Whig* explained that the war had driven him mad, implying that he was not of sound mind and therefore the decision was not rational. "Mr. Ruffin's mind had been very perceptibly affected since the evacuation of Richmond and the surrender of the Confederate armies."[82] The *Savannah Daily Herald* noted that Ruffin "had been much dejected" since the defeat of Richmond and Lee's surrender.[83] An Atlanta newspaper went so far as to call Ruffin "deluded."[84] In conceding that Ruffin's mental state had been compromised by the ill-effects of war, southern newspapers reflected traditional explanations of suicide, that it was an act of madness—ironically, a view consonant with those expressed in northern newspapers.

Somewhat paradoxically, then, southern accounts of Ruffin's suicide pivoted to motive, implying that the steady hand of reason, not insanity, drove his decision. They focused on his refusal to live under rule by the US government. Although Ruffin's suicide note went on for pages and cited various reasons for his self-inflicted death, including his own diminished health, loss of property, and financial ruin, the southern press fixated on his defiant resistance to Yankee rule, widely reporting a quote attributed to Ruffin but not found in his note: "I cannot survive the loss of the liberties of my country."[85] A Charleston newspaper summarized this point simply: "he could never live under the United States Government and took death in preference."[86] Despite focusing on a patriotic motive for Ruffin's death, notably, these early reports of Ruffin's suicide are devoid of valorization.

The contradictory elements of contemporary southern reports of Ruffin's death—it was at once an act of madness and reasoned defiance—

reflect the mutating understanding of suicide that emerged in the South after the war. Leading up to and throughout the war, southerners denounced suicide as immoral and cowardly, as criminal and sinful. So how would a people, now defeated, view the self-murder of one of its leading lights? How could they condemn the father of secession for what seemed to most as at least understandable and to many as heroic?

Inchoate, contradictory depictions of Ruffin's death in the immediate aftermath of the war's end that merely hinted at veneration gave way within a generation to full-blown martyrdom. As the roots of the Lost Cause took hold, southern apologists heralded Ruffin as a nineteenth-century Cato, a nod to the Roman senator who took his own life rather than live under the corrupt rule of Caesar. "Cato of old killed himself rather than surrender; Ruffin of Virginia, killed himself rather than submit to government by the hated abolitionists," wrote a Virginia educator at the dawn of the twentieth century.[87] Sarah Rice Pryor similarly recollected Ruffin's death as "Cato-like."[88] But the most striking evidence that southerners had jettisoned their belief in the repugnance of suicide in the postwar years in favor of a heroic model that celebrated the defunct nation came in the creation of a new twist that emerged about Ruffin's death, completely unfounded and entirely apocryphal: that he draped himself in the Confederate flag before shooting himself in 1865. No contemporaneous news account about his death makes reference to this dramatic, nationalistic gesture. In fact, such a fabrication would have been inconceivable in 1865, at a time when southerners were just beginning to take stock of how the war had transformed the meaning of suicide. The earliest known published reference to the mythical Ruffin death scene appears in 1885 as an explanatory footnote in a letter transcribed and appearing among the wartime letters of the Tyler family. Subsequent biographers have repeated the made-up account, and it has proliferated among reputable published works on Ruffin and been accepted as fact ever since.[89] Ruffin, a Confederate martyr who would rather die than live under Yankee rule, a fate worse than death, retains his unshakeable legacy.

James McBride Dabbs, a South Carolina author, farmer, and civil rights activist, recalled in 1962 how a friend once shared, "You know what I learned in high school? I learned that the greatest days of the South were the heroic years from 1861 to '65 during which she was committing suicide."[90] The celebration of the South's suicidal experiment as heroic emerged not in the Civil War years but later, from the efforts of the Lost Cause generation, whose proponents reimagined suicide as honorable. Traditionally conceived as an odious act of dishonor and shame, the New (White) South embraced suicide as a noble and patriotic sacrifice, constitutive of a reconceived identity grounded in white supremacy and myth.

Notes

1. Sarah L. Palmer, *Six Months Among the Secessionists. A Reliable and Thrilling Narrative of the Sufferings and Trials of Miss Sarah L. Palmer, A Native of Pennsylvania, who, at the opening of the Great Southern Rebellion, was teaching school in Knoxville, the home of Parson Brownlow* (Philadelphia: Barclay, 1864), 16–17, accessed via *Sabin Americana, 1500–1926* online database (accessed March 11, 2013).

2. *New York Herald,* January 20, 1861 (accessed April 29, 2009).

3. *Charleston (S.C.) Mercury,* July 23, 1861 (accessed April 29, 2009).

4. Richard Bell examines the political rhetoric of suicide in the context of the new nation in *We Shall Be No More: Suicide and Self-Government in the Newly United States* (Cambridge, Mass.: Harvard Univ. Press, 2012).

5. Diane Miller Sommerville, *Aberration of Mind: Suicide and Suffering in the Civil War–Era South* (Chapel Hill: Univ. of North Carolina Press, 2018).

6. "The Defence of the Funding System, [July 1795]," *Founders Online,* National Archives, last modified June 13, 2018, http://founders.archives.gov/documents/Hamilton/01-19-02-0001 (accessed August 31, 2018), original source: *The Papers of Alexander Hamilton,* vol. 19, *July 1795–December 1795,* ed. Harold C. Syrett (New York: Columbia Univ. Press, 1973), 1–73.

7. "The Warning No. III, [21 February 1797]," *Founders Online,* National Archives, last modified June 13, 2018, http://founders.archives.gov/documents/Hamilton/01-20-02-0330, (accessed August 31, 2018), original source: *The Papers of Alexander Hamilton,* vol. 20, *January 1796–March 1797,* ed. Harold C. Syrett (New York: Columbia Univ. Press, 1974), 517–20. Additional references to political suicide by Hamilton include: "New York Ratifying Convention. Remarks (Francis Childs's Version), [27 June 1788]," *Founders Online,* National Archives, last modified June 13, 2018, http://founders.archives.gov/documents/Hamilton/01-05-02-0012-0034, original source: *The Papers of Alexander Hamilton,* vol. 5, *June 1788–November 1789,* ed. Harold C. Syrett (New York: Columbia Univ. Press, 1962), 94–104; "New York Ratifying Convention. Remarks (Melancton Smith's Version), [27 June 1788]," *Founders Online,* National Archives, last modified June 13, 2018, http://founders.archives.gov/documents/Hamilton/01-05-02-0012-0036, original source: *The Papers of Alexander Hamilton,* vol. 5, *June 1788–November 1789,* ed. Harold C. Syrett (New York: Columbia Univ. Press, 1962), 109–12; "From Alexander Hamilton to Samuel Jones, [21 January 1789]," *Founders Online,* National Archives, last modified June 13, 2018, http://founders.archives.gov/documents

/Hamilton/01-05-02-0071, original source: *The Papers of Alexander Hamilton,* vol. 5, *June 1788–November 1789,* ed. Harold C. Syrett (New York: Columbia Univ. Press, 1962), 244–46; "The Stand No. I, [30 March 1798]," *Founders Online,* National Archives, last modified June 13, 2018, http://founders.archives.gov/documents/Hamilton/01-21-02-0225, original source: *The Papers of Alexander Hamilton,* vol. 21, *April 1797–July 1798,* ed. Harold C. Syrett (New York: Columbia Univ. Press, 1974), 381–87; "From Alexander Hamilton to James A. Bayard, 6 April 1802," *Founders Online,* National Archives, last modified June 13, 2018, http://founders.archives.gov/documents/Hamilton/01-25-02-0315, original source: *The Papers of Alexander Hamilton,* vol. 25, *July 1800–April 1802,* ed. Harold C. Syrett (New York: Columbia Univ. Press, 1977), 587–89.

8. "From John Adams to John Taylor, 17 December 1814," *Founders Online,* National Archives, last modified June 13, 2018, http://founders.archives.gov/documents/Adams/99-02-02-6371 (accessed August 31, 2018). Note: This is an Early Access document from *The Adams Papers.* It is not an authoritative final version. Select references to political or national suicide in early America include: *Letters of Delegates to Congress,* vol. 14, *October 1, 1779–March 31, 1780,* John Armstrong Sr. to Horatio Gates, February 16, 1780, p. 424; *Letters of Delegates to Congress,* vol. 8, *September 19, 1777–January 31, 1778,* Eliphalet Dyer to John Sullivan, October 11, 1777, p. 105; *Letters of Delegates to Congress,* vol. 11, *October 1, 1778–January 31, 1779,* Paper Currency, January 20, 1779, p. 490; *Letters of Delegates to Congress,* vol. 9, *February 1, 1778–May 31, 1778,* Joseph Reed to Jonathan Bayard Smith, February 8, 1778, p. 58, all found online at "A Century of Lawmaking for a New Nation: U.S. Congressional Documents and Debates, 1774–1875" website.

9. Bell, *We Shall Be No More.*

10. *Cincinnati Daily Commercial,* May 6, 1861, in *Northern Editorials on Secession,* ed. Howard Cecil Perkins, vol. 2 (1942; reprint, Gloucester, Mass.: Peter Smith, 1964), 829.

11. *Littell's Living Age* 68 (March 23, 2861): 763.

12. *Richmond (Va.) Daily Dispatch,* November 12, 1862. All citations to the *Daily Dispatch* are from the online source sponsored by the University of Richmond (accessed April 20, 2009). On debates within the secession conventions, consult Charles B. Dew, *Apostles of Disunion: Southern Secession Commissioners and the Causes of the Civil War* (Charlottesville: Univ. of Virginia Press, 2001).

13. *Richmond (Va.) Daily Dispatch,* February 25, 1861. George W. Brent, a Unionist from Alexandria, likewise condemned the secession movement as national suicide. *Richmond (Va.) Daily Dispatch,* March 9, 1861, and "Virginia Secession Convention," March 8, 1861, https://secession.richmond.edu/documents/index.html?keyword=suicide&element=p&formType=Keyword&Submit=&start=1&order=date&direction=ascending&id=pb.1.518 (accessed March 5, 2013). See also Samuel Woods, "Virginia Secession Convention," March 19, 1861, at https://secession.richmond.edu/documents/index.html?keyword=suicide&delegates=woodss%2C&

formType=Delegates&Submit=&start=1&order=date&direction=ascending&id =pb.2.57 (accessed March 5, 2013).

14. Pleasant A. Stovall, *Robert Toombs: Statesman, Speaker, Soldier, Sage: His Career in Congress and on the Hustings—His Work in the Courts—His Record with the Army—His Life at Home* (New York: Cassell, 1892), 226, accessed via Google Books, April 18, 2008. See also *Atlanta Journal-Constitution,* May 15, 1861, Georgia USGenWeb Archives Project (accessed May 5, 2009).

15. Jonathan Worth to D. G. Worth, May 15, 1861, quoted in Charles Royster, *The Destructive War: William Tecumseh Sherman, Stonewall Jackson, and the Americans* (New York: Vintage, 1993), 175.

16. Jonathan Worth to Barzillai G. Worth and T. C. Worth, April 26, 1862, in *The American Civil War: Letters and Diaries* online database (Alexandria, Va.: Alexander Street) (accessed January 30, 2007).

17. "The Great Union Speech of Alexander H. Stephens, vice-president of the Southern Confederacy," n.d., https://www.loc.gov/resource/rbpe.24402000/?st =text (accessed July 7, 2019). Unionists battling secessionists in Georgia, Louisiana, and North Carolina also employed the language of suicide in describing the move for southern independence: *Macon Telegraph,* April 25, 1861; *New Orleans Times,* June 25, 1865; *Fayetteville Observer,* March 18, 1861.

18. *New York Herald,* February 8, 1861 (accessed April 29, 2009).

19. *New York Herald,* April 12, 1861 (accessed April 29, 2009).

20. *Liberator,* August 30, 1861 (accessed February 21, 2013).

21. For a thorough treatment of attitudes toward suicide from the eighteenth century through Reconstruction, consult Sommerville, *Aberration of Mind,* 235–261.

22. *Carrollton (La.) Sun,* May 22, 1861.

23. *New York Journal of Commerce,* quoted in the *Richmond (Va.) Daily Dispatch,* December 13, 1860 (accessed October 2, 2008).

24. On suicide in American law, see Howard I. Kushner, *American Suicide: A Psychocultural Exploration* (New Brunswick, N.J.: Rutgers Univ. Press, 1991), 17–18, 26, 29–30. Following the American Revolution, coroners' juries grew increasingly reluctant to enforce the laws on the books against suicide, and some states, like Virginia, argued for the repeal of laws that provided for confiscation of suicides' property. Bell, *We Shall Be No More,* 20–21; Terri L. Snyder, "Stories of Suicide in Eighteenth-Century Virginia: Masters, Slaves, and Print Culture during the Imperial Crisis," paper presented to the Ohio Seminar in Early American History and Culture (October 14, 2005), in author's possession (page 4). Nine states retained laws against suicide through 1964. Robert E. Litman, "Medico-Legal Aspects of Suicide," *Washburn Law Journal* 6 (1966–1967): 395.

25. David Silkenat, *Moments of Despair: Suicide, Divorce, and Debt in Civil War North Carolina* (Chapel Hill: Univ. of North Carolina Press, 2011), 35.

26. Sommerville, *Aberration of Mind,* 24.

27. *Richmond (Va.) Daily Dispatch,* April 19, 1861 (accessed March 2, 2009).

28. *Liberator,* June 21, 1861 (accessed February 21, 2013).

29. Reported in *Richmond (Va.) Daily Dispatch,* October 10, 1861.

30. Daniel Steele, *The Cause, the Crime, and the Cure of Our National Suicide. A National Fast Day Sermon, Delivered in The Baptist Church, Springfield, September 26, 1861* (Springfield: Samuel Bowles, 1861), 11, 10, available at the David M. Rubenstein Rare Book and Manuscript Library, Duke University, Durham, North Carolina.

31. Ibid., 18, 19.

32. Egbert C. Smyth, *Our Country Not Forsaken of God. A Sermon Preached to the Students of Bowdoin College in the Congregational Church, Brunswick, June 23, 1861 by Egbert C. Smyth* (Brunswick: A. G. Tenney, 1861), 9, accessed via *Sabin Americana, 1500–1926* online database (accessed March 10, 2013).

33. Rev. B. Sadtler, *A Rebellious Nation Reproved. A Sermon Preached by Rev. B. Sadtler, Pastor of St. John's Evangelical Lutheran Church, Easton, Pa., on the Day of Humiliation, Fasting and Prayer, September 26, 1861* (Easton, Pa.: Davis and Eichman, 1861), 8, accessed via *Sabin Americana, 1500–1926* online database (accessed March 10, 2013).

34. Irving Hall, "Speech of Joseph Holt," New York City, September 10, 1861, in *The Rebellion Record: A Diary of American Events, with Documents, Narratives, Illustrative Incidents, Poetry, Etc.*, ed. Frank Moore (New York: D. Van Nostrand Publishers, 1869), 26, accessed via *Sabin Americana, 1500–1926* online database (accessed March 11, 2013).

35. *Richmond (Va.) Daily Dispatch,* May 22, 1861 (accessed March 2, 2009).

36. *Macon (Ga.) Telegraph,* November 2, 1863.

37. Milton S. Latham, *Speech of Hon. Sen. Milton S. Latham of California, Delivered in the U.S. Senate, February 1, 1861 on the President's Message,—'The mission of peace from Virginia'* (Washington, D.C.: Henry Polkinhorn, 1861), 11, accessed via *Sabin Americana, 1500–1926* online database (accessed March 10, 2013).

38. Joseph Holt, *Letter from the Hon. Jos. Holt, Upon the Policy of the General Government, The Pending Revolution, Its Objects, Its Probable Results if Successful, and the Duty of Kentucky in the Crisis* (Washington, D.C.: Henry Polkinhorn, 1861), 23, accessed via *Sabin Americana, 1500–1926* online database (accessed March 10, 2013). See also Joseph Holt, "Letter from Joseph Holt to J. F. Speed, May 31, 1861," in *Letters of the Hon. Joseph Holt, the Hon. Edward Everett, and Commodore Charles Stewart on the Present Crisis,* ed. Edward Everett and Charles Stewart (Philadelphia: W. S. and A. Martien, 1861), 45, in *The American Civil War: Letters and Diaries* online database (Alexandria, Va.: Alexander Street) (accessed January 30, 2007).

39. Steele, *The Cause, the Crime, and the Cure of Our National Suicide,* 10.

40. "Article VI.—The Church and the Country," *Princeton Review* (April 1, 1861): 336.

41. [Robert Dodge], *A Book for Every Soldier's Knapsack: Tracts for the War. Secession: The Remedy and Result* (New York: James Miller, 1861), 41, accessed via *Sabin Americana, 1500–1926* online database (accessed March 10, 2013).

42. Reverend John C. Lord, *Causes and Remedies of the Present Convulsions: A Discourse* (Buffalo, N.Y.: Jospeh Warren, 1861), 21, accessed via *Sabin Americana, 1500–1926* online database (accessed March 10, 2013).

43. Anonymous, *The Ides of March; or, Abraham Lincoln, Private Citizen. Being a Sequel to the End of the Irrepressible Conflict. By a Merchant of Philadelphia* (Philadelphia: King and Baird, 1861), 22, accessed via *Sabin Americana, 1500–1926* online database (accessed March 10, 2013).

44. *New York Herald,* May 14, 1862.

45. James A. Hamilton, *State Sovereignty: Rebellion Against the United States by the People of a State Is Its Political Suicide* (New York: Baker and Godwin, 1861), 24, accessed via *Sabin Americana, 1500–1926* online database (accessed March 10, 2013).

46. Nahum Capen, *The Indissoluble Nature of the American Union, Considered in Connection with the Assumed Right of Secession. A Letter to Hon. Peter Cooper, New York* (Boston: A. Williams, 1862), 26, accessed via *Sabin Americana, 1500–1926* online database (accessed March 10, 2013).

47. *Liberator,* February 19, 1864 (accessed February 21, 2013). Apparently neither the duke of Argyle nor Cooper was aware of the ability of starfish to regenerate limbs. The use of the starfish analogy is thus flawed.

48. *New York Herald,* January 3, 1861 (accessed April 29, 2009).

49. The author of the first quote appeared as "Hill," and could have been either Joshua Hill or Benjamin Hill, both of whom attended the Georgia secession convention. *Raleigh (N.C.) Daily Register,* February 9, 1861, accessed via the Gale News Vault online database (accessed March 10, 2013). The *Richmond (Va.) Daily Dispatch* attributed the quote to "Mr. [H. B.] Troup" (December 20, 1860). Quote on France also located at *Moore's Rural New Yorker,* January 5, 1861, 10. While many southerners viewed secession as an act of political suicide, it is likely a majority viewed it as a justifiable act of independence, much like American patriots had done in 1776 in declaring independence from Britain.

50. Rev. William A. Hall, *The Historic Significance of the Southern Revolution: A Lecture Delivered by Invitation in Petersburg, Virginia, March 14 and April 29, 1864. And in Richmond, Virginia, April 7 and April 21, 1864* (Petersburg, Va.: A. F. Crutchfield, 1864), 44–45.

51. "Address of Congress to the People of the Confederate States," in *Richmond (Va.) Daily Dispatch,* March 21, 1865 (accessed March 20, 2013); and *Weekly Intelligencer* (Atlanta, Ga.), April 12, 1865, accessed via the Atlanta Historic Newspaper Archive (accessed April 30, 2012).

52. *Richmond (Va.) Examiner,* January 28, 1865, excerpted in *New York Herald,* February 1, 1865 (accessed April 29, 2009).

53. Royster, *The Destructive War,* 185.

54. Charles Sumner, *The Works of Charles Sumner,* vol. 7 (Boston: Lee and Shepard, 1875), 526.

55. On theories of reconstruction, consult James M. McPherson, *Battle Cry of Freedom: The Civil War Era* (New York: Oxford Univ. Press, 1988), 698–703;

Charles H. McCarthy, *Lincoln's Plan of Reconstruction* (1901; reprint, New York: AMS Press, 1966) (Sumner's plan on pages 196–212); Herman Belz, *Reconstructing the Union: Theory and Policy during the Civil War* (Ithaca, N.Y.: Cornell Univ. Press, 1969) (Sumner's plan on pages 56–65); Eric L. McKitrick, *Andrew Johnson and Reconstruction* (Chicago: Univ. of Chicago Press, 1960), 93–119 (Sumner's plan on pages 110–13). For Sumner's quote, see *The Works of Charles Sumner,* vol. 6 (Boston: Lee and Shepherd, 1874), 302.

56. See, for example, Michael MacDonald and Terrence R. Murphy, *Sleepless Soul: Suicide in Early Modern England* (Oxford, UK: Clarendon Press, 1900), 15–16, 109–43; Victor Bailey, *"This Rash Act": Suicide across the Life Cycle in the Victorian City* (Stanford, Calif.: Stanford Univ. Press, 1998), 67–77.

57. "State Suicide," *Atlantic Monthly* 12, no. 72 (October 1863): 519–29, quotations on 519, 520, 521, 519. Reporting on Sumner's theory of state suicide can be found at "Senator Sumner and State Suicide," *Army and Navy Journal* (December 2, 1865): 227–28.

58. *Macon (Ga.) Telegraph,* December 22, 1866.

59. *Georgia Weekly Telegraph,* March 26, 1866.

60. Ibid., March 15, 1867, 6, accessed via Georgia Historic Newspapers online database (accessed March 20, 2013).

61. Jonathan Worth, "Letter from Jonathan Worth to Benjamin Sherwood Hedrick, February 26, 1867," in *The Correspondence of Jonathan Worth,* ed. Joseph Grégoire de Roulhac Hamilton, vol. 2 (Raleigh, N.C.: Edwards and Broughton, 1909), 900.

62. *Lynchburg Republican,* November 2, 1864, quoted in McPherson, *Battle Cry of Freedom,* 836.

63. Sarah E. Gardner, *Blood and Irony: Southern White Women's Narratives of the Civil War, 1861–1937* (Chapel Hill: Univ. of North Carolina Press, 2004), 92–95; David W. Blight, *Race and Reunion: The Civil War in American Memory* (Cambridge, Mass.: Belknap Press, 2001), 259–62, 282–91; Caroline E. Janney, *Remembering the Civil War: Reunion and the Limits of Reconciliation* (Chapel Hill: Univ. of North Carolina Press, 2013), 145–48; Alan T. Nolan, "The Anatomy of the Myth," in *The Myth of the Lost Cause and Civil War History,* ed. Gary W. Gallagher and Alan T. Nolan (Bloomington: Indiana Univ. Press, 2000), 14–17, 19–21, 25–30.

64. Bell, *We Shall Be No More,* 264.

65. *Savannah (Ga.) Daily News and Herald,* October 22, 1867.

66. Benjamin Hill, speech, Atlanta, Georgia, September 5, 1876, in *Senator Benjamin H. Hill of Georgia: His Life, Speeches and Writings,* ed. Benjamin H. Hill Jr. (Atlanta: T.H.P. Bloodworth, 1893), 469, accessed via Google Books (accessed March 20, 2013).

67. E. S. Riley Jr., "Com. Preble's 'Infernal,'" *Southern Magazine* 12 (January 1873): 30–35, accessed via Google Books (accessed March 21, 2013). On *Southern Magazine* and other similar Lost Cause magazines, consult Gaines M. Foster,

Ghosts of the Confederacy: Defeat, the Lost Cause, and the Emergence of the New South (New York: Oxford Univ. Press, 1985), 49–50.

68. The UDC was not founded until 1894, so this undated publication must have appeared at the turn of the century. On the UDC's efforts to control the narrative of the Civil War, consult Gardner, *Blood and Irony,* 118–58.

69. Mrs. Alexander H. Major, "A Crape Veil," in *Reminiscences of the Women of Missouri during the Sixties* (N.p.: United Daughters of the Confederacy, Missouri Division, n.d.), 294–98. The nobility of southern white women juxtaposed to brutish and amoral federal soldiers during Reconstruction was a common Lost Cause-era trope. Gardner, *Blood and Irony,* 102–4.

70. Ibid.

71. Sommerville, *Aberration of Mind,* 246–61.

72. *Daily Arkansas Gazette* (Little Rock, Ark.), May 15, 1867; *Atlanta (Ga.) Daily Intelligencer,* May 10, 12, 1867; *Weekly Atlanta (Ga.) Intelligencer,* May 15, 1867.

73. *Savannah (Ga.) Daily News and Herald,* October 25, 1867; *National Police Gazette,* October 26, 1867.

74. *Pulaski (Tenn.) Citizen,* December 21, 1871.

75. On reports of postwar suicide mania, see *Tri-Weekly Republican* (Americus, Ga.), May 12, 1870, 2. For additional postwar newspaper accounts commenting on the increase of suicides and describing them as epidemics or mania, see the *Thomasville (Ga.) Times,* May 3, 1879, and August 5, 1876; *Weekly Sumter Republican* (Americus, Ga.), October 1, 1875; *Albany (Ga.) News,* February 28, 1873; *Daily Phoenix* (Columbia, S.C.), April 17, 1868; *Savannah (Ga.) Daily News and Herald,* February 11, 1868; *Charleston (S.C.) News and Courier,* July 10, 1883; *National Police Gazette,* October 26, 1867, 23; *Macon (Ga.) Telegraph,* August 2, 1865; *New Orleans Times,* July 12, 1866. Additional sources that commented on the rise of late nineteenth-century suicides include William Mathews, "Civilization and Suicide," *North American Review* 152, no. 413 (April 1, 1891): 470, 477; and Horace Mellard DuBose, "Suicide—Its Causes and Cures," *Quarterly Review of the Methodist Episcopal Church, South* 21 (1884): 36. The war generated widespread emotional and psychological distress among soldiers and civilians. See Sommerville, *Aberration of Mind.*

76. *Harper's Weekly,* July 29, 1865.

77. *Flag of Our Union,* July 15, 1865, reprinted in *Ballou's Dollar Magazine,* September 1, 1865.

78. *Davenport (Iowa) Daily Gazette,* June 22, 1865.

79. *North American and U.S. Gazette* (Philadelphia), June 28, 1865.

80. *Portland (Maine) Transcript,* July 1, 1865.

81. *New York Times,* June 23, 1865.

82. *Richmond (Va.) Whig,* June 20, 1865, reprinted in the *Atlanta (Ga.) Daily Constitutionalist,* June 29, 1865, *Alexandria Gazette and Virginia Advertiser,* June 21, 1865, and *Louisville (Ky.) Daily Journal,* June 25, 1865.

83. *Savannah (Ga.) Daily Herald,* June 27, 1865.

84. *Atlanta (Ga.) Daily Intelligencer,* July 2, 1865.

85. *Louisville (Ky.) Daily Journal,* June 25, 1865; *Atlanta (Ga.) Daily Constitutionalist,* June 29, 1865; *Savannah (Ga.) Republican,* July 11, 1865.

86. *Charleston (S.C.) Daily Courier,* June 30, 1865.

87. Henry Ellis, "Edmund Ruffin: His Life and Times," in *The John P. Branch Historical Papers of Randolph-Macon College,* vol. 3 (Richmond: Richmond Press, 1909), 123; "New Supervisors," *Virginia Journal of Education* 14 (September 1920): 20. On white southerners' invocation of Roman suicides like Cato following the Civil War, see Margaret Malamud, *Ancient Roman and Modern America* (Chichester, UK: Blackwell, 2009), 89.

88. Mrs. Roger A. [Sarah Agnes Rice] Pryor, *My Day: Reminiscences of a Long Life* (New York: Macmillan, 1909), 162.

89. Lyon G. Tyler, ed., *The Letters and Times of the Tylers,* vol. 2 (Richmond: Whittet and Shipperson, 1885), 647.

90. Davis W. Houck and David E. Dixon, eds., *Rhetoric, Religion and the Civil Rights Movement, 1954–1965* (Waco, Tex.: Baylor Univ. Press, 2007), 490.

5

Warrior Turned Reformer

Emory Upton and the Modernization of the American Army

James R. Hedtke

The Civil War was a pivotal event in American history. The war led to the abolition of slavery and the preservation of the Union. It opened political discourse on the meaning of equality in American society and served as the catalyst for industrialization, urbanization, immigration, and modernization. America's deadliest war also brought into question the preparedness and organization of the US Army to engage in modern warfare. After the Civil War, an obscure officer from western New York, Emory Upton, became the driving force for reform in the US Army. Upton was not one of the well-known and celebrated generals to emerge from the Civil War; however, his writings and suggested reforms to military policy and organization led to the development of the modern American army.

Upton was born on a farm near Batavia, New York, on August 27, 1839. He was the tenth child and sixth son of Electra and Daniel Upton. Upton's parents were strict Methodists and were zealous in their faith. They embraced temperance as well as abolition and were active participants in the Underground Railroad. Daniel and Electra imbued in their children a deep love and respect for God. They also provided their children with a sense of duty and responsibility to improve and reform society.[1] Upton's upbringing fostered the development of his unimpeachable character and his desire to reform a flawed world.

At the age of fourteen, Upton had an epiphany. After he read a book on the life of Napoleon, he made the decision to become a soldier.[2] To accomplish his goal, Upton decided to attend West Point. Congressman Benjamin

Pringle advised the young man that he needed more formal education before he could receive an appointment to the military academy.[3] In 1854, Upton followed his older brothers to Ohio's Oberlin College to prepare for entry into West Point.

Oberlin emphasized discipline, responsibility to God and community, as well as the need to reform an imperfect society. It was an integrated institution and espoused the abolition of slavery. The school's mission reinforced the values that Upton received from his parents. His experience there convinced him that the world was a dark place and that he must be an agent of truth and reform.[4]

Upton saw Oberlin as a stepping stone to admittance to the US Military Academy. His purpose was to secure a practical education that would allow him to pass the admission tests into West Point.[5] He lived a disciplined life, arising at 5 A.M. every morning. He refused to sleep with a pillow in fear that he would become round-shouldered. He even wagered a friend that he would attain the rank of general before he reached the age of forty-five.[6]

In 1856, Congressman Pringle awarded Upton an appointment to West Point. Upton was just sixteen years old when he entered the military academy, but his arduous schedule at Oberlin had prepared him well for military life. At West Point, Upton remained true to his beliefs and convictions. The same year, he became the first cadet to announce publically that he was an abolitionist. Upton's open support for abolition incurred the wrath of southern upperclassmen.

The antagonism reached a crescendo after John Brown's October 1859 raid on the federal arsenal at Harper's Ferry, Virginia. Cadet Wade Hampton Gibbes of South Carolina made disparaging remarks about Upton having had sexual relations with black female students while attending Oberlin. This insult led to a duel between the two cadets one evening after formation. Upton emerged from the fight with a facial cut that left a permanent scar on his upper right cheek. Gibbes escaped unscathed from the confrontation. The bloodied Upton won the respect of his classmates, but the Military Academy remained deeply divided on the issue of slavery.[7]

The Civil War had already begun when Upton graduated from West Point on May 6, 1861. He finished in the top ten in his class, ranking eighth out of forty-five cadets. He received a commission as a second lieutenant in the 5th U.S. Artillery. Eight days later, Upton was promoted to first lieutenant. At this point in the war, there was a great need for professional officers to train the raw citizen soldiers who swelled the ranks of the

Union army. Upton soon found himself training and drilling the volunteers who formed the 12th New York Infantry. Many of the men in this unit hailed from Genesee County and had been Upton's neighbors.

Upton feared that he might be forced to train volunteers while the war passed him by. He applied for a transfer and became the aide-de-camp to Brigadier General David Tyler of the 1st Division, Department of Northeastern Virginia. Upton had his first taste of combat on June 17, 1861, while conducting a reconnaissance mission near Vienna, Virginia. He next engaged Confederate troops in the firefight near Blackburn's Ford, Virginia, on July 18, 1861.[8]

Three days later, Upton participated in the First Battle of Bull Run. Early in the morning, General Tyler's division advanced to Blackburn's Ford, where Upton aimed and fired one of the opening salvos of the battle. Upton then guided the 1st Massachusetts and the 2nd and 3rd Michigan across Bull Run Creek. In the charge, a musket ball wounded Upton in his left side and arm. Despite his wounds, he remained on the field of battle delivering orders from General Tyler. Later in the day, he had his horse shot out from under him while rallying the 69th New York. He quickly and calmly commandeered another mount and continued to perform his duty throughout the battle.

Although General Tyler officially commended Upton for his courage and gallantry under fire, the young soldier was deeply disturbed by the Union defeat at First Bull Run. In a letter to his sister, Upton expressed his feelings about the battle. He wrote: "I regret to say we were defeated. Our troops fought well, but were poorly managed."[9] Upton blamed the Union defeat at Bull Run on poorly trained volunteer soldiers and unprepared officers. The loss convinced him that the US Army needed drastic reforms. He believed that a well-trained army under the leadership of competent, professional officers could have quickly ended the rebellion.[10] These views became a constant theme of Upton's writings and discourse during the war and the springboard for his proposed reforms after the conflict ended. Upton also was disturbed by the popular but mistaken belief "that because our citizens individually possess courage, fortitude and self-reliance, they must necessarily possess the same qualities when aggregated as soldiers."[11] He believed that this notion led to the "fatal delusion that an army animated by patriotism needed neither instruction or discipline to prepare it for battle."[12]

After Upton recovered from the wounds he received at Bull Run, the War Department reassigned him to the artillery. He then took command of

Battery D, 2nd U.S. Artillery. His battery defended the fortifications around Washington, D.C. In the spring 1862, his unit joined General George B. McClellan's Peninsula Campaign in Virginia. Upton's battery performed well in this operation, and both General William B. Franklin and General Henry Warner Slocum complimented Upton's work in their official reports. Upton demonstrated all of the attributes of command during the Peninsula Campaign. He was calm and collected under fire. He possessed the ability to see the whole battlefield and utilize that vision at the critical moment to his advantage. He also commanded the admiration, respect, and confidence of both his men and his superiors.

After the Union defeats on the peninsula and at the Second Battle of Bull Run (August 28–30, 1862), General Robert E. Lee decided to invade the north with his Army of Northern Virginia. Upton, who had been promoted to captain before Lee's invasion, now commanded an artillery brigade in the 1st Division of VI Corps in the Army of the Potomac. His artillery brigade consisted of four batteries and a total of sixteen guns. Upton saw his first action in the Maryland Campaign at Crampton's Gap on September 14, 1862. The accurate fire from Upton's artillery helped to force the Confederates from the gap.

At the Battle of Antietam on September 17, 1862, Upton's batteries engaged in a constant artillery duel with Confederate gunners from 2 P.M. to dusk. A brigade commander in the 2nd Division, VI Corps, wrote in his official report that Upton's guns "were of inestimable value to us, and the coolness and precision with which they were served deserve the highest commendation."[13] Upton himself enjoyed the thrill and sting of combat. He possessed the traits of a true warrior. On September 22, he wrote to his sister that "from the time we left Alexandria till the close of the battle of Antietam, I never spent any hours more agreeably or enjoyed myself better."[14]

The five-foot, eleven-inch-tall, 170-pound, blond-haired, blue-eyed Upton epitomized the professional soldier. He did not drink, curse, smoke, or gamble. He was a fervent and zealous Christian. He constantly talked and read about military tactics. On the battlefield he was both calm and courageous. General James Wilson, a friend and fellow officer, wrote that Upton "was religious, a devout and pious Christian. He was one of the purest men I ever knew as well as one of the ablest."[15]

Upton also was ambitious. In October 1862, the War Department ordered him to report to West Point as an instructor. Upton, however, feared that this would be a dead-end assignment, stifling any chance for promotion in the ranks. He believe that to gain promotion and to impact the war effort, one had to be on the front lines, not teaching in a classroom. Promotion also came faster to individuals commanding volunteer units than in the regular army.

Before the army could send him to West Point, Upton took leave and traveled to Albany, New York. There Upton lobbied New York politicians for command of the 121st New York Infantry. Colonel Richard Franchot had just resigned command of the regiment to take a seat in the US House of Representatives. Upton's efforts proved successful. At the age of twenty-three he was promoted to the rank of colonel and took command of the 121st New York.

He immediately brought discipline and professionalism to his new regiment. Upton relentlessly drilled his men to improve their skills as soldiers. He improved their health and spirit by requisitioning tents, blankets, and food from the quartermaster. He placed an emphasis on field sanitation and greatly reduced the number of soldiers reporting on the sick list. He also instituted promotion examinations for individuals seeking commissions as officers. This system helped to counter requests from New York politicians to promote individuals on the basis of their political connections rather than on their military knowledge and skill. In the postwar years this became one of the reforms Upton pushed for, and his wartime efforts bore fruit. His regiment developed a noticeable *esprit de corps,* one founded on a mutual respect between the commander and his troops. Major Douglas Campbell of the 121st New York remarked that Upton was "watchful of his men, studious of their health and comfort, kind as a woman: but in battle he was terrible."[16]

The 121st New York saw its first major action under Upton's command on May 3, 1863, near Salem Church during the Battle of Chancellorsville. General Joseph Bartlett, Upton's brigade commander, ordered his regiment to attack a Confederate position on a cleared ridge near Salem Church. The Confederates put down a murderous fire on the New Yorkers as they attacked the Rebel position. The southerners repulsed the attack and inflicted staggering losses on the 121st New York. Nearly 61 percent of Upton's regiment was killed, wounded, or taken prisoner.

His defeat at Salem Church reinforced Upton's belief once again that the army needed reform. It also taught him several valuable lessons. The most important of these was that daytime frontal assaults must be carefully planned and new tactics were needed to make them succeed. Bravery of troops alone could not overcome incompetent leadership or ill-suited tactics when attacking an entrenched defensive position.

On July 1, 1863, the first day of the Battle of Gettysburg, Upton became the commander of the 2nd Brigade, 1st Division, VI Corps, Army of the Potomac. He considered his promotion an important stepping stone in his quest to become a general. His brigade arrived at Gettysburg on July 3 and saw no action during the three-day battle.

Upton's troops did not see large-scale combat again until the evening of November 7, 1863. Lee's army had established a bridgehead on the northern bank of the Rappahannock River that endangered the Army of the Potomac. Upton's troops spearheaded a nighttime attack on the Confederate defensive position. He used guile, bayonets, and darkness to drive the southerners from their works. Upton and his troops seized the pontoon bridge, cutting off the Confederates from their escape route. Upton's brigade captured seven colors, 103 officers, 1,337 enlisted men, 1,225 small arms, and four cannon.[17] The hard-earned lessons learned at Salem Church helped Upton achieve this lop-sided victory at Rappahannock Station.

After the victory at Rappahannock Station, Upton hoped that he would be promoted to general. Major General George Gordon Meade, commander of the Army of the Potomac, bluntly told Upton that he needed political influence to become a general. Upton secured letters of recommendation supporting his promotion to general from eight brigadier generals and seven major generals, including Meade,[18] who argued that Upton should be promoted "on account of the distinguished and gallant service he has rendered during the war."[19] Major General John Sedgewick, commander of the VI Corps, wrote to the War Department that "Colonel Upton would make an excellent brigade commander, and I earnestly hope he will be appointed."[20] Upton, who regularly complained about officers who solicited recommendations from politicians for military promotions, also lobbied New York senator Edwin Morgan about a vacant brigadier generalship in New York. Despite these efforts, Upton failed to gain his generalship. Ironically, he concluded from this experience, as before, that political patronage and state sovereignty undermined military effectiveness. Such interventions promoted incompetent individuals to leadership positions in the army. After the Civil War, Upton sought to remediate both of these practices with military reforms.

Upton's star rose and gained an opportunity to influence military tactics in the spring of 1864 when President Abraham Lincoln appointed Ulysses S. Grant as general-in-chief of all Union armies. Grant made his saddle his office, and his headquarters was with the Army of the Potomac. His overall strategy was to attack with all Union armies simultaneously engaging their Confederate opponents. The mission of the Army of the Potomac was to attack and destroy Lee's army. The Overland Campaign, commenced in May 1864, was the plan to achieve this objective.

The Battle of the Wilderness (May 5–7) was the first engagement of the Overland Campaign. Stymied by Lee's forces, Grant decided to abandon the conflict in the Wilderness and outflank Lee by marching southeast and occupying the crossroads at Spotsylvania Court House (May 8–21). Lee uncovered Grant's plans and arrived at Spotsylvania first. The Confederates established a formidable system of breastworks there and braced themselves for the inevitable Union assault.

The center of the Confederate line at Spotsylvania contained a large salient, a bulge in a defensive line vulnerable to attack, that resembled a mule shoe. The Confederates created the salient to incorporate a small hill in their line so that Union artillery could not use it to shell the southern position. A small pine woods two hundred yards away made the salient more vulnerable because it could mask Union troop movements. Grant's problem was that to take the salient he would have to launch a frontal attack. Such assaults had a high rate of failure in the Civil War because of the increasing accuracy of rifle fire and the effective use of short-range artillery from entrenched positions.

During the war, Upton devoted considerable attention to developing tactics for assaulting entrenched positions. He considered this one of the greatest challenges in modern linear warfare. It was also his best opportunity to make a contribution to reforming military tactics. His plan was to attack quickly the fixed position and deliver maximum firepower on it. He proposed an infantry attack in column to dislodge the defenders. The column would be composed of three infantry regiments (roughly three thousand men) abreast in each of four successive lines. The first line would overwhelm the defenders in the outermost trenches and then spread out to the right and left to create further penetration. The second line would occupy the trenches seized by the first line and fire on enemy reinforcements. The third line would advance in support of the second line. The final line would remain in reserve and exploit any breakthroughs. This line would also protect against any counterattack.[21]

Upton had outlined such an attack in column to both Grant and Meade during the spring 1864 campaigns. Grant decided to employ Upton's idea against the "mule shoe" on the evening of May 10. The Union commanders allowed Upton to select twelve regiments for the assault. Upton conducted a reconnaissance of the area with his regimental officers and carefully instructed each of them about the role their troops would play in the attack. Such careful preparation and attention to detail were unusual prior to most frontal assaults.

At 6 P.M. on May 10, Union artillery signaled the start of the attack at Spotsylvania. Upton issued the order for the men to move forward, and the troops double-timed across the open space from the pine woods to the Confederate entrenchments. The first line pierced the rebel defense and captured two lines of southern entrenched positions. Upton had proved his point; the column was an effective tactic for making frontal assaults.

The attack stalled, however, when Lee rushed reinforcements to the breakthrough while adjacent Union troops failed to advance in support of Upton's column. With the attack blunted, Grant ordered Upton's force to withdraw under the cover of darkness to Union lines. Upton's twelve regiments suffered nearly one thousand casualties while inflicting about the same number of killed, wounded, and missing on the Confederates. During the attack his troops also captured about twelve hundred southern prisoners.[22]

Grant was so impressed with Upton's tactics and leadership that he immediately promoted the twenty-four-year-old colonel to brevet brigadier general of volunteers. President Lincoln confirmed Upton's appointment on May 11, 1864. Upton was pleased that he received his promotion on the basis of "gallant and distinguished services" rather than political patronage.[23]

General Grant attempted another attack on the "mule shoe" on May 12 using more troops than employed by Upton. This assault also ended in failure. Unable to dislodge the Confederates from their position, Grant once again tried to outflank Lee's army. The Overland Campaign continued to North Anna (May 23–26) and then down to Cold Harbor (May 31–June 12). The campaign finally ended in mid-June when the Army of the Potomac forced Lee's army into the fortifications of Petersburg, and Grant laid siege to the city.

The Overland Campaign proved to be a critical event in Upton's career. He had become a general and employed the tactic of assault by column. He saw the need for leadership based on merit rather than political patronage. He had also seen his brigade bled white. He lost about 60 percent of his men in the campaign.[24] Upton never questioned the valor and devotion of the citizen-soldier, but he remained worried about the competence of their leaders. He expressed this concern in a letter he sent to his sister on June 4, 1864, the day after the horrific bloodletting at the Battle of Cold Harbor. He wrote:

> I am disgusted with the generalship displayed. Our men have, in many instances, been foolishly and wantonly sacrificed. Assault after assault has been ordered upon the enemy's entrenchments when they knew nothing about the strength or position of the enemy. Thousands of lives might have been spared by the exercise of a little skill; but as it is, the courage of the poor men is expected to obviate all difficulties. I must confess that, so long as I see such incompetency, there is no grade in the army to which I do not aspire.[25]

Since the Union defeat at the Battle of First Bull Run, Upton had contemplated the importance of reforming the US Army. The tragic loss of life during the Overland Campaign confirmed its necessity. According to friend and biographer Peter Michie, by 1864 "tactics became the theme of Upton's daily conversation, engrossed his mind almost to the exclusion of everything else and he drew from every battlefield its important lesson."[26]

In the late summer of 1864, Grant transferred the VI Corps to General Philip Sheridan's army in the Shenandoah Valley to engage Lieutenant General Jubal Early's Confederate forces. On September 19, Upton distinguished himself again at the Battle of Opequan Creek. Early's forces attacked Sheridan's troops and drove a gap between the VI and XIX Corps. In the Union counterattack, Confederate fire killed Upton's division commander, Brigadier General David Allen Russell. Upton immediately assumed command of the division, continued the assault, and drove the southerners across the countryside. As Upton urged his men forward, a Confederate shell exploded near him. A fragment from the shell ripped into his thigh and exposed his femoral artery.[27]

When General Sheridan arrived at Upton's position and saw the serious nature of his wound, he ordered Upton to the rear to receive medical treatment for his injury. Once Sheridan left the area, Upton ordered his staff surgeon to apply a tourniquet to stop the flow of blood. He then mounted a stretcher and had the bearers carry him from brigade to brigade while he issued orders to his officers. He did not leave the battlefield until nightfall. The next day, Sheridan informed him that he had received a brevet promotion to major general.

Upton returned home to Batavia, New York, to convalesce from his wound. After such a serious injury, most individuals would have resigned their commission and basked in the glory of their achievements. During his stay in Batavia, he continued to think about and work on tactical reforms for the infantry. In December, General James Wilson presented Upton with an extraordinary opportunity that brought him back to the field of battle even though his wound had not fully healed.

Grant and Sherman had created the Cavalry Corps of the Military Division of the Mississippi and placed General James Wilson in charge of the unit. Grant allowed Wilson to choose officers from the Army of the Potomac to fill his top command positions. Wilson knew Upton from their days together as cadets at West Point, and he wanted Upton to command one of his cavalry divisions. Upton accepted Wilson's offer. He took command of the 4th Division of the Cavalry Corps even though he was still limping from his wound.

The mission of the new Cavalry Corps was to capture Selma, Alabama, and Columbus, Georgia, as well as to drive Lieutenant General Nathan Bedford Forrest's vaunted cavalry from the region. On the night of April 2, 1865, Wilson and Upton launched a two-pronged attack on Selma with dismounted cavalry. This powerful and mobile force equipped with the new seven-shot Spencer repeating carbines overwhelmed the Confederate defenders in a nighttime attack. Wilson's cavalry corps captured this important industrial center in the heart of the Confederacy and defeated Forrest's cavalry for the first time.[28]

On April 16, Upton led the attack against Columbus. Under the cover of darkness, he sent his dismounted troops to capture the Confederate works that protected the bridges into the city. Once he breached the southern defenses, Upton ordered mounted cavalry to seize the city itself. By 10 P.M. he had captured Columbus as well as fifteen hundred prisoners and twenty-four cannon.[29] In an unprecedented military maneuver, Upton had launched a successful night attack against a fortified city using only cavalry troops.

The Cavalry Corps finished the war with an unblemished record. In the last six weeks of the conflict, the Corps won every battle and captured three thousand prisoners, fifty-two artillery pieces, and thirteen battle flags.[30] They also captured Alexander H. Stephens, the Confederacy's vice president.[31]

As for many other soldiers, the Civil War proved to be the defining point in Emory Upton's life. Only twenty-five years old at the end of the conflict, he nevertheless had amassed an extraordinary wartime record. Upton had acquired a unique breadth of experience commanding artillery, infantry, and cavalry units in combat. He had applied new infantry tactics at the Battle of Spotsylvania. His experience in the Civil War convinced him that the army was in desperate need of reform at all levels. Political patronage, state sovereignty, poor leadership, undisciplined troops, and outdated tactics all led to unacceptably high casualty rates in the Civil War. He believed that the United States could not repeat this experience if it hoped to fight and win future wars. The new driving force and purpose in his life became military reform. His competence, varied military experience, and intense determination made him uniquely qualified to undertake the task.

At the conclusion of the war, Upton reverted back to his rank of lieutenant colonel in the regular US Army. The War Department assigned him to the Department of Missouri. His commander, General John Pope, placed him in charge of the District of Colorado. At his headquarters in Denver, he initiated reforms that reduced corruption and spent federal funds more efficiently. With few threats from the Native Americans in his district, he had ample time to work on reformulating the tactics used by the army.

Upton believed that the army, in line with the increasingly accurate rifles employed during the war, must alter its tactical methods in attacking entrenched positions. Accordingly, in 1866 he published *Infantry Tactics: Double and Single Rank Adapted to American Topography and Improved Fire-Arms.* In his revised tactics, he emphasized the use of skirmishers, soldiers firing and moving individually, as a screen behind which the main body of troops would advance on the target. Skirmishers would advance in basic units of four soldiers and fire at enemy positions from behind the natural shelter of ravines, rocks, and trees. The field commander would determine the number of "fours" necessary to secure every stage of the advance with overwhelming and accurate fire on the entrenched enemy. After the skirmishers secured the advance route, a single line of assault troops would then overwhelm the defenders.

In the summer 1866, Upton presented his ideas at West Point to a board of officers convened by the War Department. The board unanimously approved the use of his tactics for the army. General Grant himself welcomed Upton's tactical reforms. In February 1867, he wrote to Secretary of War Edwin M. Stanton that "I have seen the system applied to company and battalion drills and am fully satisfied of its superior merits and adaptability to our service."[32] The War Department convened a second board when some officers who were not on the original board disagreed with his ideas. The second board also favored his tactics, and on August 11, 1867, the War Department adopted his new system for the US Army and the militias of the United States.[33] By 1873, tactical manuals for the infantry, artillery, and cavalry were all based on his original work.

Although Upton's tactics were adaptations to linear warfare, they did impact military thinking beyond the late nineteenth century. Upton's "fours" became the precursor of squad-based tactics used by the modern army. He also established a dialogue among military planners that tactics must change to accommodate the development of new weapons and varied topography. The effective employment of his tactics also required well-trained soldiers led by professional, competent officers.

In 1868, Upton married Emily Martin of Willowbrook, New York. He found Emily's delicate features and deep faith in God attractive. He took a one-year leave of absence from the service to court and marry her. The couple was married on February 19, 1868, at Willowbrook and then embarked on a European honeymoon. While in Europe, Emily contracted an infection in her lungs, to which she succumbed on March 28, 1870. According to Peter Michie, Upton mourned the loss of Emily for the rest of his life.[34] To mask the pain and despair caused by his young wife's untimely death, he consumed himself in his work to reform the army.

In June 1870, President Grant selected Upton to be the commandant of the US Military Academy. This assignment placed Upton in the ideal position to raise the level of professionalism needed by officers to employ his tactics. He did not permit the ritual of hazing while he was stationed at West Point and cultivated a sense of honor and integrity among the cadets. He removed complacent, old professors and replaced them with young officers who exemplified his zeal, intellect, and discipline. He met personally with every cadet who violated regulations and stressed the need to follow every order with precision. During his five years at West Point, he was responsible for the instruction of 389 cadets.[35] This core group of officers fought in the Spanish-American War and World War I. His military thought, professionalism, and discipline served as the model for an entire generation of officers and influenced the future development of the US Army.

While Upton was at West Point, he developed a close mentor-protégé relationship with William Tecumseh Sherman, then the army's general-in-chief. Mindful of the need for strategic reform in the US Army, and frustrated by his lack of promotion, Upton suggested to Sherman a plan to achieve both goals. He proposed a tour of Europe to study the military organization and practices of the armies on the continent. Based on his observations, he would make recommendations to reform the American army. Sherman embraced his proposal and suggested the tour include Asia. The War Department allocated funds for the venture, and in

August 1875 Upton and two other officers departed San Francisco for their journey.

For almost eighteen months Upton trekked across Asia and Europe gathering information on the military policies and organization of foreign armies. In some instances his observations proved to be prescient to twenty-first century Americans. He wrote his sister that the Afghans "have warlike manners and little political stability. They possess an eye for an eye mentality. They acknowledge no law and from cradle to grave are born and bred for war."[36] About Persia, Upton commented: "Their leader lives in great palaces while the mass of population dwells in hovels. The leadership shows no concern for the masses."[37]

In December 1877, Upton submitted his report to the War Department detailing his observations and recommendations for reform. In 1878, D. Appleton and Company published the report in book form as *The Armies of Asia and Europe.* His 446-page work recommended a vast reorganization of the army as well as a major rethinking of US military policy. He used his observations and comparisons gathered on the tour to reinforce his experiences from the Civil War. In a letter home, Upton concluded that "our military organization is so worthless that I now feel a thousand pages would not suffice."[38]

In 1878, Sherman sent Upton to Fort Monroe in Virginia. There, Upton served as the superintendent of studies at the Artillery School of Practice. While stationed at Fort Monroe, he began work on another book manuscript, *The Military Policy of the United States,* that promised to approach army reform from a different perspective. He endeavored to write a complete military history of the United States beginning with the Revolutionary War. His purpose was to demonstrate "the enormous and unnecessary sacrifice of life and treasure, which has attended all our armed struggles."[39] He researched and wrote chapters on this subject until his death in 1881. The War Department published his unfinished work posthumously in 1904.

In his two works on military reform, Upton suggested many changes that impacted the development and organization of the American army. One of his most important recommendations was that the US government develop a professional, national army under the leadership of competent officers. He espoused federal rather than state control of the military and professional officers rather than amateurs. He reasoned that the intrusion of states into the national military resulted in "waging wars on the theory that we are a confederacy instead of a nation."[40] He believed that state interference into national wars led to both an inefficient and ineffective fighting force. As a result, wars became longer, deadlier, and more costly to wage. Upton's deep sense of responsibility and duty also led him to see faulty military policy as immoral. He wrote that "whenever [battles] may be lost, it is the people who suffer and the soldiers who die, with the knowledge and the conviction that our military policy is a crime against life, a crime against property, and a crime against liberty."[41]

Upton proposed an army based on a three-tiered system. The first tier would be the regular army composed of professional soldiers and officers. The second tier was the National Volunteers. This tier would be organized in peacetime with each congressional district providing a two hundred-man battalion to this reserve force. The national government would provide professional officers and financial support for each battalion. The state militia would be the final tier. States would support the militias and they would only be used in the last resort to execute laws, suppress rebellions, and repel invasions. The secretary of war assumed command of all tiers when called into national service.[42] The organizational structure of the modern American army reflects Upton's recommendations. Today, the regular professional US Army, the Reserves, and the National Guard comprise America's fighting force.

In *The Armies of Asia and Europe* Upton called for the United States to establish a war academy to "educate officers in the art of war and to prepare them for staff and to hold high command."[43] Upton argued that every great nation had a war academy for its generals and staff officers. The constant reeducation of officers would provide an effective, efficient professional leadership corps in touch with the latest tenets of military science. In his address at the laying of the cornerstone of the Army War College building in Washington on February 21, 1903, Secretary of War Elihu Root paid homage to Upton for championing the necessity of the institution. Today the Army War College in Carlisle, Pennsylvania, is the army's top leadership school. It offers a master's of strategic studies degree to senior military leaders. Notable graduates of the Army War College include Dwight D. Eisenhower, Norman Schwarzkopf Jr., and Tommy Franks. In her work *Soldiers and Scholars: The U. S. Army and the Uses of Military History, 1865–1920,* historian Carol Reardon concluded that "Col. Emory Upton, a strong believer in military professionalism, deserves a high place in the ranks of the US Army's most influential reformers in the post-war years, and his contributions to military education belong near the top of the list of his accomplishments."[44]

Upton also recommended the establishment of a General Staff headed by a chief of staff in *The Armies of Asia and Europe.* The General Staff would supervise the army, prepare war plans, manage the flow of information, and conduct as well as coordinate military activities with the navy. Upton wrote that members of the General Staff should have the "highest professional training and the widest experience of any staff department in the army."[45]

It would be organized so that members would be rotated from line to staff as well as the reverse. The chief of staff would serve as the main military adviser to the president and the secretary of war. This arrangement would provide a direct line of communication between civilian leadership and military command in the field. Congress adopted Upton's proposal when it passed the General Staff Act in 1903, twenty-two years after his death. Congress took action on his reforms after the Dodge Commission (appointed by President William McKinley in 1898) found serious flaws in how the War Department conducted the Spanish-American War. During World War I, the General Staff expanded to five divisions to handle the increased workload—the Executive, War Planning, Purchase and Supply, Storage and Traffic, and Operations divisions. The National Security Act of 1947 provided for a Joint Chiefs of Staff that replaced the General Staff as the president's and secretary of defense's main advisors on military matters.

The twenty-first-century American army is to a significant degree the product of Upton's calls for reform in the decades following the Civil War. The professional, national army of today, run by a competent staff of officers constantly educated at war colleges, remains Upton's foremost legacy to the country. The military and the US Congress also adopted other military reforms Upton advocated. The military dropped short-term enlistments of three to six months in favor of longer terms of service. This allowed the army time to train soldiers properly before inserting them into combat. Promotions based on merit and the interchangeability of staff and line appointments both led to a more professional, competent officer corps. The army also adopted Upton's call for compulsory retirements as well as examinations for promotion. The modern American military modeled its use of nighttime attacks to achieve surprise and victory after his successes at Rappahannock Station, Selma, and Columbus.

Unfortunately, Upton did not live to see most of his reforms go into effect. General William Tecumseh Sherman presciently informed Upton that "The time might not be now, but will come when these [reforms] will be appreciated, and may bear fruit even in our day."[46] In *Upton's Regulars: The 121st New York Infantry in the Civil War,* Salvatore G. Cilella Jr. concludes correctly that Upton "was a man ahead of his time. His philosophy and proposed reforms were not applicable to an isolationist nation."[47]

In 1881, Upton took command of the 4th Artillery, stationed at the Presidio in San Francisco. By this time he had become disgruntled and discouraged. He had prematurely lost his beloved wife. He had not received the promotion he thought he deserved. His call for military reform had fallen on deaf ears in both Congress and the War Department. He also was suffering physical and psychological problems probably caused by a slow-growing tumor in his frontal sinuses. His sinus condition brought about severe headaches that rendered him incapable of concentrating on his duties. The pain caused him to lapse into bouts of depression and deprived him of rational thought. On the evening of March 14, 1881, he wrote a short letter to his sister Sara and a one-line note of resignation with an explanation to the adjutant general. He then picked up his Colt .45 and shot himself in the head. The talented life of Emory Upton had reached an abrupt end at the age of forty-two.

In 1904, President Theodore Roosevelt encouraged Secretary of State Elihu Root to publish Upton's unfinished *Military Policy of the United States.* The mediocre performance of the US Army in the Spanish-American War had led to an outcry for military reform, and Upton's work soon became the bible for military reformers who led the "Preparedness Movement" in the early twentieth century.[48] As the winds of war swirled around Europe, the army adopted many of Upton's reforms and moved this branch of the service into the modern era. In assessing Upton's contributions to the modern army, Andrew J. Bacevich wrote, "to a greater extent than any other officer since his time, Upton has determined the way our Army thinks. . . . Even those who took issue with Upton did so on the terms he established."[49] If Upton was not the father of the modern American army, then he unquestionably served as its most important and vocal proponent.

In 1895, General James H. Wilson wrote the introductory note for Peter Michie's biography of Upton, *The Life and Letters of Emory Upton.* Wilson's tribute to his former division commander speaks to the significance of Upton's life and achievements. He wrote: "so long as the Union has such soldiers as he to defend it, it will be perpetual."[50] Upton could not have asked for a finer or more apposite eulogy.

Notes

1. Peter S. Michie, *The Life and Letters of Emory Upton, Colonel of the Fourth Regiment of Artillery* (New York: D. Appleton, 1885), 2.

2. Merritt Starr, "General Emory Upton—His Brothers, His Career," *Oberlin Alumni Magazine* 18 (May 1922): 14.

3. Stephen E. Ambrose, *Upton and the Army* (Baton Rouge: Louisiana State Univ. Press, 1964), 5.

4. James Harris Fairchild, *Oberlin: The Colony and the College* (Oberlin: E. J. Goodrich, 1883), 11–53.

5. Michie, *The Life and Letters of Emory Upton,* 5.

6. Ibid., 7.

7. Morris Schaff, *The Spirit of Old West Point, 1858–1862* (Boston: Houghton Mifflin, 1907), 142–48.

8. Michie, *The Life and Letters of Emory Upton,* 50.

9. Ibid., 53.

10. Emory Upton, *The Military Policy of the United States* (1904; reprint, Washington, D.C.: Government Printing Office, 1912), 227–62.

11. Ibid., 243.

12. Ibid.

13. Michie, *The Life and Letters of Emory Upton,* 65.

14. Ambrose, *Upton and the Army,* 20.

15. Richard Barry, "Emory Upton, Military Genius," *New York Times Magazine,* June 16, 1918, 2.

16. Ambrose, *Upton and the Army,* 69.

17. Michie, *The Life and Letters of Emory Upton,* 85.

18. Ambrose, *Upton and the Army,* 27.

19. Michie, *The Life and Letters of Emory Upton,* 114–15.

20. Ibid.

21. George T. Stevens, *Three Years in the Sixth Corps: A Concise Narrative of Events in the Army of the Potomac from 1861 to the Close of the Rebellion, April, 1865* (New York: D. Van Nostrand, 1870), 131–32.

22. Michie, *The Life and Letters of Emory Upton,* 99.

23. Isaac O. Best, *History of the 121st New York State Infantry* (Chicago: J. H. Smith, 1921), 42–79.

24. Michie, *The Life and Letters of Emory Upton,* 107.

25. Ibid., 107.

26. Ibid., 190.

27. Barry, "Emory Upton, Military Genius," 12.

28. James Harrison Wilson, *Under the Old Flag: Recollections of Military Operations in the War for the Union, the Spanish War, the Boxer Rebellion, etc.,* 2 vols. (New York: D. Appleton, 1912), 2:221–30.

29. US War Department, *The War of the Rebellion: A Compilation of the Official Records of the Union* and *Confederate Armies,* 128 vols. (Washington, D.C.: Government Printing Office, 1880–1901), ser. 1, vol. 49, part 1, 478.

30. Starr, "General Emory Upton," 33.

31. Ambrose, *Upton and the Army,* 51.

32. Michie, *The Life and Letters of Emory Upton,* 197.

33. Emory Upton, *Infantry Tactics, Double and Single Rank Adapted to American Topography and Improved Fire-Arms* (New York: D. Appleton, 1868), ii–iv.

34. Michie, *The Life and Letters of Emory Upton,* 235–41.

35. Association of Graduates, *The Register of Graduates and Former Cadets of the United States Military Academy West Point, New York* (West Point, N.Y.: Association of Graduates, 2005), 4–53.

36. Michie, *The Life and Letters of Emory Upton,* 345.

37. Ibid., 400–402.

38. Starr, "General Emory Upton," 34.

39. Upton, *The Military Policy of the United States,* vii.

40. Ibid., xiii.

41. Ibid., xi.

42. Ibid., v.

43. Emory Upton, *The Armies of Asia and Europe* (New York: D. Appleton, 1878), 319.

44. Carol Reardon, *Soldiers and Scholars: The U.S. Army and the Uses of Military History, 1865–1920* (Lawrence: Univ. Press of Kansas, 1990), 36.

45. Upton, *The Armies of Asia and Europe,* 319.

46. Upton, *The Military Policy of the United States,* v.

47. Salvatore G. Cilella Jr., *Upton's Regulars: The 121st New York Infantry in the Civil War* (Lawrence: Univ. Press of Kansas, 2009), 463.

48. Richard C. Brown, "General Emory Upton—The Army's Mahan," *Military Affairs* 17 (Autumn 1953): 129.

49. Andrew J. Bacevich, "Emory Upton: A Centennial Assessment," *Military Review* 61 (December 1981): 22–23.

50. Michie, *The Life and Letters of Emory Upton,* xxviii.

6

Ulrich Bonnell Phillips and World War I

Finding "*pax plantation*" at Camp Gordon, Georgia

John David Smith

In October 1917, the *Atlanta Constitution* reported that "Thousands Pour into Camp Gordon; Many are Negroes."[1] The newspaper referred to US Army Cantonment No. 123, or Camp Gordon, Georgia. The US Army established this facility as a boot camp in July 1917 in Chamblee, in DeKalb County, about fourteen miles northeast of Atlanta in the area known as Silver Lake.[2] It quickly became the largest military training camp in the South.

Soon after Camp Gordon opened its doors, a most unlikely person, the forty-year-old historian Ulrich Bonnell Phillips (1877–1934), joined the base's nonmilitary staff as a volunteer officer for the Young Men's Christian Association (YMCA). In 1917 Phillips, then teaching at the University of Michigan, was completing a book manuscript that eventually became his widely acclaimed and influential *American Negro Slavery: A Survey of the Supply, Employment and Control of Negro Labor as Determined by the Plantation Régime* (1918). Phillips, who had spent most of the World War I years preparing his book for publication, left Ann Arbor for the fall semester, taking a sabbatical to conduct additional research in the South and to add the finishing touches to his project. But Phillips inexplicably changed course, joining the Camp Gordon staff in October.

According to John Herbert Roper, Phillips evolved during this period "from a Progressive analyst of class struggle to a more astute social analyst."[3]

Paul Lawrie maintains that Progressive Era historians and social scientists like Phillips considered the "Negro Problem" as determining "the place of the Negro in the nation's industrial past, present, and future. The wartime state transformed African Americans into industrial factors on a national scale for the first time in American history." Phillips worked at a time when social scientists were shifting their analysis of minority peoples from one based on biology to sociocultural models of race. Resembling other Progressives, his racial ideology exhibited an "abiding tension between progression and regression," a tension "exacerbated by rapid industrialization, migration and war."[4]

This essay tests Roper's and Lawrie's arguments by examining Phillips's experiences during World War I at Camp Gordon. This service contributed to his understanding of blacks in white-run, regimented organizations, bringing to mind encounters between white officers and African American enlisted men who served in the U.S. Colored Troops during the Civil War. Phillips's work at Camp Gordon additionally confirmed his understanding of slavery, plantation paternalism, and the management of subject peoples, all the while underscoring his obsession with racial control, management, order—in short, the maintenance of the status quo in the New South.

By World War I, Phillips, a native Georgian, had established himself as one of the leading historians of the South, already having published five books and several landmark scholarly articles on southern economic history and African American slavery. He taught at the University of Wisconsin from 1902 to 1908 before moving to Tulane University. In 1911 Tulane's dean, fearful that Phillips might leave for another school, described him as "one of the two or three most brilliant scholars in American history to-day." With much prescience he cautioned that Phillips's publications "have made him known on both continents. I think it would be a calamity to the University for us to lose him."[5] That year Phillips indeed left New Orleans for a professorship at Ann Arbor.

His Michigan years, 1911 to 1928, were Phillips's most productive. There he came to dominate first the field of slavery studies, then southern history, and finally to leave his imprint as an interpretive historian who cast his native South as "a land with a unity despite its diversity, with a people having common joys and common sorrows, and, above all, as to the white folk a people with a common resolve indomitably maintained—that it shall be and remain a white man's country."[6] When Phillips changed universities again, in 1929, this time leaving Michigan for Yale University, a colleague remarked that "his pungent personality, his acute criticism and trenchant comment on current events will be greatly missed." Replacing him would be difficult, "as great teachers make a great university, buildings and winning football teams to the contrary."[7]

Phillips left no explicit statement of his attitudes toward the world war, although a Yale colleague, Ralph Henry Gabriel, found Phillips's war work with the YMCA unsurprising. He considered it fully in keeping with Phillips's "near-religious messianic activism."[8] According to Merton L. Dillon, Phillips generally stayed "aloof" from the saber-rattling and propaganda of his colleagues at Ann Arbor and at other universities. That said, Phillips "was as much as an Anglophile as any," having written in 1917, upon election as a fellow in the Royal Historical Society, "Identification with anything authentically British is particularly gratifying."[9] As a graduate student at Columbia University, Phillips had mastered affecting a British accent to mask his southern linguistic roots.[10] No doubt Phillips considered volunteering with the YMCA to work with black recruits his contribution to the war effort.

Although the May 1917 Selective Service Act authorized the military draft registration of blacks as well as whites, race riots in East St. Louis, Illinois, and Houston, Texas, delayed the first African Americans from being called up until October. The US Army desperately needed recruits, regardless of skin color, but African American soldiers in the Great War were "often ignored when not maligned." White southerners feared the prospect of large numbers of armed blacks stationed in military camps in their region. "They believed that the uneasy and sometime violent status quo which they maintained might not withstand the wartime upheaval." The conscription of blacks, a contributor to *The New Republic* explained, "brings the South face to face with the necessity of overhauling its scheme of racial relationships."[11] Ultimately the army drafted more than 367,000 blacks, 200,000 of whom served overseas. African Americans constituted approximately one of every ten soldiers in the American Expeditionary Force. Around 90 percent of the black doughboys, however, served as stevedores, performing fatigue labor and unloading supplies.[12] Black recruits assigned to southern camps experienced firsthand what a contemporary described as the "recrudescence of [the] South's intolerance," what a black combat veteran termed "the prejudices, insults and duplicity of his white American ally."[13]

The army segregated the black troops into separate units from the moment they entered the military training centers. This held special significance in southern cantonments like Georgia's Camp Gordon. "Soldiers training in Jim Crow states would be bound by Jim Crow laws, in camp as well as out."[14] Although it assigned no black officers to Camp Gordon, the facility had six black YMCA officers and several black noncommissioned officers. The NAACP's magazine *The Crisis* reported that 25 percent of the blacks in the camp were illiterate. "Examining and Exemption boards have sent up numbers of colored men who never should have been passed," its editor reported.[15]

As at other US Army bases during the Great War, black soldiers at Camp Gordon suffered numerous indignities. They received inadequate medical care (including failure to receive standard vaccinations for typhoid and physical examinations for tuberculosis, and the assignment of soldiers infected with venereal disease to fatigue labor), served under white commissioned officers, and performed a disproportionate amount of fatigue labor (especially loading and unloading of supplies). The army assigned white sergeants experienced in supervising blacks in agricultural work to train blacks at the camp. "The white chain gang boss, then, would be an ideal man to oversee the work of black privates," wrote John Dittmer, whose account of the social conditions of black troops at Camp Gordon, decidedly separate and unequal, differs dramatically from the roseate one Phillips would write. Dittmer's research suggests that the blacks experienced interracial violence and suffered because the army refused to allow Atlanta blacks to provide the soldiers with necessary social services. He noted that they continually received "rebuffs from the . . . white YMCA and Red Cross officers."[16]

Phillips's work at Camp Gordon constituted part of a larger national mobilization effort. The US Army had thirty-six major cantonments designed to train full divisions of 36,000 men each.[17] The army largely completed these tent and barrack camps by the winter of 1917–1918. Camp Gordon constituted one of sixteen temporary military training camps hurriedly established upon America's entrance into World War I. It was ready to occupy troops in five months and became the most substantial training facility in the region. The first recruits, who came from Georgia, Florida, Alabama, and Tennessee, arrived on September 2, 1917. They eventually formed the 82nd Division of the national army, later known as the "All American" division. It fought with distinction in the St. Mihiel and Meuse-Argonne offensives. Phillips held the unit in the highest esteem.[18]

Camp Gordon was a massive facility. It consisted of 2,400 acres with 1,635 buildings. At the height of its service (August 1918), the base's barracks held 47,489 men; at its lowest point (December 1918), Camp Gordon contained 15,063 soldiers. Its corral space held 7,688 horses and mules. By 1921 the government had salvaged and abandoned the base.[19] At any one time, 40,000 men occupied Camp Gordon; over the course of the war it served 100,000 soldiers. By late 1917 Camp Gordon also hosted more than 9,000 black draftees, the largest number of African Americans assigned to any army base in the nation. It inducted black enlistees from every county in Georgia.[20]

At Camp Gordon the YMCA offered troops religious and literacy training, entertainment, library and mail services, and recreational activities, including intramural boxing.[21] Statistics from one month alone, February 1918, document that Camp Gordon's YMCA hut received some 700,000 visits by soldiers, many of which were by repeat guests. This number suggests "almost the entire population of the camp [visited] every single day. During that time 692,000 letters were written, $58,780 worth of money orders were sold, and 1,850 books were circulated, besides a much larger number of magazines and papers."[22] A volunteer described the camp as "Cosmopolitan . . . in every sense of the word for there were descendants of all tongues and races assembled for a common purpose."[23] Phillips paid special attention to the large number of black recruits billeted there.

The YMCA volunteers assigned to the post supervised the activities and offered immigrant and African American recruits basic education, including training in French and history. The *Atlanta Constitution* pointed out that black troops received the same amusements as white soldiers—moving pictures, lectures, and regimental stunts.[24] The YMCA assigned building number 154 as its designated hut for black troops, determined to transform it into "as home like as possible for the fellows." The agency established an elementary education program for the men, providing such basic literacy as teaching them to sign their names and to write "several words."[25] But the newspaper omitted one significant detail: the YMCA huts were segregated, and segregation in them "was strictly enforced."[26]

Nearby Atlanta University, an African American school established in 1865 by the American Missionary Association, provided books for the training facility's African American in-camp library, and the city's black newspaper, the *Atlanta Independent,* conducted a fund drive to supply the black soldiers with newspapers to read. Even before Camp Gordon became operational, members of Atlanta's black community organized the Colored Committee to plan entertainment for its African American trainees while the city's black churchmen invited soldiers to dinner with members of their congregations. The city's Social Charity Club, comprised of leading blacks, devoted itself to the uplift of the base's African American recruits. In the spring of 1918, one thousand black soldiers from Camp Gordon joined fifteen thousand black Atlantans in a War Savings Stamps drive parade.[27] Camp Gordon also featured an extensive recreation program for its African American troops. By November 1917 its ambitious athletic program included baseball, rugby, basketball, volleyball, soccer, quoits, and medicine ball. The Atlanta Cubs, the city's all-black baseball team, opened its 1918 season against a team composed of African American recruits from Camp Gordon.[28]

An all-white Committee on Colored Cooperation, not the Colored Committee, supposedly coordinated Camp Gordon's educational, recreational, and social programs for blacks with Atlanta's black community. According to Harry H. Pace, secretary of the Colored Committee, "Whenever an attempt was made by the Colored Committee to do something which they [the Committee on Colored Cooperation] believed to be in line with their wishes it was blotted and eventually stopped. The result is that nothing has been done for Colored Soldiers at Camp Gordon who came into the city of Atlanta." In practice the YMCA fell short of harnessing the support of Atlanta's black community, alienating it instead. In October 1917, for example, whites excluded Camp Gordon's black soldiers, along with Atlanta's African American community, from a major patriotic parade. The *Atlanta Independent* charged that the black troops "were snubbed and treated like scullions. . . . They were not wanted—actions spoke louder than words."[29]

Phillips, a close student of class and especially race relations in the Old and New Souths, thus encountered a racial tinder box at Camp Gordon. The presence of such a large contingent of armed African Americans captured the attention of white Atlantans. Local whites considered the assignment of blacks to Camp Gordon most worrisome, fearing mutiny and rebellion by armed blacks akin to the Houston race riot of August 1917 that resulted in the hanging of nineteen black soldiers and the sentencing of forty-one others to life imprisonment.[30]

The *Constitution* commented that fortunately Camp Gordon's commanders "are men who know how to deal with this *problem.* They are stern disciplinarians, most of them southern men, and with their proven abilities and their past experiences, these officers can be depended upon to protect the peace." Beyond this, the newspaper assured its readers that only black recruits from Georgia would receive training there. "They will, in other words, be at home." The editor went on to admonish readers that it was essential "that all must be just to the negro recruits. Police and citizens alike must treat them justly. With firm men and experienced disciplinarians in charge, the situation will be kept well in hand and no trouble will be experienced. And the negroes must themselves feel that they are on trial today as never before in history. If they make good their covenant with their government they will deserve and receive credit. If they do not, they will bring opprobrium on their whole race."[31]

A black clergyman, the Reverend D. W. Cannon, educational secretary and general missionary of the Baptist Convention of Georgia, responded to the *Constitution*'s editorial, reminding readers that many whites found offensive the idea of black men in uniform "and, of course, when trouble [between the races] arises the papers and the police give the negro the worst of it, regardless of the conditions under which the trouble arose." While Cannon agreed that their military experiences at Camp Gordon would test the black recruits, he assured readers that "our boys will deport themselves as becometh soldiers going out to do and die for the Stars and Stripes." That said, he urged the *Constitution*'s editor to admonish whites "that these soldiers are human and know when they are treated right and feel as keenly as anybody else an unnecessary insult." It was in the best interest of whites to treat the black troops fairly, Cannon continued, because "in some crisis across the sea, these same black boys who they fear and the wisdom of whose presence they question, may eventually have to save the shattered remnants of some company of their own white sons who may have fallen into some trap set by the wily and resourceful Germans."[32]

Despite Reverend Cannon's words, the presence of so many black soldiers at a southern military base continued to preoccupy whites. In November 1917 the *Constitution* ran a long feature story designed to convince white Atlantans that they had little to fear from Camp Gordon's African American troops. In her report Isma Dooly, a young reporter for the *Constitution* and a supporter of the conservative National Civic Federation, drew on the well-worn trope of the South's loyal slaves during the Civil War. "Many of the men [at Camp Gordon] were the grandsons of those negroes who had protected the defenseless and innocent on the plantations and in the small communities during the war of the confederacy." She went on to compliment the military for assigning southern white officers to the black units, "for the white southern men—especially the man who is serving his country—knows how to lead these dependent ones."[33]

Dooly also praised the "colored" YMCA for its educational and humanitarian work among the black troops. She quoted J. B. Watson, a black field secretary of the YMCA, who described the recruits as a diverse group, including virtually every white stereotype of contemporary blacks. "I suppose they are an average set of Georgia negroes from every point of view, if you can get an average out of four thousand. They are from the city and country. The musician, the artisan and the college man are all there, and also the crap-shooter and the booze-fighter. The cotton and corn growers from south Georgia mix freely with the butlers, the chauffeur and hotel men from the cities; but they all look alike in khaki." Dooly ended her story on an upbeat note. Despite reservations by blacks and whites about the experiment of training blacks in the South's camps, it appeared to her that military service generally was an uplifting experience for the blacks, physically, mentally, and morally.[34] And, according to Dooly, this experience resulted at least in part from the training that the YMCA provided on military bases like Camp Gordon.

Phillips first served as the YMCA's associate secretary (and later its educational director); he also taught English and French. The *Constitution* welcomed Phillips back to Georgia as a native son, lauding him as a "Famous Educator," an expert on "the history and traditions of the negro race." Phillips, the paper reported,

> is a southerner to the manor born, liberal, big-hearted, jovial. He came south, with his family, in his automobile, on a brief respite from university work in order to do research work, and reaching Atlanta a week ago, went to Camp Gordon purely as a matter of curiosity. While there he became impressed with the wonderful opportunities for educational work among the soldiers, especially among the colored, and he volunteered his services, which were quickly accepted by the war work council. He then received an indefinite leave from his university, drove out to the camp and entered enthusiastically into this new educational work.[35]

Although largely removed from his research and writing, Phillips nonetheless found the work with recruits stimulating and rewarding.[36] In November 1917 he informed his Michigan colleague Carl H. Van Tyne that "This camp work is the most inspiring thing I have ever experienced."[37] In addition to teaching and planning programs, Phillips supervised construction and maintenance of camp buildings. "It would do you good to sit on the side lines and see me hustle," he joked. "Do I find time for educational and other human work? Yes, in crevices. Shall I be able to read proofs on my 'Slavery,' when they shortly begin to come? Damifino. Shall I get to bed tonight? Maybe, if I stop this letter right here."[38]

In December 1917, Phillips assumed responsibility for all educational programs, including classes in English, German, French, and history. The camp offered entertainment most nights. The *Constitution* described Camp Gordon as "a soldier city" with more than thirty thousand men, about one-third of whom were immigrants, hence the importance of presenting classes in English and, in terms of entertainment, the significance of "offering something different and something snappy and attractive every night."[39] Phillips reported to Dean J. R. Effinger at Michigan that his duties at Camp Gordon included serving as "an automobile messenger . . . an introducer of male quartettes, saxophone bands, prestidigitators and spellbinders, a silencer of the noisy, a trainer of the crude into the arts and graces of more or less polite society, a heartener of the downhearted, an intermediary between private and officer, a fountain of knowledge in the fields of strategy, world politics and the reason for things in general, and a doer of a little of everything else including a bit of pulpit oratory. My job is in fact mostly made up of *et ceteras*. Egad, it's a bully one!"[40] The *Constitution* reported a scene at Camp Gordon's train station, describing Phillips as "a tall, ruddy-faced man [who] brought postal cards and stamps to a mob of eager, apprehensive troopers after the clerk had closed the office; dramatically he delivered himself of the last cards as the train pulled from Atlanta heading to the coast and shipment to war."[41]

In a New Year's letter to the *Michigan Alumnus*, Phillips provided additional glimpses into the diverse range of his war work at Camp Gordon:

> I am steadily and speedily on the go from early morn till very dewy eve in my double capacity of educational secretary (they've dropped the "associate" from my title) and superintendent of buildings; but I keep in fitter condition than for many years past. My life is a meeting of emergencies in a constant succession. Yesterday was a fair sample. It began with recruiting carpenters and laborers and showing their foremen and the plumber and the painter their appointed work. Next with my own hands (once fair) I robbed an idle furnace of its grate bars and put them into another whose custodian had let the ashes

accumulate with regrettable results. Next was the induction into office of a new educational secretary for one of the unit buildings and the coaching of a corporal of many tongues who had just been detailed from Division Headquarters, at our request, to labor with the hundreds of troops in every battalion whose accustomed languages are other than English and to raise their morale by teaching them our country's cause. Then I rode a truck to a pile of random lumber and helped the driver to load 2 x 6's for an extension to one of our buildings, and en route inspected some of the work in progress. Hard upon this followed what proved an altercation with the camp 'phone manager over the shifting of certain instruments, and a search of the express office for consignments of Christmas presents for the troops. This was fruitless in itself but yielded a stamp-selling machine (five ones for a nickel) ordered for our service; but the apparatus when unpacked proved to have been broken in transit and for the present useless. Interspersed were sundry 'phone calls and momentary conferences as I was caught on the wing. One dealt with the organization of a new class in French, another with an order from the general in command making attendance on classes in English mandatory upon all troops deficient therein, a third on French signboards now being painted for the camp, etc., etc. After a futile inquiry for certain soldiers, as yet unknown, who walked off with a neat stack of our weather boarding, I snatched a genuinely quick lunch, broke away from buttonholing colleagues at mess, and made a dash to Atlanta with two grate bars in my tonneau which I carried to a foundry to serve as patterns for a dozen new ones. Followed a conference with the executive secretary of the Southeastern Department on the firing of an incompetent and trouble-making member of our staff, another with our architect, then the purchase of two cars of lumber, two hundred feet of stove pipe, a quantity of Cornell wall-board, a half gross of "Soldier's Spoken French," and sundry other matters before I dined with my wife in town, quite briskly and drove back to camp, thirteen miles, having picked up several soldiers and the aforesaid stovepipe for the trip. The rest of the evening was taken up with a staff conference, a bit of chauffeuring about camp (nine passengers one trip clustered closely in my five-passenger car), the jotting of my intended schedule for the morrow, and the writing of several imperatively necessary letters. In bed I started to read the *Atlantic Monthly,* but sleep cut that

> off. Today, New Year's, my workmen have taken a half holiday, which permits me to ramble a bit in this letter. Tomorrow will be much like yesterday, and many morrows to come. Next week, however, I expect the proofs for my book, "American Negro Slavery" to begin to arrive. When I shall read and revise them is a question without an answer.[42]

Despite his diverse and hectic duties at Camp Gordon, while in Georgia Phillips continued his historical work, determined to track down plantation records "when affairs permit" during his southern sojourn.[43] In April 1918 he delivered an informal talk on "The Plantation Product of Men" at the Georgia Historical Association's annual meeting in Atlanta.[44] Claiming that his duties as educational director prevented him from presenting a formal paper, Phillips spoke without notes.[45] Significantly, he drew upon his experiences with black troops at Camp Gordon in his encomium of the Old South's planter elite and their world.

Phillips described the plantation as important in southern history as much for being "the factory system applied to agriculture" as for imparting a distinctive "imprint upon the South," what he considered "a philosophy which we must pass on in our turn." Phillips identified a nexus between social conditions in a World War I-era Georgia army base and those that existed under plantation slavery. For example, he said that a senior officer admonished a newly minted officer not to believe what his soldiers said, but rather to rely on their noncommissioned officers, who, like slave foremen of old, understood their charges. "At Camp Gordon it is a pleasure to be with the negroes," Phillips explained, "for they are, for the most part, plantation negroes, and it is easy to manage them. Those who know the type, know when and where to count on it, and when otherwise."[46] Phillips then summarized his arguments about the social role of the plantation and the planters—themes that had their roots in his previous essays and soon would appear full blown in *American Negro Slavery.*

He defined the plantation broadly—as an agricultural workplace, as a homestead, and as a training school. Phillips credited planters with playing several roles for their slaves and for their communities—as magistrates, as administrators and, drawing on a Progressive Era analogy, as settlement workers in modern cities. "They served as patterns of life as well as preceptors in the training of a backward people," Phillips explained. He waxed nostalgic for the sense of "neighborliness" present on the plantation but absent in twentieth-century America. Unlike what he termed "the curse of modern industrialism," plantation agriculture provided care and supervision of the work force from sunup to sunset. The planters' economic self-interest—they owned the factors of production—motivated them as owners and managers to care for their workers. Planters and plantation mistresses generally created a sense of "intimacy and cordiality" between themselves and their slaves.[47]

The historian observed the same comradeship between whites and blacks at Camp Gordon as allegedly had existed between masters and their slaves. In camp, he explained, "white and black enlisted men from the same county meet in warm friendliness. The cordiality between the two elements dates from plantation times." Those prone to "view the old Southern regime from afar off with a theorist's eye are likely to think it was an agency of race alienation." But no, Phillips insisted, "the grouping of persons of the two races in the intimate relationship of possession tended strongly to counteract that antipathy which all races feel toward each other." "The possession was not wholly of the slave by the master," he explained, "but also of the master by the slave."[48]

Phillips considered plantation life an apt analogy for the military. Like soldiers, the slaves worked in squads trained by discipline and routine. He credited the plantation regime with producing "types of men and women, white and black, that are distinctive in the world." Phillips insisted that the plantation "made for strength of character and readiness to meet emergencies, for patience and tact, for large mindedness, gentility, and self-control." He yearned for those traditions—elements too often lost "in the whirl of modern life." Yet Phillips saw evidence around him—at Camp Gordon and elsewhere in the New South—that the positive qualities of "the old regime" were being fostered, allowing the South to "remain in long future times as wholesome, constructive, and strong as she has been in the past."[49] Phillips's informal talk before the Georgia Historical Association thus served as a trial run of sorts for the preface of his *American Negro Slavery* that he drafted while serving with the black troops at Camp Gordon.

In November 1918, after having performed "*et ceteras*" at Camp Gordon for more than a year, Phillips moved in yet another unlikely direction; he received a commission as a captain in the US Army's Military Intelligence Division (MID), Army General Staff, Washington, D.C.[50] This was an unusual move because Phillips had no previous military experience and, because of his wife and two children, his Selective Service Local Board had classified him as 2-A, a deferred status for men with dependents.[51]

Despite his enthusiasm for military intelligence, Phillips's work for MID ended as abruptly as it had begun. On February 10, 1919, the army, apparently no longer needing his services, unceremoniously discharged him. Phillips thus returned to Michigan for the start of the spring 1919 semester.[52] By then his new book *American Negro Slavery* already was receiving rave reviews. For example, Philip Alexander Bruce judged it "a monument of research, and equally so of fair and discriminating presentation." In 1919, Bruce, unaware of future fierce historiographical debates over slavery and Phillips's declining reputation, wrote, "I venture to say that you have said the final word."[53]

Significantly, Phillips had composed the preface to *American Negro Slavery* during his stint at Camp Gordon. As his talk before the Georgia Historical Association made clear, his experiences with black troops informed, meshed closely with, and confirmed his interpretations of both slavery and contemporary race relations. He considered his service at Camp Gordon akin to conducting anthropological-sociological field research among African Americans. According to Roper, at the army base Phillips "watched his surroundings, this community, with singular fascination."[54] Phillips even recorded some of what he saw at Camp Gordon in photographs, a medium he considered both "modern" and "scientific."[55] Roper explains: "Blacks were everywhere, cooking, on sanitation detail, in construction, basically performing the indispensable dirty work of running an army machine. Yet, however degrading the work, there remained one fact: everybody in the United States Army must learn to handle firearms; every soldier's basic first training is infantry. So all those smiling, cooperative, obedient, black soldiers had fighting knowledge and many were carrying arms."[56] Phillips differed from those white Atlantans who had expressed reservations about the prospect of armed blacks. His observations of Camp Gordon's African American troops convinced him that the future course of race relations in the region would be bright if southern white paternalism, like that practiced by the "best" southern slaveholders of old, prevailed. What Phillips saw at the military camp put to rest, at least in his mind, visions of race war in the region.

Phillips's observations of the men of the two races interacting socially (although "of course quartered separately"), he recalled in the preface to *American Negro Slavery*, "reënforced my earlier conviction that Southern racial asperities are mainly superficial, and that the two great elements are fundamentally in accord. That the harmony is not a new thing is evinced by the very tone of the camp."[57] That Phillips compared chattel slavery with life in the rigidly segregated US Army suggests that he believed, even a half-century after emancipation, that African Americans continued to work best under white management. Like slaves, the black soldiers reportedly excelled at performing rote tasks such as military drill under the discipline of white officers and black noncommissioned officers. According to Phillips, the black men exhibited

> the same easy-going, amiable, serio-comic obedience and the same personal attachments to white men, as well as the same sturdy light-heartedness and the same love of laughter and of rhythm, which distinguished their forbears. The non-commissioned officers . . . show a punctilious pride of place which matches that of the plantation foremen of old; and the white officers who succeed best in the command of these companies reflect the planter's admixture of tact with firmness of control, the planter's patience of instruction, and his crisp though cordial reciprocation of sentiment. The negroes are not enslaved but drafted; they dwell not in cabins but in barracks; they shoulder the rifle not the hoe; but the visitor to their company streets in evening hours enters nevertheless a plantation atmosphere.[58]

Phillips noted approvingly that when relaxing in their barracks (significantly he termed it "the quarter"), the black troops sang "Down by the Riverside." This "old-time unmartial" spiritual contained the refrain "I ain' go' study war no mo' / I ain' go study war no mo' / Study war no mo'!" Not only did the black soldiers sing but, according to Phillips, they also gambled. He claimed to have heard through a barracks "window the mention of two bits as a wager, and an earnest adjuration of 'sebben or lebben.'" To these familiar Jim Crow-era white stereotypes of blacks, Phillips added: "The grim realities of war, though a constant theme in the inculcation of discipline is as remote in the thought of these men as is the planet Mars. Yet each of their lieutenants is justly confident that his platoon will follow whithersoever he may lead." In Phillips's opinion, "It may be that the change of African nature by plantation slavery has been exaggerated. At any rate a generation of freedom has wrought less transformation in the bulk of the blacks than might casually be supposed."[59] Reviewing Phillips's *American Negro Slavery,* the black scholar W.E.B. Du Bois, one of Phillips's most consistent and vocal critics, found astounding that a historian in 1918 considered the mass of African Americans unchanged from the fourteenth to the twentieth century. When Phillips listened to the black troops at Camp Gordon, Du Bois observed, all he heard was "the throwing of dice."[60]

Echoing Du Bois, Adriane Lentz-Smith recently has charged that Phillips's descriptions of Camp Gordon underscore the degree to which racism both blinded him to the progress by African Americans since emancipation and deafened him to the cries of Jim Crow-era blacks for true freedom and justice. As Lentz-Smith observes correctly, "Phillips heard the singing" at Camp Gordon "but he did not actually listen." He was unattuned both to *why* the men sang—the burdens their people had experienced before, during, and after emancipation—and to *what* they sang. "To truly hear African Americans," she explains, "Phillips would have had to listen past his prejudices, to understand black people as fully human, and to see black troops as men, not children." Ignoring their struggles and accomplishments since emancipation, Phillips overlooked how African Americans had grown and changed. "The system of Jim Crow that Phillips had helped to construct had waged war on black citizenship since the late nineteenth century," Lentz-Smith maintains. To the soldiers "Down by the Riverside" may have signified a range of emotions, from defiance to despair, but, Lentz-Smith adds, "it was never the unthinking, unchanging 'old-time' song that Phillips imagined."[61]

Of course, both Du Bois and Lentz-Smith are correct. In 1918 Phillips misread virtually all manifestations of African American agency, cultural expression, manhood, self-assertion, and self-respect. Just as he failed to recognize brutality on the part of masters and resistance on the part of slaves, Phillips's racial bias blinded him to the accomplishments by and the meaning of black military service to the men he engaged with at Camp Gordon. Yet both critics, like most of Phillips's detractors, missed how his albeit limited and selective engagement with black troops at Camp Gordon influenced his racial thought, how this experience left him sanguine for race relations in the post–World War I South. While historians rightly denounce Phillips's well-documented condescension, elitism, and racism, he nevertheless was cautiously optimistic for peaceful race and social relations and degrees of assimilation in the post–World War I world.

Although not uncritical of aspects of plantation life, since 1903 Phillips repeatedly had espoused the importance—economically and socially—of organizing black laborers on plantations, rather than on small, independent farms. And Phillips had campaigned on and off for years for the reestablishment of the plantation system as the solution to the South's economic and racial problems. Differentiating between slavery (which he considered an inefficient and archaic labor system) and the plantation (which he judged a modern, efficient locus for organizing agricultural laborers, a blend of the modern factory and the social settlement house), Phillips called for the return of what he termed "patriarchal plantations" and the phasing out of independent black-run farms. Such a move, Phillips explained in the *Sewanee Review* and elsewhere, "is therefore a movement of progress from the stagnation of demoralized industry in the recent past toward a more effective system for the future. Together with the recent growth of cotton factories, it indicates that the South is now becoming more fully alive to the spirit of specialized and systematized industry which is elsewhere prevalent in modern America."[62]

Phillips argued that close interracial association between blacks and whites held the key to southern economic progress and racial harmony. "The South has long been held in a false position of hostility to the negro, while in actual truth the conservative thinking, God-fearing element among the Southern people have been and still remain the most substantial, practical, and valuable friends that their black neighbors have ever had." Whites needed efficient, reliable black labor, Phillips explained, while blacks required the example and precept white tutelage conferred. "The average negro," Phillips remarked, "has many characteristics of a child, and must be guided and governed, and often guarded against himself, by a sympathetic hand." Relocating blacks to moderately sized plantations, Phillips concluded, would allow the African American "to take his place in the modern world of specialized and organized industry and yet have the protection from the harsher features of the modern strife, which will be afforded him by the patriarchal character of the system of which he is a part."[63]

Roper suggests that Phillips's Camp Gordon experiences confirmed his belief that the plantation model would resolve the problem of racial discord in the New South. It alone would allow for "peaceful coexistence" between the races and remove the temporary racial tensions that resulted from Reconstruction. Roper has incisively pinpointed Phillips's four-part schema of southern race relations: First, "the long decades of antebellum *pax plantation.*" Second, "an interregnum of 'asperities'" during and after Reconstruction. Third, "a present marked by *pax Camp Gordon.*" Fourth, "a future of *pax plantation.*" Roper added, however, that Phillips's vision for plantation-based racial harmony hinged "on the conservative elite getting its message of *back to the farm* to the masses, black and white."[64]

Although Phillips had long subscribed to his belief in "*pax plantation*," his return "home" to Georgia 1917–1918 and his YMCA military service at Camp Gordon convinced him even more so of its relevance, utility, and wisdom. The black doughboys' dignified, disciplined, and, to his mind, "managed" behavior at Camp Gordon confirmed for Phillips the need for white paternalistic racial control in the modern South. "Demonstrations," Roper maintains, "of decorous black behavior in camp were a special boon for the historian: his own best hopes and dreams were borne into reality by Negro soldiers; now he could bend to the task of proselytizing others."[65]

As Phillips put his finishing touches on *American Negro Slavery* and performed his seemingly endless "*et ceteras*" at Camp Gordon, he drew a parallel between the discipline, organization, and order of army life and what he famously termed "the plantation régime." "Plantation slavery had in strictly business aspects at least as many drawbacks as it had attractions," Phillips admitted in his book. "But in the large it was less a business than a life; it made fewer fortunes than it made men."[66] In his opinion the black troops made good soldiers because their ancestors had been good slaves.

Phillips's military experiences as a YMCA volunteer led him to resolve "the tension between assimilation and segregation" that Lawrie identified.[67] They reinforced his attitude toward blacks (or so-called inferior peoples), confirmed his aversion to radical change, and strengthened his belief in the economic assimilation and social segregation of African Americans. Phillips's military work validated his longstanding commitment to racial and class hierarchy, especially the circumscribed place of blacks in American life. His day-to-day work with African Americans reaffirmed—did not challenge—his almost two decades of research on their life and labor as slaves. Denying the capacity of blacks for marked growth and change, Phillips envisioned no "New Negro" in 1920s America. Instead he looked back longingly to the old Negro of slavery times. For him, the experiences of African American recruits at Camp Gordon proved that twentieth-century blacks succeeded best under white management. To Phillips's mind, "the black was a ready ally in a war to save civilization"—both overseas and in the New South.[68]

Notes

An earlier version of this essay appeared as "Finding '*pax plantation*' at Camp Gordon, Georgia: Historian Ulrich Bonnell Phillips and World War I," *Journal of the Gilded Age and Progressive Era* 13 (October 2014): 564–99, © Society for the

History of the Gilded Age and Progressive Era, reprinted with deletions, minor emendations, and permission.

1. "Thousands Pour into Camp Gordon; Many are Negroes," *Atlanta Constitution,* October 5, 1917, 1.

2. T. F. McCarthy, *"A Year at Camp Gordon": United States Cantonment, No. 123* (Wilkes-Barre, Pa.: T. F. McCarthy, 1920), 10; Camp Gordon Historical Marker Number 044-91, http://www.hmdb.org/marker.asp?marker=14570 (accessed March 22, 2012); Todd Womack, "World War I in Georgia," in *New Georgia Encyclopedia,* http://www.georgiaencyclopedia.org/nge/Article.jsp?id=h-3223 (accessed June 27, 2011). The cantonment was located at the present site of Airport Drive. It was named for Confederate lieutenant general and later Georgia governor and US senator John Brown Gordon.

3. John Herbert Roper, "Introduction to the ROSE Edition," in Ulrich Bonnell Phillips, *Georgia and State Rights* (1902; reprint, Macon, Ga.: Mercer Univ. Press, 1984), xxiv.

4. Paul Raymond Din Lawrie, "'To Make the Negro Anew': The African American Worker in the Progressive Imagination, 1896–1928" (Ph.D. diss., University of Toronto, 2011), 255, 205, 255.

5. [Dean ?] to E. B. Craighead, February 8, 1911, Ulrich B. Phillips Personnel File, Tulane University Archives.

6. Ulrich B. Phillips, "The Central Theme of Southern History," *American Historical Review* 34 (October 1928): 31.

7. Arthur S. Aiton, "Professor Phillips Goes to Yale," *Michigan Alumnus* 35 (September 14, 1929): 794.

8. John Herbert Roper interview with Ralph Henry Gabriel, March 13, 1975, Ulrich B. Phillips Papers, Southern Historical Collection, Louis Round Wilson Special Collections Library, University of North Carolina at Chapel Hill.

9. Merton L. Dillon, *Ulrich Bonnell Phillips: Historian of the Old South* (Baton Rouge: Louisiana State Univ. Press, 1985), 102.

10. Roper interview with Gabriel, Phillips Papers; Roper, "Introduction to the ROSE Edition," xvii.

11. Edward M. Coffman, *The War to End All Wars: The American Military Experience in World War I* (1968; reprint, Lexington: Univ. Press of Kentucky, 1998), 69, 231; "Negro Conscription," *The New Republic,* October 20, 1917, 318.

12. Lawrie, "'To Make the Negro Anew,'" 128, 169.

13. W. Allison Sweeney, *History of the American Negro in the Great World War* (1919; reprint, New York: Negro Universities Press, 1969), 81; Sergeant Greenleaf B. Johnson, "The Events of the Times: The Negro's Part in the War in Democracy," *Washington Bee,* January 18, 1919, 1.

14. Richard Slotkin, *Lost Battalions: The Great War and the Crisis of American Nationality* (New York: Henry Holt, 2005), 49.

15. "The War," *The Crisis* 15 (March 1918): 242.

16. John Dittmer, *Black Georgia in the Progressive Era, 1900–1920* (Urbana: Univ. of Illinois Press, 1977), 194–96.

17. Allan R. Millett and Peter Maslowski, *For the Common Defense: A Military History of the United States of America* (New York: Free Press, 1984), 336.

18. See Ulrich B. Phillips, review of *Official History of 82nd Division American Expeditionary Forces, "All American" Division, 1917–1919,* in *American Historical Review* 26 (October 1920): 151–52.

19. Nancy K. Bristow, *Making Men Moral: Social Engineering during the Great War* (New York: New York Univ. Press, 1996), 236; Georgia Historic Marker, 044-91, erected 1988, Chamblee, Georgia. See http://www.hmdb.org/PhotoFullSize.asp?PhotoID=47293 (accessed July 3, 2011).

20. "The War," *The Crisis* 15 (December 1917): 85; A. M. Trawick, "Southern Race Questions in War Times," in *The Human Way: Addresses on Race Problems at the Southern Sociological Congress, Atlanta,* ed. James E. McCulloch, 2nd ed. (Washington: Southern Sociological Congress, [1918]), 120; Dittmer, *Black Georgia in the Progressive Era,* 195. Dittmer notes that after September 1917 only Georgia blacks trained at Camp Gordon. See page 194n.

21. "Prof. Phillips Heads Educational Program," *Atlanta Constitution,* December 6, 1917, 7. On YMCA-sponsored boxing matches at Camp Gordon, see McCarthy, *"A Year at Camp Gordon,"* 126–27, and Richard C. Lancaster, *Serving the U.S. Armed Forces 1861–1986: The Story of the YMCA's Ministry to Military Personnel for 125 Years* (Schaumburg, Ill.: Armed Services YMCA of the USA, 1987), 62 (photograph).

22. Frederick Harris, ed., *Service with Fighting Men: An Account of the Work of the American Young Men's Christian Associations in the World War,* 2 vols. (New York: Association Press, 1922), 1:388.

23. McCarthy, *"A Year at Camp Gordon,"* Introductory.

24. "Thousands Pour into Camp Gordon; Many are Negroes," 1.

25. Bristow, *Making Men Moral,* 150.

26. Arthur E. Barbeau and Florette Henri, *The Unknown Soldiers: African-American Troops in World War I* (1974; reprint, New York: Da Capo, 1996), 40.

27. Bristow, *Making Men Moral,* 150–51, 153, 154.

28. Ibid., 150–51, 153.

29. Ibid., 154–55.

30. See Robert V. Haynes, *A Night of Violence: The Houston Riot of 1917* (Baton Rouge: Louisiana State Univ. Press, 1976).

31. "The Negroes in Camp," *Atlanta Constitution,* August 30, 1917, 6 (emphasis added).

32. "Negro Minister Bespeaks Race Harmony in Places Where Colored Troops Train," *Atlanta Constitution,* September 9, 1917, A4.

33. Isma Dooly, "Negroes Trained at Camp Gordon New War Front," *Atlanta Constitution,* November 11, 1917, 6.

34. Ibid.

35. "Famous Educator Joins Gordon Staff," *Atlanta Constitution,* October 13, 1917, 11.

36. Dillon, *Ulrich Bonnell Phillips: Historian of the Old South,* 103–4.

37. Phillips to Claude H. Van Tyne, November 4, 1917, Claude H. Van Tyne Papers, Michigan Historical Collections, Bentley Historical Library, University of Michigan.

38. Phillips to Van Tyne, December 20, 1917, Van Tyne Papers.

39. "Prof. Phillips Heads Educational Program," *Atlanta Constitution,* December 6, 1917, 7.

40. U. B. Phillips to J. R. Effinger, n.d., *Michigan Alumnus* 24 (December 1917): 151–52.

41. Clipping from *Atlanta Constitution,* n.d., paraphrased in Roper, "Introduction to the ROSE Edition," xxvii.

42. Ulrich B. Phillips to the General Secretary [January 1, 1918], *Michigan Alumnus* 24 (February 1918): 283–84.

43. Ulrich B. Phillips to William Watts Ball, June 24, 1918, William Watts Ball Papers, Rare Book, Manuscript, and Special Collections Library, Duke University.

44. "Minutes of the Second Annual Meeting," *Proceedings of the Second Annual Session of the Georgia Historical Association, Atlanta, Ga., April 6, 1918* [Athens, Ga., n.p., 1918], 5–6.

45. Ulrich B. Phillips, "The Plantation Product of Men," in *Proceedings of the Second Annual Session of the Georgia Historical Association, Atlanta, Ga., April 6, 1918* [Athens, Ga., n.p., 1918], 12n.

46. Ibid., 12–13.

47. Ibid., 13–14.

48. Ibid., 14.

49. Ibid., 14–15.

50. "Dr. Phillips Is Made Captain in the Army," *La Grange (Ga.) Graphic,* November 7, 1918, 1.

51. William H. Esslinger to Whom It May Concern, October 31, 1918, Army Official Military Personnel Files, Record Group 319, Records of the Army Staff, National Personnel Records Center, National Archives and Records Administration, St. Louis, Missouri (hereafter Army OMPF Files). Esslinger was a member of the Selective Service Local Board for County of Washtenaw, Michigan.

52. Separation Order, February 10, 1919, Army OMPF Files.

53. Philip Alexander Bruce to Ulrich B. Philips, March 11, 1919, Ulrich Bonnell Phillips Papers (MS 397), Manuscripts and Archives, Yale University Library.

54. John Herbert Roper, *U.B. Phillips: A Southern Mind* (Macon, Ga.: Mercer Univ. Press, 1984), 111.

55. Four photographic images Phillips captured of Camp Gordon include photographs of men, possibly recruits, standing along a train at Camp Gordon (#44302), black civilians, possibly recruits, lined up outside a camp structure

(#44303), soldiers in a Camp Gordon courtyard near barracks (#44304), and men, possibly recruits, walking from a train at Camp Gordon (#44305). These images are available at Yale University Library's Manuscripts and Archives Digital Image Database: http://images.library.yale.edu/madid/showThumb.aspx?qs=76&qm=15&q=ulrich+phillips (accessed June 5, 2012). On Phillips and photography of African Americans and the built environment, see Patricia Bellis Bixel and John David Smith, *Seeing the New South: Race and Place in the Photographs of Ulrich B. Phillips* (Columbia: Univ. of South Carolina Press, 2013).

56. Roper, *U.B. Phillips: A Southern Mind,* 111.

57. Ulrich Bonnell Phillips, *American Negro Slavery: A Survey of the Supply, Employment and Control of Negro Labor as Determined by the Plantation Régime* (New York: D. Appleton, 1918), [ii].

58. Ibid.

59. Ibid., [ii–iii].

60. W.E.B. Du Bois, review of Ulrich B. Philips, *American Negro Slavery: A Survey of the Supply, Employment and Control of Negro Labor as Determined by the Plantation Régime,* in *American Political Science Review* 12 (November 1918): 723. On the Phillips-Du Bois relationship, see John David Smith, "Du Bois and Phillips: Symbolic Antagonists of the Progressive Era," *Centennial Review* 24 (winter 1980): 88–102. Jonathan Rosenberg provides an excellent analysis of the meaning of the war to black activists, including Du Bois. See *How Far the Promised Land? World Affairs and the American Civil Rights Movement from the First World War to Vietnam* (Princeton: Princeton Univ. Press, 2006), chapter 1.

61. Adriane Lentz-Smith, *Freedom Struggles: African Americans and World War I* (Cambridge, Mass.: Harvard Univ. Press, 2009), 2.

62. Ulrich B. Phillips, "The Plantation as a Civilizing Factor," *Sewanee Review* 12 (July 1904): 257, 260. Phillips made the same arguments in "The Economics of the Plantation," *South Atlantic Quarterly* 2 (July 1903): 231–36; "Making Cotton Pay," *The World's Work* 8 (May 1904): 4783–92; and "The Decadence of the Plantation System," *Annals of the American Academy of Political and Social Science* 35 (January 1910): 37–41. He continued to note the ubiquity of the plantation following World War I in "Plantations with Slave Labor and Free," *American Historical Review* 30 (July 1925): 738–53.

63. Phillips, "The Plantation as a Civilizing Factor," 264, 266.

64. Roper, *U.B. Phillips: A Southern Mind,* 112.

65. Ibid., 113.

66. Phillips, *American Negro Slavery,* 401.

67. Lawrie, "'To Make the Negro Anew,'" 255.

68. Roper, "Introduction to the ROSE Edition," xxvii.

7

The Man and the Martyr

Abraham Lincoln in African American History and Memory

James Oliver Horton and Lois E. Horton

On April 14, 1876, a crowd gathered on the east side of Capitol Hill in Washington, D.C., to witness the unveiling of the Freedmen's Memorial dedicated to the memory of Abraham Lincoln and his role in Black freedom. President Ulysses S. Grant, his cabinet members, justices of the Supreme Court, the Japanese minister, and other distinguished guests were arrayed behind the speaker's stand, and the marine band opened the proceedings with a rendition of "Hail Columbia." With Professor John Mercer Langston presiding, African Methodist Episcopal bishop John M. Brown offered a prayer and the Honorable J. Henri Burch of Louisiana read Lincoln's Emancipation Proclamation. In response, the crowd cheered, and the band played the French revolutionary hymn "La Marseillaise." James E. Yeatman, president of the Western Sanitary Commission, the white wartime relief society that had overseen the Freedmen's Monument project, then took the stand to explain his organization's role. He told the story of Charlotte Scott, a freedwoman who had, immediately after the assassination of President Lincoln, decided that African Americans should build a monument to his memory. She entrusted her $5 contribution to her former owner, a wartime refugee from Virginia, who gave it to the general commanding a military post in St. Louis. The general suggested that the Western Sanitary Commission take charge of the project. From this modest beginning, supporters raised contributions to build the memorial. Most of the contributors were African Americans, many of them soldiers who had fought for their freedom in the Civil War.[1]

A cannon salute, strains of "Hail to the Chief," and audience applause greeted President Grant's unveiling of the monument. Frederick Douglass, abolitionist speaker and newspaper editor, formerly enslaved, then took his place on the speaker's platform, addressing the assemblage as "Friends and Fellow-Citizens." It was the eleventh anniversary of Lincoln's assassination, and Douglass was the most widely known Black man in America. They were there to pay respects, he said, and to express "our grateful sense of the vast, high, and preeminent services rendered to ourselves, to our race, to our country, and to the whole world by Abraham Lincoln."[2]

Douglass's opinion of Lincoln had not always been so favorable. In the early years of the Civil War, the president had refused to support efforts by many of his officers to shelter enslaved people who entered US lines, fearing that such actions might drive the loyal slave states into the Confederacy. Lincoln warned US commanders to prevent slave insurrections, even as they waged war on the rebellious slaveholders. In August 1861, John C. Frémont, commander of the Western Department of the Army, declared martial law in Missouri in response to intense Confederate guerrilla action there and issued an order freeing those enslaved by all disloyal Missouri slaveholders. Lincoln revoked the order and removed him from command. Lincoln also directed US military units to respect the Fugitive Slave Act of 1850 and to return to their owners enslaved people who escaped to Union lines. Douglass had reacted angrily to Lincoln's actions, declaring him "the most dangerous advocate of slave-hunting and slave-catching in the land."[3]

African Americans understood that they could count few American political leaders as friends, particularly national leaders in presidential politics. Thus, as the 1860 presidential election approached, they expected little of the candidates. Surely the Democratic candidate Stephan A. Douglas, whose longstanding opposition to antislavery was well known, was no friend of Black people. John Bell of the middle ground Constitutional Union Party was little better, and John C. Breckinridge, the standard-bearer of the southern Democrats who broke from the national party to more strongly support the proslavery position, was even worse. In that election Abraham Lincoln, the Republican candidate, was the only reasonable hope for African Americans, but few were excited about his candidacy. During the summer before the elections, Black abolitionist leader H. Ford Douglas of Illinois toured the East, addressing free Black people and white abolitionists. Like most African Americans, he was not encouraged by the fact that there were four nonabolitionist choices on the ballot that fall.

Speaking at a Fourth of July abolitionist gathering in Framingham, Massachusetts, he asserted that African Americans had no real choice among the candidates. "So far as the principles of freedom and the hopes of the black man are concerned," he told his audience, "all these parties are barren and unfruitful." Some Black people leaned toward Lincoln as the lesser of the evils, but Douglas argued that Lincoln was no abolitionist by any measure. "I want to know if any man can tell me the difference between the anti-slavery of Abraham Lincoln, and the anti-slavery of the old Whig party, or the [conservative, white supremacist old style] anti-slavery of Henry Clay," he demanded. He then declared, "Why, there is no difference between them."[4]

John S. Rock, a Black doctor and lawyer from Boston, was somewhat more hopeful that a Republican president might lead the nation in the right direction on the slavery question, but he was not overly optimistic. "I think they are doing good work," he told a meeting of the Massachusetts Anti-Slavery Society in the winter of 1860. He drew applause as he quipped, "The idea of 'no more slave States' is good. The fewer the better." Yet he cautioned against placing too much faith in any Republican, for the party "aims to place white men and white labor against black men and black labor." In this regard Rock and many others believed that for African Americans, "Such Republicanism is no better than [the] Democracy."[5]

Rock and others who shared his views were reacting to many of Lincoln's public statements on slavery and race. Although Lincoln professed to believe that slavery was wrong, they found the policies he favored equivocal. Lincoln took a strong stand against the 1854 Kansas-Nebraska Act that allowed for the spread of slavery into the western territories through Douglas's policy of popular sovereignty, but he was careful not to condemn slaveholders. In Peoria, Illinois, he told an audience, "I have no prejudice against the Southern people. They are just what we would be in their situation." It was the existence of slavery in the South, he believed, that made southern supporters of slavery what they were, and he suggested colonization as the solution to the problem of slavery. While he admitted the impracticality of such a plan, he told his audience, "My first impulse would be to free all the slaves and send them to Liberia—to their native land."[6]

In his 1858 run for the US Senate against Stephen A. Douglas, Lincoln's arguments opposing slavery included positions even more troubling to African Americans. During the Lincoln-Douglas debates, which drew national attention and thousands of spectators to seven sites across Illinois,

Lincoln warned that slavery's presence, and especially its spread out of the South into the West, threatened the nation. At the debate in Alton, Illinois, he asked rhetorically, "What has ever threatened our liberty and property save and except this institution of Slavery?" Contrasting his position with Douglas's, Lincoln again called for restricting slavery's spread by limiting the institution to the southern states where it already existed. He believed this was the most certain way to blunt its danger to the union. Lincoln argued that the Founding Fathers intended to restrict slavery and called his approach "the old fashioned way, the way in which the fathers themselves set us the example."[7]

Lincoln's position was congruent with the Republican Party's free soil stance, but African Americans had hoped that he would more fully embrace abolition. Instead, he conceded southern slaveholders the constitutional right to the protection of their human property and seemed to accept the theory of white supremacy that rationalized it. In Charleston, Illinois, Lincoln told the crowd what they wanted to hear, but he angered Black people by denying them social and political rights. He drew cheers from the audience as he declared, "I will say then that I am not nor ever have been in favor of bringing about in any way the social and political equality of the white and black races." Making his stance even clearer, he added, "I am not nor ever have been in favor of making voters or jurors of [N]egroes, nor of qualifying them to hold office, nor to intermarry with white people." Then to defend himself further against Douglas's charge that his position on race and slavery would ultimately lead to intermarriage, Lincoln assured the crowd, "I do not understand that because I do not want a [N]egro woman as a slave I must necessarily want her for a wife."[8]

Two years later, as the 1860 presidential election approached, African Americans in the six northern states where they could vote weighed their options carefully. Frederick Douglass had no illusions that a Lincoln presidency would bring an abolitionist administration to power, but he hoped a Republican victory would be viewed as a triumph "over the wickedly aggressive pro-slavery sentiment of the country." Such a victory might be a first step toward raising the legitimacy of abolition in the eyes of American voters and encouraging its growth. He hoped that a Republican in the White House might help move the nation in an antislavery direction.[9]

Nevertheless, Lincoln's prospective rise to the White House did not convince African Americans that Republicans were necessarily their allies. Even beyond Lincoln's words, there was overwhelming evidence that the party did not support Black rights. Many Republican leaders courting white northern voters had made it clear that a stand against the spread of slavery was not an endorsement of racial equality. As Lyman Trumbull, Republican senator from Illinois, assured his supporters, "We the Republican Party, are the white man's party." Ohio's Republican governor John Greiner went even further, saying, "We have no Sambo in our platform. . . . We object to Sambo. We don't want him about. We insist that he shall not be forced upon us. We don't want him in Ohio, or in the territories. . . . We decline the task of looking after his welfare."[10]

Such efforts by Republicans to distance themselves from abolitionists, however, did little to reassure southern voters. Most found even Democrat Stephan A. Douglas unreliable on the slavery issue. In a public letter to the *Milledgeville Weekly,* Joseph E. Brown, "the ploughboy" governor from northern Georgia, charged that Lincoln signified "the mere instrument of a great triumphant party, the principles of which are deadly hostile to the institution of slavery." Lincoln did not carry a single southern state and won the presidency with less than 40 percent of the popular vote. By the time he took office, seven southern states had already withdrawn from the United States, calling their new nation the Confederate States of America. Republicans made great efforts to present themselves as moderates, but during the secession crisis white southerners nonetheless believed the White House was in the hands of radical abolitionists.[11]

In the early days of his presidency, Lincoln resisted abolitionists' urgings that he meet southern secession with a fatal strike at slavery. His inaugural address in March 1861 made clear that he would never accept secession, but he assured the slaveholding states that he had no plans to interfere with slavery where it currently existed. On the contrary, he said that he would do all he could to bring about a peaceful solution to this national crisis. Lincoln's assurances did little to convince slaveholding southerners, but they did alarm Black people. One African American called the new chief executive merely "the fag end of a series of proslavery administrations" that had occupied the White House during the preceding decades.[12]

As the new president settled into the White House, African Americans and their white abolitionist allies were determined to prod the administration toward some antislavery action. Conservative supporters of the seceding South were equally determined to sustain their influence. Although Lincoln hoped to resolve the national crisis without warfare, in April Confederate forces fired on Fort Sumter in South Carolina, and the US garrison surrendered. Within days the president issued a call for seventy-five thousand volunteers to put down the rebellion, and war had begun.

With the opening of hostilities, four additional southern states, Virginia, Arkansas, Tennessee, and North Carolina, withdrew from the United States to join the Confederacy. Virginia fractured over the issues of secession and slavery, as the western part of the state broke away and in late June was admitted to the United States as the new state of West Virginia. Despite internal differences and suspicions about the new Republican administration, four slave states, Delaware, Kentucky, Maryland, and Missouri, remained loyal to the United States. Thus, Lincoln found himself squeezed between abolitionist demands and his fears that any move against slavery in the seceding states might drive the loyal slave states into the Confederacy.

As the war flared during the summer and fall of 1861 the demand for trained soldiers became one of Lincoln's chief concerns. This situation was greatly exacerbated by the fact that almost one-third of the nation's army officer corps, including important West Point-trained men, had resigned their US commissions to join the Confederacy. African Americans immediately volunteered for military service. In the face of a harsh new fugitive slave law in 1850, Black men had become increasingly militant and had begun preparing themselves for a war against slavery. In the mid-1850s they had formed Black militia companies–the Massasoit Guard in Massachusetts, the Attucks Guards in Ohio and in New York–enlisting and drilling Black men in northern cities and towns. J. J. Simmons, the leader of a New York City Black militia unit, vowed to march through the South at the head of a determined force with "a bible in one hand and a gun in the other." Yet, Lincoln's War Department rejected the service of African Americans. Government officials and most American whites, including the president himself, questioned the ability of enslaved and formerly enslaved men to fight. Slavery, some argued, would make them too submissive and cowardly to be good soldiers.[13]

Frederick Douglass was among those Black people angered and insulted that the descendants of African American heroes of past wars could have their military courage or ability questioned. "Colored men were good enough . . . to help win American independence," he thundered, "but they are not good enough to help preserve that independence against treason and rebellion." Then he asked, "Why would Lincoln attempt to fight the rebels with only one hand?" During the first year of the war, the US Army expanded from just over 16,000 men to over 714,000, but more troops were needed. As casualties mounted and military recruiting grew ever more difficult, some even in the federal government found Douglass's question increasingly pertinent.[14]

Lincoln, however, continued to court the loyal slave states. When his military commanders attempted to shelter fugitives from slavery who escaped to US military lines, he ordered them returned to their masters. He did attempt to encourage loyal slave owners to free their enslaved people with an offer of compensated emancipation, but none agreed. Finally, in the spring and summer of 1862, Congress took control of the issue and prohibited the military from returning fugitives. It also answered a long-standing abolitionist entreaty and abolished slavery in the District of Columbia, providing nearly $1 million to compensate slave owners in the nation's capital for their losses. In addition, Congress authorized the enlistment of Black people into the military, but President Lincoln still hesitated. Yet, that summer he announced to his cabinet plans to proclaim the emancipation of all people owned by rebellious Confederates. On the advice of Secretary of State William Henry Seward, Lincoln was careful not to appear to be acting out of weakness and waited for a US victory before publicly announcing his plans. The opportunity came in the fall. On September 17, US forces repelled a Confederate invasion at Antietam, Maryland, and forced Robert E. Lee's army to withdraw southward to Virginia. Lincoln made his announcement five days later. He told the nation that on January 1, 1863, he would issue an emancipation proclamation declaring free all enslaved people of those still in rebellion against the United States.[15]

Across the nation, African Americans awaited the new year of 1863 with anticipation, skepticism, and great hope. For most Black people, Lincoln remained an enigma, his beliefs about slavery uncertain and his actions unpredictable. During his time as president he had shown signs of changing some of his pre-presidential racial biases, but he seemed always to fall short of their expectations. In August 1862, for example, he had been the first American president to invite a delegation of African Americans, including abolitionist H. Ford Douglas of Illinois, formerly enslaved New York abolitionist minister Henry Highland Garnet, and formerly enslaved abolitionist speaker and writer William Wells Brown, to meet with him at the White House. However, at that historic meeting he had disappointed and angered them by saying that Black people were a burden on the nation. He contended that Black and white people would never be able to live together on the basis of equality in America, that the races "should be separated," and that African Americans should leave the nation and be settled in Africa or the West Indies.[16]

As the new year approached, Black Americans were almost afraid to hope that the president would make the bold statement against slavery that he had promised. Throughout the North, in small towns and large cities, African Americans held mass meetings to await the momentous hour. Lincoln received copies of the proclamation to review during late morning, but the traditional New Year's Day receptions occupied him until early afternoon. Rereading the document, he was overcome with the gravity of the occasion and paused to gather his nerves before affixing his signature. He told those present, "I never, in my life, felt more certain that I was doing right, than I do signing this paper." Obviously understanding the document's historic importance, he continued, "If my name ever goes into history it will be for this act, and my whole soul is in it."[17]

Word did not reach the abolitionist stronghold of Boston until after 10 P.M. Frederick Douglass, Black abolitionist Dr. John Rock, Ralph Waldo Emerson, Harriet Beecher Stowe, Oliver Wendell Holmes, and a host of other abolitionists, Black and white, were among the three thousand who had gathered in Tremont Temple that morning to anxiously await news of the proclamation. When the word of Lincoln's signing finally came, the exhausted crowd gained new life, greeting it with prayers of thanksgiving, hymns of praise, and shouts of joy. Wherever Black people heard the news they broke into wild celebration, singing, dancing, praying, giving impromptu orations on freedom, and telling heartrending stories of family and friends still held in slavery. They understood that the proclamation itself was only a halfway measure, because it applied only to enslaved persons still held by rebels not under the US government's control; but they also understood that the Emancipation Proclamation had transformed the war's purpose. The war had become a holy crusade to end slavery. The proclamation also announced the federal intention to finally recruit Black troops. Under the headline "Proclamation Day in Boston," William Lloyd Garrison's newspaper, *The Liberator,* declared, "The first day of January, 1863 has now taken rank with the fourth of July, 1776 in the history of the country." With this proclamation African Americans began to see Lincoln as the "Great Emancipator."[18]

As the proclamation changed the war, the war itself was changing Lincoln. Part of his change was attributable to the role African American troops played in the war and to his association with Frederick Douglass.

Lincoln and Douglass first met at the White House in August 1863. Douglass was recruiting Black troops for the government and was in Washington to confer with federal officials about the unequal pay and treatment imposed on African Americans. He met with members of Congress and Secretary of War Edwin M. Stanton before visiting the White House, where Lincoln received him. The two men discussed a number of matters, including the need to equalize the pay of Black soldiers, who were paid about half of what whites of comparable rank were paid. At first Lincoln seemed unsympathetic, telling Douglass that "the employment of colored troops at all was a great gain to the colored people . . . that they ought to be willing to enter the service upon any condition." Douglass recalled that Lincoln seemed to believe the inferior pay provided to Black soldiers was "a necessary concession to smooth the way to their employment at all as soldiers." After a lengthy exchange, however, Douglass thought that Lincoln had changed his opinion on pay equity.[19]

As Douglass remembered it, the president agreed that "ultimately they would receive the same [pay]." The formerly enslaved Douglass considered the president a man much like himself, sincere, self-educated, and self-made, and believed him to be worthy of "the prefix *Honest* to the name Abraham Lincoln." The Black leader came away from the meeting not sure that he would receive all that he had hoped for, but not totally disappointed. Lincoln had not promised outright to equalize the pay and treatment of Black soldiers. Yet, Douglass was much impressed that the president had treated him as an equal and attentively listened to his arguments.[20]

The struggle for equal pay continued, with a few Black soldiers writing directly to President Lincoln about their situation. Many years later, Harriet Tubman, a fugitive from slavery in Maryland, legendary underground railroad conductor, and Civil War scout and spy, recalled that she and other African Americans were furious with Lincoln for tolerating this inequality. She reported having visited Mrs. Lincoln but never wanting to see the president. In retrospect she considered Lincoln an ally, but during the war she was highly critical of him and his administration. As she explained, "You see we colored people didn't understand den he was our frien'. All we know was dat de first colored troops from Massachusetts only got seven dollars a month, while de white regiment got fifteen. We didn't like dat. But now I know all 'bout it, an' I'se sorry I didn't go see Massa Lincoln and tank him." Finally, in March 1865, as the war neared its end, Congress authorized equal pay for all Black soldiers. In acknowledgment of the injustice Black troops had suffered, their pay increase was made retroactive to their actual dates of enlistment.[21]

By the spring of 1865, Abraham Lincoln could no longer reassure slaveholders that he was no threat to slavery. In his first inaugural address he had pledged not to interfere with slavery in the slave states, but by the time of his second inaugural in 1864, the president linked the hardships of war to the sinfulness of slavery, the "peculiar and powerful interest" which was "somehow, the cause of the war." He suggested that the evil of slavery had brought the punishment of the Almighty upon the nation through the ordeal of war. Perhaps, he speculated, America's punishment would be continued "until all the wealth piled by the bond-man's two hundred and fifty years of unrequited toil shall be sunk, and until every drop of blood drawn with the lash, shall be paid by another drawn with the sword." Douglass and many other African Americans maintained a realistic appraisal of Lincoln the adroit politician, but they were increasingly impressed with "the solid gravity of his character."[22]

Lincoln invited Douglass to the White House reception after the second inaugural address, a gesture of respect for an African American unprecedented in presidential history. White House officials initially were unprepared to accept a Black man at such an affair, and denied him entrance. Douglass talked his way into the gathering, assuring them he was a guest of the president. Then, as he entered the room, Lincoln publicly acknowledged Douglass, announcing to the crowd, "Here comes my friend Douglass." Taking Douglass's hand he said, "I am glad to see you. I saw you in the crowd today, listening to my inaugural address; how did you like it?" Then, adding a final personal touch, Lincoln said, "there is no man in the country whose opinion I value more than yours." Douglass complimented the speech, whereupon Lincoln thanked him.[23]

The president had met with other African Americans during his time in the White House, but never on such an equal footing as with Douglass. As an employee in the Lincoln household, Elizabeth Keckley, a Black dressmaker and personal servant to Mary Todd Lincoln, reported being treated respectfully by the president and his wife. She remembered one occasion when Lincoln arrived at the White House to find her engaged in preparing the First Lady for a social event. It was the first time Keckley had seen him since his inaugural speech and she was anxious to congratulate him on a job well done. As she related the incident, "I went up to him, proffering my hand with words of congratulation. He grasped my outstretched hand warmly, and held it while he spoke: 'Thank you. Well, Madam Elizabeth.'" Keckley explained, "he always called me Madam Elizabeth." Lincoln went on to relate his ambivalence at having won a second term in the White House. "I don't know whether I should feel thankful or not. The position brings with it many trials. We do not know what we are destined to pass through. But God will be with us all. I put my trust in God." The president had good reason to be apprehensive about his second term–the war was dragging on and casualties were mounting almost as rapidly as criticisms of his war policies. Lincoln's casual intimacy with this employee was noteworthy. It matched his generally relaxed and casual manner and was not at all surprising, except that this employee was African American.[24]

The Black abolitionist speaker and women's rights activist Sojourner Truth had been so impressed with the Emancipation Proclamation in 1863 that she became determined to meet Lincoln personally. On her extensive trip from Michigan, through Boston, and south to Washington, D.C., she added campaigning for Lincoln's reelection to her antislavery and freedmen's aid activities. In the fall of 1864, however, Truth was not prominent enough to be able to have an audience with the president on her own. Finally, with the aid of a white abolitionist friend, Lucy Coleman, who worked through Elizabeth Keckley, Truth managed to gain an early morning appointment with Lincoln. She and Coleman were kept waiting for three and a half hours, and when they finally went in to see the president, they noted the change in his manner from the relaxed and joking man he had been with his male visitors to the tense and anxious man who greeted them. He called the tall, elderly Sojourner Truth "Auntie" and signed her autograph book: "For Auntie Sojourner Truth, October 29, 1864." He was annoyed, according to Coleman, when Truth praised him as "the Great Emancipator." Coleman concluded that Lincoln "believed in the white race, not in the colored, and did not want them put on an equality." When Sojourner Truth later recounted this meeting, she told a much more favorable version of her treatment by Lincoln, one seemingly more congruent with her elevated stature in the antislavery community. It was this more favorable version that convinced Harriet Tubman that she had judged Lincoln too harshly.[25]

Lincoln's behavior toward Black people may not always have been consistent with his antislavery reputation, but his racial opinions had changed from the days of the debates with Stephen A. Douglas in the late 1850s to the time of his open cordiality with Frederick Douglass. For instance, after 1863 he dropped his earlier plans for the colonization of African Americans outside the United States. Lincoln's change of heart became clear after Confederate commander Robert E. Lee surrendered his forces to US general Ulysses S. Grant at Appomattox Court House, Virginia, on April 9, 1865. After Lee's surrender, African Americans wondered about the shape of the anticipated peace. On April 11, in Washington, a celebratory torchlight parade of thousands stopped at the White House and called for Lincoln. With Elizabeth Keckley looking on, and his young son Tad holding a light to illuminate his text, the president appeared to answer their questions as he spoke optimistically to the crowd. "We meet this evening, not in sorrow, but in gladness of heart," he told them. This was the start of what he hoped would be "a righteous and speedy peace whose joyous expression can not be restrained." He continued with comments on Black freedom and on the status of African Americans as free citizens. He seemed willing to seriously consider abolitionists' demands that enslaved people not only be freed but that they also be given the vote.[26]

A decade earlier Lincoln had publicly dismissed African Americans' right to vote, hold public office, or serve on juries; now he seemed willing to support those rights for at least a select number. Speaking specifically about the conditions for the readmission of Louisiana to the United States, Lincoln acknowledged approvingly that the new state constitution had opened public schools to Black people and had empowered the legislature to give them the right to vote. "I would myself prefer that [the franchise] were now conferred on the very intelligent, and on those who serve our cause as soldiers." Lincoln was sure that a new spirit of freedom would affect the nation, even the South. "The colored man too," he said, "in seeing all united for him, is inspired with vigilance, and energy, and daring." In this speech, however, the president stopped just short of advocating a complete overturning of the Supreme Court's ruling in the 1857 Dred Scott case that had advanced the opinion that African Americans were not and could never be full American citizens.[27]

Black people were gratified and encouraged by Lincoln's words on this grand occasion. Yet, Keckley worried that the president, as the lamplight set him clearly against the dark background, was saying things that many southerners found shocking. She later recalled thinking, "What an easy matter would it be to kill the President as he stands there!" Keckley's worries were well founded, since in the audience that night was John Wilkes Booth, a popular Shakespearian actor and an ardent southern sympathizer. Booth had shared drinks earlier that evening with a friend to "drive away the blues" brought on by Lee's surrender, and in his despair, he would not fully accept the Confederate defeat. Listening to the president, he became increasingly distressed. Finally, when Lincoln spoke in support of franchising some Black people, it was too much for Booth to bear. He left the White House grounds with his companion, denouncing any plan that might result in Black citizenship. "[N]ow by God, I'll put him through," Booth exclaimed, adding, "That's the last speech he'll ever make."[28]

Three days later Booth made good on his threat. He shot Lincoln as he attended a performance of *Our American Cousin* at Ford's Theatre with Mary Todd Lincoln. The president died the next day. Shock settled over Washington, and soon the city was wrapped in black crepe. African Americans were especially moved by what most considered a personal loss. One Black woman upon hearing the news of Lincoln's assassination proclaimed in anguish, "My good President! I would rather have died myself! I would rather have given the babe from my bosom! Oh Jesus! Oh Jesus."[29]

Black people mourned their president in churches, at community meetings, in spontaneous gatherings across the North, and even in the South under threats of white reprisal. In New York City, African Americans protested when officials refused to allow them to take part in the city's funeral procession for the late president. In a speech to Black New Yorkers, Douglass denounced the city council's action and praised Lincoln as their fallen hero. Editors at the *New York Evening Post* understood what Lincoln had come to mean to African Americans: "Our late President was venerated by the whole colored population with a peculiar degree of feeling . . . and [they] looked upon him as the liberator of their race. We have accepted the services of colored citizens in the war and it is disgraceful ingratitude to shut them out of our civil demonstration." The newspaper also published a letter by Black minister John Sella Martin, who argued that Lincoln had formed a special relationship with African Americans, whom "he had lifted by the most solemn official acts to the dignity of citizens and defenders of the union." Lincoln, he argued, would have wanted African Americans to be "allowed the honor of following his remains to the grave." Under intensifying pressure, both locally and from Washington, the city council relented. As a result, two thousand Black mourners participated in the city's funeral procession, although they were forced to the rear ranks.[30]

African Americans observed Lincoln's death in many ways. Thousands stood along the route in silent tribute as the train bore his body to his home state of Illinois. Most were realistic about Lincoln and understood that he had been a conservative antislavery man at best for almost all of his life. Yet, they appreciated and became devoted to the memory of the abolitionist that he had become by the time of his death. By the time Douglass delivered his message to the crowd at the unveiling of the Freedmen's Memorial in Washington in 1876, Lincoln was, for most, the "Great Emancipator." He had become a white martyr for Black freedom, an image that remained strong among African Americans through the rest of the nineteenth and most of the twentieth century.

Most African Americans felt a great affection for the martyred Lincoln, and parades and memorials commemorating his life and work became a mainstay of Black cultural life. At the end of the nineteenth century, Booker T. Washington, principal of the Tuskegee Institute, one of the most important African American colleges of the era, told a large gathering in Philadelphia what Lincoln meant to him personally. Washington, born into slavery in Virginia in 1856, had been freed as a result of the Emancipation Proclamation. There was no doubt in his mind that Lincoln had freed him. In his "Abraham Lincoln Memorial Address" in February 1899, Washington introduced himself as "one whom the Great Emancipator found a piece of property and left an American citizen."[31]

Washington charged African Americans with the responsibility of completing the work begun by Lincoln. The president had freed the enslaved people, Washington told his audience, now it was the job of every Black American to take every opportunity available to rise to the highest level of educational and economic achievement. Lincoln himself was the inspiration, having risen from poverty, and Washington spoke directly to this self-made man: "Yes, in answer to your proclamation, Father Abraham, we are coming, ten million strong—we are coming by the way of the college, by the way of agriculture, the shop, the factory, the trades, the household arts. With this foundation, if God is right and the Bible is true, there is no power that can permanently stay our progress."[32] During the early twentieth century, Lincoln the martyr became an icon for many Black families. His picture was often one of only two pictures of white faces that routinely hung in African American homes, the other being a depiction of Jesus Christ. He also became a symbol of freedom for twentieth-century civil rights activists. In 1905 a group of twenty-nine Black leaders, calling themselves the Niagara Movement, met near Buffalo, New York, to create a national civil rights organization. They were responding to racial violence in the early years of the century. In 1908 there was a vicious race riot in Lincoln's hometown of Springfield, Illinois, that raged for several days, with white mobs beating and killing many African Americans and driving thousands from the city. The following year on February 12, 1909, the centennial of Lincoln's birth, the Niagara Movement joined with other civil rights activists, both white and Black, to issue a call for a national conference on the question of race in America. From this effort emerged the National Negro Committee, which would become the National Association for the Advancement of Colored People (NAACP).[33]

Official celebrations of Lincoln's one hundredth birthday focused almost exclusively on his role as savior of the union. African Americans and their white civil rights allies pressed for a national remembrance of Lincoln the emancipator, but they were generally ignored. In Springfield, Illinois, although Booker T. Washington was invited to address the gathering, other African Americans were excluded from the official centennial ceremonies by the all-white Lincoln Centennial Association.

Ironically, Washington was unable to attend because of a previous speaking commitment in New York, but he did send a letter that was read aloud to the crowd. Although no African Americans were in attendance, part of his message was directed at his fellow Black people. "No matter where members of my race reside," he wrote, "we should resolve from this day forward that we will lead sober, industrious, frugal, moral lives, and that while being ambitious, we shall at the same time be patient, law-abiding and self-controlled as Lincoln was." His message to white Americans held special relevance for this particular occasion. "[N]o man who hallows the name of Lincoln will inflict injustice upon the [N]egro because he is a [N]egro," Washington advised the white listeners to his letter.[34]

Ultimately, Illinois African Americans organized their own commemoration, explaining that they intended to honor Lincoln despite these un-Lincoln like policies. They condemned the Lincoln Centennial Association's racial discrimination and shunned those whites who excluded them, saying, "we don't care that much about mixing with the other race."[35]

Except for its invitation to Booker T. Washington, the racial policy of the Centennial Association was in keeping with the times. Just a month before the Lincoln centennial, Georgia had passed legislation restricting Black voting, becoming the last southern state to do so. The NAACP took note and urged that Lincoln's birthday be an occasion for "taking stock of the nation's [racial] progress." It argued that Lincoln would be "disheartened and discouraged" by America's racial direction in the new century.[36]

Meanwhile professional Black historians attempted to drive this point home by writing and teaching what was called Negro history. In their work, Lincoln generally played a central role in the story of freedom in America. Carter G. Woodson, often called the father of Black history, was born in Virginia in 1875 to formerly enslaved parents. He earned a Ph.D. in history from Harvard University and in 1915 founded the Association for the Study of Negro Life and History, publishing the first issues of the *Journal of Negro History* the following year. In a series of important books, Woodson told the story of race in America, a distinctive history unlike that written by the vast majority of American historians at the time. In 1926 he instituted the first Negro History Week, choosing days in February that coincided with the birthdays of two heroes in Black history–Abraham Lincoln and Frederick Douglass.

During the twentieth century, however, African Americans were not of one mind on the issue of the martyred Lincoln's standing as the Great Emancipator. As was true during his lifetime, some African Americans generations later focused on the shortcomings of Lincoln the man. In the July 1922 edition of *The Crisis,* editor W.E.B. Du Bois centered his attention on Lincoln's inconsistency. He was "peace-loving, [yet] a fighter; despising Negroes and letting them fight and vote; protecting slavery and freeing the slaves. He was a man," Du Bois told his readers, "a big, inconsistent, brave man." In the same issue of *The Crisis* a story about John Brown and his 1859 raid on Harper's Ferry claimed that Brown "had more to do with the emancipation of the Negro than did even Lincoln." The author argued that slavery had been ended by public opinion, and Lincoln was "not a leader of public opinion on the slavery question."[37]

Reader reaction was swift and strong. Calling his words "unkind and uncalled for," some attacked Du Bois and the magazine for what they saw as an unwarranted attack on "Father Abraham," freedom's own martyr. In the September issue of *The Crisis,* Du Bois acknowledged that "many of my readers were hurt by what I said of Lincoln in the July *Crisis.*" He then went on to observe that it was hard for people who loved Lincoln's memory to face the fact that the martyr was, above all, a man. "They want to dream their heroes true . . . with no feet of clay; and they are astonished, angered, hurt if some one speaks the grim, forgotten truth." According to Du Bois, there was much to admire about Lincoln, the man who had pulled himself up out of poverty, ignorance and racial bigotry. As Du Bois explained, the lesson in this was that "the world is full of people born hating and despising their fellows." It was important, he argued, to remain realistic about our heroes. He urged his readers to remember that Lincoln in 1858 had been opposed to racial equality and Black voting.[38]

To those who shared Lincoln's early willingness to tolerate slavery and his racial intolerance, Du Bois felt it was important to say, "He was one of you and yet he became Abraham Lincoln." He agreed with his readers that Lincoln was "great and good," but he reminded them that he was but a man and should not be held up as more than a man. "The scars and foibles and contradictions of the Great do not diminish but enhance the worth and meaning of their upward struggle." In the end, despite his understanding of Lincoln's shortcomings and weaknesses, Du Bois reassured his readers that just as "it was the bloody sweat that proved the human Christ divine; it was his true history and antecedents that proved Abraham Lincoln a Prince of Men."[39]

During the twentieth century this more realistic appraisal of Lincoln, the man, came to define the African American memory of him, his times, and the Emancipation Proclamation. Yet, African Americans continued to focus on even this imperfect tool of freedom as a touchstone for those who would look beyond race to the meaning of America's founding. When confronting racial prejudice, the memory of Lincoln provided inspiration. The national Lincoln Memorial was an important reaffirmation of that promise, but its dedication in 1922 was a reminder of the ambivalent African American memory of the man for whom it was named. The Lincoln Memorial Commission at first did not include African Americans in the dedication ceremony. Only at the last minute did they call on Tuskegee principal Dr. Robert Moton to speak to the gathering. When he spoke, Moton addressed a segregated audience, with Black people seated in a special section in the back, roped off and designated "Colored Only." Military ushers enforced the segregated seating.[40]

If, as some believed, Lincoln had issued his proclamation and made his final speech as a prelude to full African American citizenship, clearly there was a great distance yet to go. This obvious racial insult, while completely in keeping with the demands of the segregated South that surrounded Washington and that characterized the city itself, was especially infuriating in the aftermath of the massive Black contribution to the First World War, a campaign billed as the war to save the world for democracy. African Americans who attended the ceremony in honor of the president many people still called the Great Emancipator were undoubtedly aware of the massive racial violence returning Black soldiers met in 1919. They had found equal treatment for the first time in their lives in France and elsewhere in Europe, but hostile whites attempted to return them to their racial place in America. This was also a time of escalating Ku Klux Klan activity, with its expansion to areas outside the South. Racial violence was a prominent fact of life even as Lincoln's memory was honored in this impressive ceremony. Whites reportedly lynched fifty-one African Americans in 1922.[41]

During the 1930s, the memory of African American soldiers' experiences during and after World War I continued to spur the civil rights movement to attack racial injustice. The NAACP brought suit against discriminatory policies at the University of North Carolina, against unequal pay for Black teachers in Montgomery County, Maryland, and against Missouri for its failure to provide equal educational facilities for its Black citizens. In these efforts Lincoln's name was often evoked as a battle cry for justice. John Wesley Dobbs, a retired railway mail clerk and the leader of the Black Masonic Order in Atlanta, rallied his members with a speech that recalled the significance of January 1, 1863. He told the story of emancipation, adding that all Black people should "pause to commemorate that historic event with profound gratitude to God and to Abraham Lincoln."[42]

Throughout this period the Great Emancipator and martyr for freedom was revered in the memories and traditions of African Americans. When, in 1939, the Daughters of the American Revolution denied the use of Constitution Hall to Marian Anderson, a world-renowned African American singer of spirituals and lieder songs, First Lady Eleanor Roosevelt resigned from the organization and arranged for the concert to take place at Lincoln's memorial. The site of Anderson's triumph became a fitting platform for seventy-five thousand Americans, both Black and white, to demonstrate their commitment to freedom.[43]

Through the mid-twentieth century people continued to evoke the name of Abraham Lincoln in the fight for civil rights, equality, and freedom. In Black memory, Lincoln had come to symbolize all those martyred in the struggle. Thus, the Lincoln Memorial was a logical choice for Martin Luther King's "I Have a Dream" speech that climaxed the 1963 March on Washington. "Five score years ago," King declared, "a great American, in whose symbolic shadow we stand today, signed the Emancipation Proclamation. The momentous decree came as a great beacon of hope to millions of Negro slaves who had been seared in the flames of withering injustice. It came as a joyous daybreak to end the long night of their captivity."[44] African

Americans thus had taken control of Abraham Lincoln's image and molded his legacy to tasks that might complete the mission they believed he began with the Emancipation Proclamation. The symbolic Lincoln had become an important, politically useful weapon in the civil rights movement.

The passage of the national Civil Rights Act in 1964 and the national Voting Rights Act in 1965 promised the victory of civil rights. President Lyndon Baines Johnson's Great Society program reduced poverty, but racial inequality persisted. Inner cities erupted in racial violence, and some of America's most influential Black leaders, including Malcolm X and Martin Luther King Jr., were assassinated. During this time American youth were being drafted, wounded, and killed in the unpopular Vietnam War, and a rise of Black militancy paralleled growing antiwar activity. Part of this militancy was a challenge to popular assumptions about American heroes and to the traditional narratives of American history.

Abraham Lincoln was among the heroes who came under increased scrutiny during the late 1960s. Journalist and historian Lerone Bennett, who had been critical of Lincoln in his 1961 edition of *Before the Mayflower: A History of Black America,* wrote an article for *Ebony* magazine entitled "Was Lincoln a White Supremacist?" In this 1968 article Bennett answered the question in the affirmative and painted the Great Emancipator as a self-serving opportunist whose proclamation was only a military and political device, not a document issued out of concern for Black suffering. Further, in a book published in 2000 Bennett argued that the Lincoln whom Black people had come to see as a martyred hero was only forced into glory.[45]

Other historians proved less critical of Lincoln than Bennett, but few accepted him as the Great Emancipator of earlier times. By the twenty-first century, African Americans had once again come to a more realistic balance between the man and the martyr. Such prominent historians as Eric Foner, Henry Louis Gates Jr., and David W. Blight generally agreed that Lincoln's great strength was his capacity to change—to learn from the evidence before him and to understand the justice of greater racial equality. Like Frederick Douglass, his critic and his friend, contemporary African Americans could generally appreciate the progress Lincoln made in his life from antislavery moderate to abolitionist and advocate of racial justice.[46]

The election of Barack Obama in 2008 as the forty-fourth (and first African American) president of the United States elevated the importance of the symbolic Abraham Lincoln. Obama, whose father was an African man from Kenya and whose mother was a white woman from Kansas, grew up in Hawaii and was a senator from Illinois when he ran for president. He emphasized his connection to Lincoln during his campaign and at his inauguration: he called slavery America's original sin, vowed to strive for unity in the creation of a more perfect union, and retraced part of Lincoln's journey by train to the nation's capital to begin his presidency. Cementing his symbolic kinship with Lincoln, as well as his tie to the civil rights movement of the mid-twentieth century, Obama held a star-studded inauguration eve gala at the Lincoln Memorial.[47]

Barack Obama's two-term presidency fostered great hopes for racial progress and met with a fierce backlash of racial resentment. During and after his administration, political activists drew attention to the long history of racial inequalities and its many consequences, including police violence against Black people and the modern explosion of Black incarceration. Protest demonstrations turned once again to the hope for a just and lasting peace that Lincoln had expressed in his Second Inaugural Address. They still celebrated his Emancipation Proclamation, but many persons of color no longer viewed him as the Great Emancipator. For most, Abraham Lincoln symbolized the nation's promise of freedom and justice and remained a beacon of hope for a promise yet unfulfilled.

Notes

This essay appeared originally as the 45th Annual Fortenbaugh Memorial Lecture, Lincoln Institute, Gettysburg College, Gettysburg, Pennsylvania, 2006, and appears here with minor emendations and permission.

1. *Oration by Frederick Douglass, delivered on the occasion of the unveiling of the freedmen's monument in memory of Abraham Lincoln, in Lincoln Park, Washington, D.C., April 14th, 1876* (Washington, D.C.: Gibson Brothers, printers, 1876), 17–18.

2. Ibid.

3. W. M. Brewer, "Lincoln and the Border States," *Journal of Negro History* 34 (January 1949): 46–72; David W. Blight, *Beyond the Battlefield: Race, Memory, and the American Civil War* (Amherst: Univ. of Massachusetts Press, 2002), 80.

4. James M. McPherson, *The Negro's Civil War: How American Negroes Felt and Acted during the War for the Union* (New York: Vintage, 1965), 5–6.

5. Ibid.

6. "Speech on the Kansas-Nebraska Act at Peoria, Illinois," in *Abraham Lincoln, Slavery, and the Civil War: Selected Writings and Speeches,* ed. Michael P. Johnson (Boston: Bedford/St. Martin's, 2001), 45; "Slavery and the Repeal of the

Missouri Compromise, Peoria, Illinois, October 16, 1854," in *Abraham Lincoln: Word for Word,* ed. Maureen Harrison and Steve Gilbert (San Diego: Excellent Books, 1994), 105–44, 116.

7. "Seventh Lincoln-Douglas Debate, October 13, 1858," in Johnson, ed., *Abraham Lincoln,* 79.

8. "Fourth Lincoln-Douglas Debate, August 21, 1858," in Johnson, ed., *Abraham Lincoln,* 73.

9. See William S. McFeely, *Frederick Douglass* (New York: Norton, 1991), 208–11. In 1860, Black people could vote in Maine, New Hampshire, Vermont, Massachusetts, Rhode Island, and New York. In New York, however, Black voters, but not white voters, had to meet a property requirement.

10. Leon F. Litwack, *North of Slavery: The Negro in the Free States, 1790–1860* (Chicago: Univ. of Chicago Press, 1961), 269–70; Earl B. Wiley, "Governor John Greiner and Chase's Bid for the Presidency in 1860," *Ohio History* 58 (July 1949): 245–73, 262.

11. Reprinted from *The Federal Union* (Milledgeville, Ga.) December 11, 1860.

12. Donald Yacovone, ed., *Freedom's Journey: African American Voices of the Civil War* (Chicago: Lawrence Hill Books, 2004), 299.

13. James Oliver Horton and Lois E. Horton, *In Hope of Liberty* (New York: Oxford Univ. Press, 1997), 263; C. Peter Ripley, ed., *The Black Abolitionist Papers,* 5 vols. (Chapel Hill: Univ. of North Carolina Press, 1985–1992), 4:319n20.

14. *New York Tribune,* February 12, 1862; *Douglass' Monthly,* September, 1861; Hondon B. Hargrove, *Black Union Soldiers in the Civil War* (Jefferson, N.C.: McFarland, 1988).

15. In September 1861, for example, Lincoln overturned General John C. Frémont's emancipation order in Missouri.

16. David W. Blight, *Frederick Douglass and Abraham Lincoln* (Milwaukee, Wisc.: Marquette Univ. Press, 2001), 10.

17. Quoted in Doris Kearns Goodwin, *Team of Rivals: The Political Genius of Abraham Lincoln* (New York: Simon and Schuster, 2005), 499.

18. Goodwin, *Team of Rivals*; John Hope Franklin, *The Emancipation Proclamation* (Garden City, N.Y.: Doubleday, 1965); *The Liberator,* January 9, 1863.

19. Frederick Douglass, *Life and Times of Frederick Douglass* (1892; reprint, London: Collier, 1969), 348.

20. Douglass, *Life and Times,* 348; McFeely, *Frederick Douglass,* 229.

21. Kate Clifford Larson, *Bound for the Promised Land: Harriet Tubman, Portrait of an American Hero* (New York: Ballantine, 2004), 369, 136n. The most likely possibility is that Harriet Tubman met Mary Todd Lincoln through an association with Mrs. Lincoln's Black dressmaker and personal servant, Elizabeth Keckley.

22. "Second Inaugural Address, Washington, D.C., March 4, 1865," in Johnson, ed., *Abraham Lincoln,* 320–21, 321; Douglass, *Life and Times of Frederick Douglass,* 348.

23. Douglass, *Life and Times of Frederick Douglass,* 366.

24. Elisabeth Keckley, *Behind the Scenes* (New York: G. W. Carleton, 1868), 157.

25. Nell Irvin Painter, *Sojourner Truth* (New York: Norton, 1996), 203–7. Quotations from Lucy W. Colman, *Reminiscences* (Buffalo, 1892), quoted in Painter, *Sojourner Truth,* 206, 207; Larson, *Bound for the Promised Land,* 227.

26. James L. Swanson, *Manhunt: The Twelve-Day Chase for Lincoln's Killer* (New York: William Morrow, 2006), 5.

27. Johnson, ed., "Last Public Address," *Abraham Lincoln,* 332.

28. Swanson, *Manhunt,* 6.

29. Benjamin Quarles, *Lincoln and the Negro* (New York: Oxford Univ. Press, 1962), 240.

30. Victor Searcher, *The Farewell to Lincoln* (New York: Abingdon Press, 1965), 139; Philip S. Foner, *History of Black Americans: From the Compromise of 1850 to the End of the Civil War* (Westport, Conn.: Greenwood, 1983), 449–50.

31. Booker T. Washington, "An Abraham Lincoln Memorial Address in Philadelphia," February 14, 1899, Philadelphia, Pennsylvania, https://teachingamericanhistory.org/library/document/an-abraham-lincoln-memorial-address-in-philadelphia/ (November 2020).

32. Ibid.

33. James Oliver Horton and Lois E. Horton, *Hard Road to Freedom* (New Brunswick, N.J.: Rutgers Univ. Press, 2001), 215; Mary White Ovington, *How the National Association for the Advancement of Colored People Began,* reprint from *The Crisis,* August, 1914.

34. Booker T. Washington, "A Letter of Regret," February 8, 1909, *Lincoln Centennial: Addresses Delivered at the Memorial Exercises Held at Springfield, Illinois, February 12, 1909* (The Illinois Centennial Commission, 1909), 68–71.

35. Barry Schwartz, *Abraham Lincoln: Forge of National Memory* (Chicago: Univ. of Chicago Press, 2000), 212.

36. Scott Sandage, "A Marble House Divided: The Lincoln Memorial, the Civil Rights Movement, and the Politics of Memory, 1939–1963," *Journal of American History* 80 (June 1993): 135–67, 139.

37. W.E.B. Du Bois, "The World and Us," *The Crisis* 24 (July 1922): 103; J. Max Barber, "A Pilgrimage to John Brown's Grave," *The Crisis* 24 (July 1922): 167–69.

38. W.E.B. Du Bois, "Again Lincoln," *The Crisis* 24 (September 1922): 199–201.

39. Ibid.

40. Sandage, "A Marble House Divided," 141.

41. Lerone Bennett, *Before the Mayflower: A History of Black America* (1961; revised ed., New York: Penguin Books, 1988), 525.

42. Geneva Tonsill, "Interview with John Wesley Dobbs (Negro)," December 2, 1939, *American Life Histories: Manuscripts from the Federal Writers' Project, 1936–1940,* United States, Work Projects Administration, Manuscript Division, Library of Congress, page 10.

43. Fran Burke, "Eleanor Roosevelt, October 11, 1884–November 7, 1962—She Made a Difference," *Public Administration Review* 44 (September–October 1984): 365–72. See also Raymond Arsenault, *The Sound of Freedom: Marian Anderson, the Lincoln Memorial, and the Concert That Awakened America* (New York: Bloomsbury, 2009).

44. Martin Luther King Jr., "Address at the March on Washington, August 28, 1963," Martin Luther King Jr. Papers Project Speeches, Address at March on Washington, https://kinginstitute.stanford.edu/king-papers/documents/i-have-dream-address-delivered-march-washington-jobs-and-freedom (accessed November 26, 2020).

45. Lerone Bennett Jr., "Was Lincoln a White Supremacist?" *Ebony* 23 (February 1968): 35–38, 40, 42; Lerone Bennett Jr., *Forced into Glory: Abraham Lincoln's White Dream* (Chicago: Johnson Publishing Company, 2000).

46. Eric Foner, *The Fiery Trial: Abraham Lincoln and American Slavery* (New York: Norton, 2010); Henry Louis Gates Jr., *Stony the Road: Reconstruction, White Supremacy, and the Rise of Jim Crow* (New York: Penguin Press, 2019), David W. Blight, *Frederick Douglass: Prophet of Freedom* (New York: Simon and Schuster, 2018).

47. Lois E. Horton and James Oliver Horton, *Hard Road to Freedom: The Story of African America,* revised ed. (New York: Oxford Univ. Press, forthcoming).

8

"If at First You Don't Secede"

War and Remembrance

Stephen J. Whitfield

No feature of the national experience has endured in memory with the intense power to divide the public like the Civil War. The Great Depression and the Second World War, though far more recent, may linger less in the consciousness of the citizenry. Because those exclamation points of modern history served to unify the nation, memories and impressions of the period of 1929 to 1945 do not generate the political anxiety that the blue-versus-gray images continue to produce. Nor have historians distanced themselves from the emotional voltage that the ordeal of the Union emits. In 1956, when David H. Donald surveyed some secondary works, he wryly calculated that "there must be more historians of the Civil War than there were generals fighting in it, and of the two groups, the historians are the more belligerent."[1] Why have the vestiges of that war proven to be so lingering and so inescapable? The most plausible answer is the simplest: the sheer tenacity of southern white consciousness. That is the theme of this essay. It is intended to contribute to the politics of memory, and even more broadly to locate the fault lines that have continued to mark civic life in the United States.

The persistence of a distinctive southern white mentality deserves to be understood as a continuous phenomenon. This regionally inflected consciousness combines truculence with grievance, don't-tread-on-me bellicosity with defensiveness, pride with bitterness. The bumper sticker that proclaims "If at First You Don't Secede" may be humorous in intent, and even a sort of self-parody of recalcitrance. The slogan nevertheless points to a political issue that still simmers. But when did this sort of regional differentiation emerge in the American polity? As far back as 1820, according to

Carl Degler, who cited the crisis over the admission of Missouri, which awakened ex-President Jefferson, as he famously stated, "like a fire-bell in the night." Were slavery banned in Missouri, some southern politicians would have been primed to smash the Union in retaliation. "All Southerners in Congress," Degler noted, "saw slavery as an institution with which they identified their region and one that ought not to be limited in the future." In their insistence on the admission of Missouri as a slave state, legislators from and in the South began to tie their regional interests to a narrow construction of the meaning of the Constitution. Thus the doctrine of states' rights was ideally designed to limit the authority of the federal government, were it to contest the legitimacy and durability of the peculiar institution.[2]

In the fervor of their commitment, in their willingness to risk the very existence of the republic, the southern states also diverged from the others in the Union. Prepared to go to the brink, the heavily Democratic region lost a fair election in 1860. The South reacted by choosing the obstinate "rule-or-ruin mentality" of secession. No other country in the Western Hemisphere ever erupted into full-scale war over the prospect of stopping the expansion of slavery. (The violent revolution in Haiti was designed to eliminate slavery itself.) How the two sides in the American Civil War could be distinguished, Lincoln explained in his Second Inaugural Address: "One of them would *make* war rather than let the nation survive and the other would *accept* war rather than let it perish. And the war came." But both sides knew, Lincoln added, that slavery had "somehow" caused the war. The crowd listening to that speech included the Confederate partisan John Wilkes Booth, the prominent actor born in the slave state of Maryland. As the military defeat of the South became certain, he feared that the president intended to install what Booth called "nigger citizenship." That prospect stirred him to join in the plot to kidnap Lincoln, who had once seen Booth perform on stage. (Booth identified with Shakespeare's Brutus.) The conspiracy was enlarged into an assassination that epitomized the lawless violence inherent in the southern animus against the ideal of equality. Booth's diary even anticipated the phrase that Confederate sympathizers adopted after the war, when he wrote that "our cause being almost lost, something decisive and great must be done."[3]

It was done, tragically; and the Lost Cause authorized a defiance that not even the sting of defeat on the battlefield could extinguish. Iconography offers a clue. Mississippi's 1890 constitution disenfranchised blacks only four years before the state adopted a new flag that flaunted the insignia of the beaten Confederacy. In 1895 Alabama adopted as its state flag the original Confederate battle insignia (consisting of the red St. Andrews cross on a white field).[4] Around the turn of the century, ten of the eleven states that had rebelled against the Union also made June 3, the birthday of President Jefferson Davis, cause for official celebration. In 1907, when a statue in his honor was dedicated in Richmond, the crowd was estimated to be as large as two hundred thousand. In the South, the birthday of General Robert E. Lee (January 19) also became a state holiday. By happenstance Martin Luther King Jr. was born on January 15. The proximity of these two dates has permitted three states—Alabama, Arkansas, and Mississippi—to absorb the shock of the civil rights revolution by tying to the recent federal holiday their own holidays honoring Lee. Of course the affinities are hardly obvious. Despite the Fourteenth and Fifteenth Amendments, Lee had publicly opposed granting the franchise to the newly emancipated slaves, a basic democratic right that King would champion a century later. In the late nineteenth century, when veterans' and women's organizations established Confederate Memorial Day, they aimed to unify the region's whites by intensifying the sense of continuity to a remembered past. Celebration of this holiday permeated the South, and it remains official in four states. "Such routinized performances are essential," W. Fitzhugh Brundage has generalized, "to the diffusion and enduring cultural authority of historical memory."[5]

Respect for the Confederate dead could easily become converted into points of honor; the fragility of hair-trigger tempers could turn expressions of pride into episodes of violence. Take *Shane* (1953), a classic Western set in Wyoming. (The novel situates the action in 1889.) Although far from the battlefields of barely more than two decades earlier, memories of the war are shown to be raw enough to inspire gunplay. Jack Wilson (Jack Palance) knows exactly how to taunt a homesteader, Stonewall Torrey (Elisha Cook Jr.), a chest-expanding son of what he refers to as "the sovereign state of Alabama." When Wilson sneers at Confederate generals like Lee and Jackson, the gunfighter can invoke self-defense when he murders in cold blood the insulted Torrey, who is a little too slow on the draw. But the Alabamian evidently prefers death to dishonor.

Those Civil War generals became the monuments men of regional consciousness. Rare was the southern town without a memorial in the square or in front of the courthouse. These tributes to military glory, these reminders of the need for vigilance against northern interference with the so-called "southern way of life," were typically constructed in the late nineteenth or early twentieth centuries. What such monuments projected were ostensibly tributes to independence, local autonomy, and valor, rather than what Vice President Alexander Stephens had hailed as the "cornerstone of the Confederacy," which was the perpetuation of human bondage and white supremacy. Stephens's lapidary mission statement, delivered in Savannah, Georgia, on March 21, 1861, has often been quoted: "The negro is not equal to the white man. . . . Slavery, subordination to the superior race, is his natural and normal condition. This, our new Government, is the first in the history of the world, based upon this great physical, philosophical, and moral truth." The fin-de-siècle flurry of activity to celebrate in stone the secessionist heroes could hardly have been coincidental when synchronized with the regional repudiation of the Fourteenth and Fifteenth Amendments. The elevation of Confederate military figures into icons thus ran parallel with the most flagrant denial of elemental rights to the descendants of those slaves. The remembered past was not to be subjected to ethical scrutiny. Questions about the morality of a slave society—or its defense by force of arms—were not to be raised, and even less so the character of postbellum race relations.[6]

What got enlarged in the process were the boundaries of the Confederacy (though none dare call it treason). Slavery had flourished in Kentucky, for example. Yet Lincoln's home state did not secede from the Union. Indeed, the future Justice Louis D. Brandeis, who was born in 1856 in Louisville, claimed that his earliest memory consisted of observing Union troops; and indeed more Kentuckians fought for the Blue than for the Gray. The state nevertheless erected far more monuments to the Confederacy (sixty-four) than to the Union (eleven).[7] That disproportionate tribute shows how misleadingly selective the operations of collective memory can be.

Or take the neighboring state of Tennessee, the home of another president, Andrew Jackson. But in that state he was not the political or military figure who was most often represented on the statues, busts, or markers. That distinction has belonged to Nathan Bedford Forrest, who was not merely (like Andrew Jackson) a slaveholder, but made a living as a slave trader, separating parents and children on the auction block. After the war he became the preeminent leader of the Ku Klux Klan. Forrest's biographer Jack Hurst described him as "the Lost Cause's avenging angel, galvanizing a loose collection of boyish secret social clubs into a reactionary instrument of terror still feared today." In "The Diamond as Big as the Ritz" (1922), the fable that F. Scott Fitzgerald devised as a metaphor for off-the-charts avarice, slavery is preserved into the age of airplanes. How does this counterfactual work? The freedmen are tricked into believing that the Confederacy had somehow managed to win the war, under the leadership of General Forrest.[8]

But nowhere in the South, as James Loewen discovered, did a statue get erected to honor General James Longstreet (other than in his hometown of Gainesville, Georgia), even though he had served under Lee at Gettysburg. Why? After the Civil War, Longstreet favored the rights of the freed men and women. So it was not until 1998 that a second statue was finally completed to honor him—at Gettysburg, Pennsylvania.[9] It is also noteworthy that, among the thousands of Civil War memorials, very few depict the blacks who served in the Union army and navy. They numbered over two hundred thousand, and their casualty rate was about double that of white troops. "Without their help," James M. McPherson has asserted, "the North could not have won the war as soon as it did, and perhaps it could not have won at all." The most famous testimony in bronze is located not in the South but in New England, where the Augustus Saint-Gaudens memorial to the 54th Massachusetts Infantry Regiment can be found on the Boston Common. This majestic monument has inspired an especially rich literature,[10] which has served to counter the celebration of the Lost Cause. The gnawing rancor that whites felt remained so pertinent to the southern *Sonderweg* that Max Weber, visiting the South in 1904, was struck by the homogeneity of white opinion. He discerned "only aimless, impotent hatred of the Yankees."[11] Such hostility was actively encouraged; historic grievances constituted scabs that both officialdom and civil society continued to rub.

Admittedly not everyone conformed. As early as 1871, the Kentuckian John Marshall Harlan, a former slaveholder who would serve with distinction on the Supreme Court, realized that "the most perfect despotism that ever existed on this earth was the institution of African slavery. . . . I rejoice that it is gone." Nor was the journalist Walter Hines Page bewitched by the effort to forge a historical justification for southern identity so rooted in resentment and defensiveness. Page urged the United Daughters of the Confederacy to redirect its efforts toward building schools, rather than erecting monuments to exalt the Confederate dead. To be so engrossed in the past was to forfeit a better future. What his native North Carolina needed, he added, were a "few first class funerals," so that the curse of the Lost Cause might be dispelled, and the shame of ignorance and provincialism expunged. "There is not a man whose residence is in the state who is recognized by the world as an authority on anything," Page grumbled.[12]

He would go on to serve as US ambassador to Great Britain under Woodrow Wilson, a president who personified the congruence of progressivism and racism. Only afterward, in the interwar period, did that peculiar combination come to be questioned, though slowly and tentatively. Even as some segments of liberalism came to challenge the assumptions of white supremacy, the white southern myth of the past endured, and even became consolidated, as part of a national consensus. "The Lost Cause developed into a full-fledged mythology across American society," David W. Blight wrote in his classic account of the postbellum hegemony of the road to reunion, paved at the expense of African American rights. "A combination of white supremacist and reconciliationist memories had conquered all others."[13]

The white southern view occupied the center of the retrospective verdict on race and region. Confederates inhabited the attic of the American imagination and memory. No better proof could be found than the astonishing popularity of the Pulitzer Prize-winning novel *Gone with the Wind* (1936). Author Margaret Mitchell traced the destiny of her heroine so compellingly that the public came down with "Scarlett fever." Less well-known is the link between her blockbuster novel and its fictional antecedent *The Birth of a Nation* (1915). In 1936, when the Reverend Thomas Dixon, a virulent racist, sent her a letter praising *Gone with the Wind,* Mitchell replied that she "was practically raised on your books and love them very much."[14] Thus the South continued to "win" the Civil War, or at least how it would be recollected, partly because so many influential white southerners felt so passionately about it. The past that they imagined and kept alive was thus vindicated outside the region, and a racially liberal perspective was muted. The color problem in the South was left largely to that region to address. Only well after the Second World War would increasing numbers of non-southern whites oppose racial segregation with approximately as much dedication as white southerners showed in defending it. Only by the mid-1960s, that is, about half a century after the release of *The Birth of a Nation,* did a scholarly view gain traction that expressed sympathy for the abolitionists, for the Radical Republicans, and for those who had been subjected for centuries to enslavement.

Meanwhile the neo-Confederate scholarship of the interwar years was typified in Frank L. Owsley. He delivered his presidential address to the Southern Historical Association in 1939, the year that the sensational film adaptation of *Gone with the Wind* was released. In asking the delegates what had caused the Civil War, Owsley answered that it could not have been slavery—despite Lincoln's Second Inaugural Address. White southerners had been denying that accusation for decades. Instead Owsley blamed the North's "egocentric sectionalism." He had contributed to *I'll Take My Stand* (1930), the canonical case for agrarian resistance to northern commercialism and industrialism. In that volume Owsley had raged against the machine in the aftermath of Confederate defeat. For a decade, he wrote, "the South, already ruined by the loss of nearly $2 billion invested in slaves, with its lands worthless, its cattle and stock gone, its houses burned, was turned over to the three million of former slaves, some of whom could still remember the taste of human flesh and the bulk of them hardly three generations removed from cannibalism. These half-savage blacks were armed," Owsley ominously added. "Their passions were roused against their former masters by savage political leaders like [Congressman] Thaddeus Stevens" of Pennsylvania, and like Senator Charles Sumner of Massachusetts, "whose chief regret had been that his skin was not black."[15] Owsley failed to reveal how he could have gained such intimate access to Sumner's interior life.

These northern fanatics presumably made John C. Calhoun look like a statesman, ensuring that "the Marx of the master class" (in Richard Hofstadter's famous phrase) could be spared criticism for helping to push the nation toward the abyss. The doctrine of the concurrent majority made Calhoun, according to a standard 1944 biography, "the supreme champion of minority rights and interests everywhere." The object of such admiration must have been spinning in his grave, however. As Hofstadter wrote in rebuttal, Calhoun "was not interested in any minority that was not a propertied minority"; and "it was minority privileges rather than rights that he really proposed to protect." Hofstadter's own criticism of the historiography of the peculiar institution ("U.B. Phillips and the Plantation Legend," published in the *Journal of Negro History,* also in 1944) punctured scholarly complacency on the subject of slavery and helped to inaugurate the revisionist momentum that has by now activated several generations of researchers.[16] They have succeeded in torpedoing neo-Confederate historiography that Owsley embodied, by exploring and underscoring the evil of what Lincoln called "the bondsman's . . . unrequited toil."

Film revealed the tardiness of this enterprise of rectification, however. *Song of the South* (1946) emanated from the nation's most influential moviemaker, Walt Disney. Set in postbellum Georgia, *Song of the South* was adapted from Joel Chandler Harris's tales—drawn from black oral history—of Uncle Remus. These tales eventually spilled over into ten volumes (1880–1918). Bursting with pastoral charm, Disney's southern plantation looked like "a paradise for lucky slaves," one movie reviewer quipped. Viewers not besotted with nostalgia must have been stunned to see "cotton-pickers straggling home after a carefree 23 hours in the field," as they "sing and chuckle as the sunset drips gold all over them."[17] Rarely has any workforce exuded such joie de vivre. The film wove live action sequences into animated sections, and would pick up two Academy Awards. But Walter White, the executive secretary of the National Association for the Advancement of Colored People (NAACP), was incredulous, and he condemned Disney's historical fantasy for presenting "a dangerously glorified picture of slavery."[18]

Although the film sets the story *after* emancipation, the white family is so elegantly attired that the complaints about the suffering of the prostrate South during Reconstruction must have been exaggerated. The movie therefore did the neo-Confederate consensus a disservice, and here the testimony of Simone de Beauvoir may be relevant in exposing how shaky the white South's remembered past had become. Traveling eastward by bus to Jacksonville, Florida, in the spring of 1947, she happened to see *Song of the South* in Texas. "The animated drawings inserted into the film do not compensate for the irritation and disgust provoked by this insipid story in Technicolor," she complained. Nor could "the idyllic countryside . . . conceal the hatred, injustice, and fear" that were "rooted" in the region.[19]

An epilogue to the troubled history of *Song of the South* occurred in 1992, when Eric Foner, who was then teaching at UCLA as a visiting professor, took his four-year-old daughter to the theme park in Anaheim. At the exhibit devoted to "Great Moments with Mr. Lincoln" in Disneyland, Foner could not help noticing that the talking animatronic figure of the sixteenth president was capable of delivering some eloquent remarks, but without making any mention of slavery. Foner acknowledged that "it's the job of the historian to be a killjoy," and he therefore lodged a protest. The reaction of the entertainment giant was an invitation to submit a different speech for Lincoln, and to rewrite the voice-over tape loop directed at visitors to the Hall of Presidents at Orlando's Walt Disney World. Its representatives "had this bland, celebratory introduction based on the idea that

America began perfect and has been getting better ever since," Foner recalled. "So I rewrote it to say that the Declaration of Independence set out some basic ideals that we still haven't quite lived up to—that this experiment in democracy is an ongoing thing." He conceded that what he provided was "a fourth-grade idea, but rather subversive from a Disney point of view."[20] Walt Disney World solved the problem by letting Lincoln recite the entire Gettysburg Address.

The centenary of the Civil War tended to reinforce the hegemony of neo-Confederate attitudes, which conflicted with the civil rights revolution. The opening event of the official commemoration, held in Charleston, almost had to be scuttled because of the refusal of the headquarters hotel to register black delegates. (President Kennedy had to intervene to achieve a compromise. Even as the pressures of the Cold War were turning the South into an embarrassment, Jim Crow required respect. The northerners were moved to the Charleston Navy Base.)[21] Early in 1961, when the Commonwealth of Virginia officially commemorated the outbreak of the conflict, Governor J. Lindsay Almond Jr. sought to establish a parallel between the contemporary issue of states' rights and what he delicately called the "unhappy difficulties" that marred the winter of 1860–1861. Almond vowed that his state would remain dedicated to "the preservation of the rights of the states under . . . the Constitution." The Civil War, he speculated, might have been avoided had "hymns of hatred" not burst from "radicals of both sides." In equating the fire-eaters with the abolitionists, Almond articulated a false symmetry. He ignored the responsibility of his own predecessors for unleashing the dogs of war rather than accepting the democratic verdict of the election of 1860. He did not hold to account the officials of the seceding states who brought upon themselves the "terrible swift sword" of Union retribution. To be sure, ex-President John Tyler, himself a Virginian, had tried through a peace convention to preserve the Union (though by then six states had already seceded). Amazingly enough, Tyler's own grandson, Lyon G. Tyler, was still alive and joined the audience in the state capitol to listen to the gubernatorial plea for sectional reconciliation. The last governor of Virginia to have been born in the nineteenth century, Almond included the demand for racial equality among the "false issues" that made a parallel between 1861 and 1961 so misleading.[22]

Almond typified the governors elected in the 1950s and 1960s who intended to keep Jim Crow intact. He warned (in 1958) that "we face the gravest crisis since the War Between the States," which is how he labeled what the public and historians outside the region have called the Civil War. The state confronted "the cold steel of federal bayonets," and he knew that Virginia would eventually have to yield to federal courts and accept desegregation. This time, Almond ruefully admitted, his "state can't secede from the Union."[23] But meanwhile the doctrine of states' rights could be championed, and the *Richmond News Leader* was quite happy to supply the rationale. The prolific editor Douglas Southall Freeman had won fame for his four-volume, Pulitzer Prize-winning biography of Robert E. Lee. But Freeman's protégé, James J. Kilpatrick, displayed such imagination and pugnacity in defying racial desegregation that the venerable editor retired from the *News Leader* in favor of his successor. As early as 1955, Kilpatrick had argued that states might interpose their own sovereignty against the verdicts of the Supreme Court, when, in exceptional circumstances, "the Federal government oversteps its constituted authority." Nowhere does the Constitution, however, mention or recognize the sovereignty of states, an omission that did not affect his case in point.[24]

Of course, the Constitutional interpretation that Calhoun had invoked had been rather decisively buried nearly a century earlier with the surrender of the Army of Northern Virginia. But Kilpatrick nevertheless was unimpressed by realism: "I don't mind taking up lost causes—it is the fate of every Southerner." The Oklahoma-born journalist accepted the indignity of denying that he had any intention "to advocate that Virginia secede from the Union."[25] History, he conceded, would not be allowed to repeat itself. But "interposition" might at least justify a refusal to enforce desegregation within the boundaries of his own state.[26] Thus the editorial page of the *Richmond News Leader* bristled with excerpts from Calhoun's writings; and one public school pupil, who grew up in Newport News, has recalled the distribution of pamphlets consisting of the arguments for nullification and interposition that the Marx of the master class had so emphatically advanced a century earlier. By 1956 the General Assembly of Virginia voted overwhelmingly to approve a Resolution of Interposition. In that same year, when Autherine Lucy tried in vain to matriculate at the University of Alabama, the ensuing riots among its undergraduates included the burning of crosses on the campus as well as the unfurling of Confederate flags. In Atlanta the State House of Representatives passed its own Interposition Resolution by the lopsided vote of 179–1, and fiercely declared *Brown* v. *Board of Education* to be unenforceable within the state of Georgia. Then the legislatures of Alabama, Louisiana, Mississippi, and South Carolina joined in, as though Calhoun has just returned to his seat in the Senate after debating Daniel Webster.[27] Even in 1963, the memory of such provocative resolutions remained fresh enough for Reverend King to denounce, from the steps of the Lincoln Memorial, the "vicious racists" of Alabama, where its governor's lips were "dripping with the words of interposition and nullification."

Even though massive resistance failed, getting the nineteenth-century past into proper focus could remain tricky. Take Shelby Foote's three-volume *Civil War: A Narrative* (1958–1974). It treats Nathan Bedford Forrest as a hero because of his military prowess, while contriving to ignore the rest of his record. That career was so disreputable that in 1986 the Memphis chapter of the NAACP recommended the renaming of the city's "Forrest Park" and the removal of the statue that had been erected in his honor in 1905. Tone-deaf, the Mississippi-born Foote objected to this assault on the sanctity of southern white memory. Blacks ought to admire Forrest instead, he asserted, and should overcome their "prejudice" against military leaders (who were, after all, traitors). Ken Burns's *The Civil War* (1990) not only reinforced but amplified this indulgence toward Forrest. The documentary did briefly note the postwar career of the grand wizard, but it claimed that he quit the Klan when it became "too violent." Left unsaid was what sort of violence, inflicted upon newly liberated blacks, Forrest (or PBS, for that matter) might have regarded as suitable. In the summer of 2015, the city council of Memphis, with a population that is 63 percent black, voted unanimously to remove the general's equestrian statue from the municipal park that is named for him, and to remove his remains. The campaign to remove the statue finally succeeded in late 2017.[28]

Of the on-camera authorities who appeared in Ken Burns's documentary, Foote chalked up the most appearances (eighty-nine).[29] By offering an interpretation that focused on its military side, Foote discounted the role of slavery and the participation of black troops in dooming the peculiar institution. Instead he promoted admiration for the valor of both sides, independent of ideology. "No soldier on either side gave a damn about the slaves," Foote remarked in 2001. Not even all those black soldiers? How any historian could have penetrated the consciousness of even white combatants remained unclear, and isn't "The Battle Hymn of the Republic" relevant? The stirring lines of lyricist Julia Ward Howe about the sacrifice of Christ ("As He died to make men holy, let us die to make men free") seem pretty transparent as a motivation for the Union forces. Against the narrowness of

Foote's view, the memoirs of Ulysses S. Grant also merit quotation. Feeling "sad and depressed" in accepting Lee's surrender, Grant could not rejoice at "the downfall of a foe who had fought so long and valiantly, and had suffered so much for a cause—though that cause was, I believe, one of the worst for which a people ever fought, and one for which there was the least excuse." Foote and the Brooklyn-born Burns therefore missed an opportunity to repudiate the lingering "vision," Foner concluded, "of the Civil War as a family quarrel among whites, whose fundamental accomplishment was the preservation of the Union and in which the destruction of slavery was a side issue and African Americans little more than a problem confronting white society."[30]

No wonder, then, that as late as the twenty-first century controversy over the display of Confederate flags and the monuments to Confederate generals has remained an irrepressible conflict, a recurring debate over the very meaning of secession. But the diehards have been losing the fight for the Lost Cause. The Democratic governor of Virginia ordered the statue of Lee in Richmond to be taken down in 2020, which is when all displays of the Confederate battle flag were prohibited in Marine Corps installations. At the same moment, HBO Max temporarily reduced its film catalog by dropping *Gone with the Wind* as "racist." Of course not every white southerner participated in the debate over symbols of insurrection, or stood on the same side. Numerous scholars have argued for the salience of the multiplicity of the South, rather than the rigidities of its ideological homogeneity; and for half a century historical scholarship has been attuned to the need to highlight diversity. Even so iconic a work as *The Mind of the South* (1941), as C. Vann Woodward so deftly demonstrated, is vulnerable to charges that W. J. Cash exaggerated the unity and continuity of his "great South."[31] The proponent of any thesis who seeks to achieve clarity of conception runs the risk of overstatement. But however persuasive a case for dissidence and difference can be made, the durability of certain features of the white South cannot be ignored. The legacy of the nineteenth-century confrontation over slavery can still be entwined with the modern struggle for civil rights.

Take the 2016 instance of a New York Republican's presidential candidacy in South Carolina, a state that Stonewall Torrey would have called "sovereign," a state that has long absorbed the burden of southern history. In 1860 South Carolina had enslaved a higher proportion of its residents (nearly 60 percent) than any other state. The first state to secede from the Union,

South Carolina also became the first to fire upon federal property (in Charleston harbor). Such bravado led one of the state's rare opponents of secession, James L. Petigru, to sigh that "South Carolina is too small for a republic, but too large for an insane asylum." Most of the narrative of *The Birth of a Nation* is situated in South Carolina, whose infuriated delegates led the walkout of southern whites in 1948, when the Democratic Party added a civil rights plank to the platform.[32] Fast-forward to 2016, when a third of Donald J. Trump's supporters in the Republican primary told pollsters that the Confederate flag should still be flying over the state capitol in Columbia. Slightly over a third still wished that the Confederacy had won the Civil War, although countering that figure were the 24 percent who were glad (or relieved) that the North had emerged victorious. (Another 38 percent of Trump loyalists, pollsters learned, remained undecided about the political and moral consequences stemming from the stillness at Appomattox.) The overall figures for Republicans in South Carolina in 2016 may be more reassuring: 36 percent expressed satisfaction that the Union remained intact. Yes, even in South Carolina a considerable plurality of views (or reluctance to adopt or admit views) prevails. Nevertheless, a third of the participants in the GOP primary would have liked secession to have succeeded.[33]

The implication is clear. One out of every three Republicans who voted in their state's primary, by wishing that the Confederacy had won, in effect wanted slavery to be preserved. That was the purpose and meaning of the rebellion that began in the winter of 1860 to 1861. At least in South Carolina, old times there were not forgotten; and for this bloc of whites the myths of the Lost Cause can still be mobilized to meet current political aims. That is why newcomers, even in the contemporary South, are commonly stunned to realize that their neighbors "are still fighting the Civil War." Partly because the desire for racial supremacy is not far below the surface, William Faulkner's small-town lawyer, Gavin Stevens, gets quoted so frequently: "The past is never dead. It's not even past."[34]

Notes

1. Stephanie McCurry, "Civil Wars—Theirs and Ours," in *Dixie Redux: Essays in Honor of Sheldon Hackney,* ed. Raymond Arsenault and Orville Vernon Burton (Montgomery: NewSouth, 2013), 76–77; David Donald, *Lincoln Reconsidered: Essays on the Civil War Era* (1956; reprint, New York: Vintage, 1956), 82.

2. Carl N. Degler, *Place over Time: The Continuity of Southern Distinctiveness* (Baton Rouge: Louisiana State Univ. Press, 1977), 36–39, 41, 42.

3. John Burt, *Lincoln's Tragic Pragmatism: Lincoln, Douglas, and Moral Conflict* (Cambridge, Mass.: Harvard Univ. Press, 2013), 418; James Shapiro, *Shakespeare in a Divided America* (New York: Penguin Press, 2020), 85, 97, 106, 108–9, 114–16.

4. James C. Cobb, *Away Down South: A History of Southern Identity* (New York: Oxford Univ. Press, 2005), 290.

5. W. Fitzhugh Brundage, ed., "Introduction: No Deed but Memory," in *Where These Memories Grow: History, Memory, and Southern Identity* (Chapel Hill: Univ. of North Carolina Press, 2000), 9.

6. Quoted in James M. McPherson, *The Struggle for Equality: Abolitionists and the Negro in the Civil War and Reconstruction* (Princeton, N.J.: Princeton Univ. Press, 1964), 61; Brent Staples, "Confederate Memorials and Racial Terror," *New York Times*, July 25, 2015, A18; Gaines M. Foster, *Ghosts of the Confederacy: Defeat, the Lost Cause, and the Emergence of the New South, 1865 to 1913* (New York: Oxford Univ. Press, 1987), 196; David Goldfield, *Still Fighting the Civil War: The American South and Southern History* (Baton Rouge: Louisiana State Univ. Press, 2002), 6, 33.

7. Philippa Strum, *Louis D. Brandeis: Justice for the People* (Cambridge, Mass.: Harvard Univ. Press, 1984), vii; Jack Hitt, "Set in Stone," *New York Times Magazine*, October 18, 2015, 48.

8. Staples, "Confederate Memorials," A18; F. Scott Fitzgerald, *Babylon Revisited and Other Stories* (New York: Charles Scribner's Sons, 1960), 87–88.

9. Eric Foner, "Selective Memory," *New York Times Book Review*, March 4, 2001, 28.

10. James M. McPherson, *The Negro's Civil War* (New York: Vintage, 1965), ix–x; Stephen J. Whitfield, "'Sacred in History and in Art': The Shaw Memorial," *New England Quarterly* 60 (March 1987): 3–27.

11. Quoted in Marianne S. Weber, *Max Weber: A Biography*, trans. Harry Zohn (New York: Wiley, 1975), 296.

12. Quoted in Alan F. Westin, "Mr. Justice Harlan," in *Mr. Justice*, ed. Allison Dunham and Philip B. Kurland (Chicago: Univ. of Chicago Press, 1964), 108, 109, and in Cobb, *Away Down South*, 91.

13. David W. Blight, *Race and Reunion: The Civil War in American Memory* (Cambridge, Mass.: Harvard Univ. Press, 2001), 251, 387.

14. Leslie A. Fiedler, *The Inadvertent Epic: From Uncle Tom's Cabin to Roots* (New York: Simon and Schuster, 1979), 59.

15. Quoted in Thomas J. Pressly, *Americans Interpret Their Civil War* (New York: Free Press, 1965), 359; Frank Lawrence Owsley, "The Irrepressible Conflict," in John Crowe Ransom et al., *I'll Take My Stand: The South and the Agrarian Tradition* (New York: Harper Torchbooks, 1962), 62, 66.

16. Charles M. Wiltse, *John C. Calhoun: Nationalist, 1782–1828* (Indianapolis: Bobbs-Merrill, 1944), 398; Richard Hofstadter, *The American Political Tradition and the Men Who Made It* (New York: Knopf, 1948), 91.

17. Manny Farber, "Dixie Corn," *New Republic,* December 23, 1946, 879; Matthew Bernstein, "Nostalgia, Ambivalence, Irony: *Song of the South* and Race Relations in 1946 Atlanta," *Film History* 8, no. 2 (1996): 222.

18. Quoted in Catherine Gunther Kodat, "Disney's *Song of the South* and the Birth of the White Negro," in *American Cold War Culture,* ed. Douglas Field (Edinburgh, UK: Edinburgh Univ. Press, 2005), 111; Jason Sperb, *Disney's Most Notorious Film: Race, Convergence, and the Hidden Histories of* Song of the South (Austin: Univ. of Texas Press, 2012), 56, 70, 75.

19. Simone de Beauvoir, *America Day by Day,* trans. Carol Cosman (1954; reprint, Berkeley: Univ. of California Press, 1999), 207–8, 232.

20. Thomas Vinciguerra, "The Historian Who Helped Keep *The Civil War* Honest," *New Yorker,* May 10, 1999, 37.

21. David W. Blight, *American Oracle: The Civil War in the Civil Rights Era* (Cambridge, Mass.: Harvard Univ. Press, 2011), 10–14.

22. Edith Evans Asbury, "Gov. Almond Perceives Parallel with Days before the Civil War," *New York Times,* February 5, 1961, 45.

23. "Virginia: 'The Gravest Crisis,'" *Time,* September 22, 1958, 17–18.

24. Joseph J. Thorndike, "'The Sometimes Sordid Level of Race and Segregation': James J. Kilpatrick and the Virginia Campaign against *Brown,*" in *The Moderates' Dilemma: Massive Resistance to School Desegregation in Virginia,* ed. Matthew D. Lassiter and Andrew B. Lewis (Charlottesville: Univ. Press of Virginia, 1998), 51.

25. Quoted in Thorndike, "Sometimes Sordid Level," 52, 54.

26. Thorndike, "Sometimes Sordid Level," 57.

27. Angie Maxwell, *The Indicted South: Public Criticism, Southern Inferiority, and the Politics of Whiteness* (Chapel Hill: Univ. of North Carolina Press, 2014), 219, 225; Thorndike, "Sometimes Sordid Level," 70–71; David Ellenson, e-mail message to author, October 15, 2015; Cobb, *Away Down South,* 290–91; Paul Gaston, "Foreword by Way of a Memoir," in Lassiter and Lewis, eds., *Moderates' Dilemma,* x.

28. Timothy S. Huebner and Madeleine M. McGrady, "Shelby Foote, Memphis, and the Civil War in American Memory," *Southern Cultures* 21 (winter 2015): 21–22; Eric Foner, *Who Owns History? Rethinking the Past in a Changing World* (New York: Hill and Wang, 2002), 197; Emily Yellin, "A Confederate General's Final Stand Divides Memphis," *New York Times,* December 22, 2017, A13.

29. Huebner and McGrady, "Shelby Foote," 14, 18, 26.

30. Quoted in Huebner and McGrady, "Shelby Foote," 18; Charles P. Roland, *The Confederacy* (Chicago: Univ. of Chicago Press, 1960), 38; Ulysses S. Grant, *Memoirs and Selected Letters* (1886; New York: Library of America, 1990), 735; Foner, *Who Owns History?* 199.

31. Nicholas Bogel-Burroughs, "Virginia Governor Plans to Order Robert E. Lee Statue Removed," *New York Times,* June 4, 2020, A17; Jenny Gross, "U.S. Marine Corps Issues Ban on Confederate Battle Flags," https://www.nytimes.com/2020/06/06/us/marines-confederate-flag-ban.html; Daniel Victor, "*Gone*

with the Wind Is Pulled," *New York Times,* June 11, 2020, C3; C. Vann Woodward, "The Elusive Mind of the South" (1969), in *American Counterpoint: Slavery and Racism in the North-South Dialogue* (Boston: Little, Brown, 1971), 264–83; Brundage, *Where These Memories Grow,* 15–20.

32. Quoted in James M. McPherson, "The War of Southern Aggression," *New York Review of Books* 35 (January 19, 1989): 16; Eric Foner, "Warped History," *Nation,* July 20/27, 2015, 6.

33. "Trump, Clinton Still Have Big Leads," February 16, 2016, www.publicpolicypolling.com (accessed February 18, 2016).

34. David W. Blight, "Epilogue: Southerners Don't Lie; They Just Remember Big," in Brundage, ed., *Where These Memories Grow,* 349; Goldfield, *Still Fighting the Civil War,* 264; William Faulkner, *Requiem for a Nun* (1951), in *Novels 1942–1954* (New York: Library of America, 1994), 535.

9

Dwight Eisenhower and Civil War Legacies

Michael J. Birkner

Americans are happy in their forgetfulness.

—Robert Penn Warren, *The Legacy of the Civil War,* 1961

Election night, November 3, 1964–one hundred years almost to the day since Abraham Lincoln won a decisive reelection victory against his Democratic opponent, General George Brinton McClellan. On a golfing vacation in Augusta, Georgia, Dwight Eisenhower watched the returns come in with increasing discomfort. The incumbent, President Lyndon B. Johnson, did not simply win reelection, he overwhelmed Arizona Republican senator Barry Goldwater, carrying every state outside the deep South except for Arizona. "I had thought," Ike wrote confidentially to an associate two days later, "that possibly a few of the central states like Kansas, Nebraska, and Iowa might have gone Republican, but the landslide spared few indeed."[1]

As the most popular living public figure in America, Ike's views on the election were of national interest. He had declined publicly to endorse any Republican aspirant for president in 1964, but once Goldwater was nominated, he made clear he would back his party's choice, even as he anticipated Goldwater would lose the election. From Augusta, on November 5 Eisenhower released a statement reminding Republicans that the party had been "hurt, but not irretrievably." Republicans had been unfairly tagged, he noted, as the adherents of the party of the "rich and the privileged." But it was time to "remind ourselves, and the country, that we are the party of Lincoln."

Eisenhower expanded on this point, emphasizing how *Republicans* were true to Lincoln's views on "humanity, liberty, dignity, and equality. We strive to emulate his common sense approach to the nation's political and economic problems, and his integrity in every action. We share Lincoln's faith in the worth of every citizen and his trust in individuals and communities to solve their own problems whenever possible; but we recognize, with him, that when the problem is beyond their capacity to solve, they must be assured of federal help, generously and intelligently given." Ike's comments may not have reflected the core beliefs of the emerging Republican Party base, which was increasingly out of sync with his notions of a middle way in politics, and for that matter, commitment to the black freedom struggle and school integration in particular. But there is no question that as Ike reflected on his party's future and the American mission, his knowledge of Lincoln and his own perspective on the great conflict of that time provided him with a usable past.

From Dwight Eisenhower's youth forward, history mattered. Growing up on the wrong side of the tracks in Abilene, Kansas, he breathed the very ether of history, given that his hometown served for a generation at least as the end point of the Chisholm Trail, across which cattle were driven from Texas ranches en route to stockyards and the railroad that would carry them to Chicago. A frontier community that was served briefly in the 1870s by Wild Bill Hickok as sheriff, Abilene had a reputation as a wild place. But by the time Dwight Eisenhower was born in 1890, it had settled down, as one writer has noted, "to become a quiet mid-American small town, with a main street of handsome Victorian homes."[2]

During Ike's childhood and teenage years, Abilene boasted fourteen churches, four schools, paved main streets, a theater, and the county courthouse. Although the Eisenhowers were not materially well off—Ike's father, David, worked as a mechanic in the local creamery—they were a respected, God-fearing family. And Ike grew up feeling he was missing nothing he needed. A good student—so good that his high school geometry teacher suggested Ike could work out the theorems on his own—Ike was by all accounts a rough and ready youth, embracing the usual range of sporting pursuits of the day, from baseball and football to hunting and fishing. He was also bookish. The Bible was central to his learning at home, but the Eisenhower family library was well stocked with a wide range of reading options, and there was the local public library to exploit as well. Ike's "first reading love," as he recalled in his memoirs, was ancient history. As a youth Eisenhower became such a devoted reader of Greek and Roman military history that he sometimes neglected his chores. Despite his mother Ida's pronounced reverence for books, she grew annoyed about this dereliction of duty and would sometimes lock the books in a closet. But when Ida went into town Ike would find the key and "sneak out the books," as he recalled in his best-selling memoir, *At Ease.*[3]

In his reading Ike developed a special interest in Hannibal, one of the world's greatest military commanders, who led Carthage's largest army against Rome in the Second Punic War. Hannibal appealed to Ike both because of his military sagacity and because "much like the young people of all times" as he put it in *At Ease,* "lost causes" aroused sympathy "more intensely than overwhelming success begets their admiration."[4] This curiosity about lost causes surely had something to do with Eisenhower's lifelong admiration for General Robert E. Lee, whose portrait hung, along with those of three other American exemplars, in the Oval Office throughout Eisenhower's presidency.

Eisenhower's keen interest in history did not go unnoticed. When he graduated from Abilene High School in 1909 one of his classmates wrote a prophecy for the school yearbook for each senior. Ike, Cecilia Curry predicted, would likely wind up as a professor of history at Yale.[5]

That is not quite how things worked out.

Upon graduating high school in 1909, Ike worked in the Abilene creamery alongside his father for nearly two years, in part to help finance his older brother Edgar's education at the University of Michigan. Edgar had agreed that he would trade places with Ike at some point, but Ike, as historian William Hitchcock notes, was "too impatient to wait for this long-term plan to unfold."[6] Hence the decision to apply both to the Naval Academy and West Point, as stipulated by his nominator, Kansas senator Joseph Bristow. It turned out he was too old to matriculate at Annapolis, but Ike gained admission at West Point after another candidate dropped out. This was a lucky break for Eisenhower, and an equally lucky break for the American people.

After a long professional apprenticeship, usually though not always in challenging and rewarding postings across the United States, Europe, and the Philippines, Eisenhower was assigned to Washington several days after the United States entered World War II. A protégé of Army Chief of Staff George Catlett Marshall, Ike soon thereafter began his meteoric rise to Supreme Command of Allied forces in Europe.[7]

Ike had read a good deal of history during his so-called wilderness years in the military, particularly during his posting in Panama (1922–1924) under the tutelage of General Fox Conner. But during the Second World War he was primarily making history, not reading it. Insofar as he had a chance to read anything unrelated to his arduous duties in Europe, Ike consumed westerns—a habit that continued for the rest of his active life.[8]

Throughout his life Eisenhower found reading westerns a pleasant diversion. By contrast, reading history and biographies of famous people influenced his personal deportment and his sense of duty. Although Ike later claimed that over time his reading interests in history expanded beyond the biographies of military chieftains, Eisenhower's favorite historical character—his *beau ideal*—was one of the most famous of all of them: George Washington. For Ike, Washington's "stamina and patience, in adversity, first, and then his indomitable courage, daring, and capacity for self sacrifice" were impressive.[9] Although he did not mention it in his memoirs, it was George Washington's sense of duty and his fulfillment of that duty that most influenced Ike's own outlook and behavior, though a case can be made that if Washington was Eisenhower's very model as a leader, Robert E. Lee was a close second. It was no accident that after World War II Eisenhower developed a warm friendship with Douglas Southall Freeman, at that time the leading biographer of *both* George Washington and Robert E. Lee. Freeman's Lee was George Washington in different garb: notable for his modesty, consideration for his soldiers, and devotion to duty. These qualities resonated with Eisenhower and regularly entered the conversation when Lee's name came up. Ike asserted that he had read every volume of Freeman's seven-volume Washington series, the last book completed by others after Freeman's death. There is little doubt that Eisenhower at least dipped into the Lee volumes as well.[10]

If Eisenhower had a special affection for Lee, it should be said that he was as much interested in the blue as he was in the gray in his Civil War reading. While based in Panama from 1922 to 1924, reading intensively under the tutelage of General Conner, Ike consumed various Civil War histories, notably Ulysses Grant's and Philip Sheridan's memoirs, as well as first-person accounts of Gettysburg in July 1863 by Frank Haskell and Arthur Lyon Fremantle. Fox Conner would ask Ike to relate what these writers thought was going on as they were engaged in military operations and how they then made sense of their experience. Under Conner's tutelage "I became even more interested in our Civil War," Ike remembered many years later, as "we spent many hours in analyzing its campaigns." More than two decades after reading U. S. Grant's report to the secretary of war submitted in July 1865, Ike told a Grant biographer named William E. Brooks how "mightily" he was impressed by Grant's plan for the defeat of the Confederacy. "My respect for Grant has been high, in spite of many bitter criticisms that I have read both of his military ability and of his personal habits." Ike added that he had long thought that no man "constantly under the influence of liquor could have pursued a single course so steadfastly, could have . . . made numbers of close decisions which involved a nice balance between risk and advantage, and could have maintained the respect of such men as Sherman, Sheridan, Meade, and above all, President Lincoln."[11] Eisenhower's respect for military prowess and personal character was not limited to southern generals.

Not surprisingly, his special interest in the Civil War was the Battle of Gettysburg—Robert E. Lee's worst battle. Ike had first visited Gettysburg during his West Point years, having his picture taken with his mates on the steps of Christ Lutheran Church on Chambersburg Street. Returning in 1918 as commander of a tank training unit, Eisenhower spent happy hours in his free time rehashing the various decision points during the battle and its impact on the course of the war.[12] Many years later, in a televised conversation with the popular historian Bruce Catton, Eisenhower recalled that summer of 1918 in Gettysburg and how he would drive himself around the battlefield in an army issued Dodge car, stopping as close as he could get to the "spot" where Abraham Lincoln delivered the Gettysburg Address. He would "just sit there and read it again," reflecting on how Lincoln had said so much of value in so few words.[13]

Of course, the question begs to be asked: what did Eisenhower's reading and thinking about Lincoln and the Civil War have to do with his statecraft? Did it matter? If it did, *how* did it matter?

Several lines from speeches Ike delivered in Gettysburg in 1963 during the centennial commemoration have been quoted as reflecting a point of view about current affairs. But connecting Ike's *historical mindedness* and *public policy*—even on such central issues as American race relations in the 1950s and 1960s—has simply not drawn the attention of scholars.

Perhaps the most surprising aspect of Eisenhower's habitual conversation about the Civil War is his persistent reference not to "the Civil War" but to the "War Between the States," or as he put it in a letter to Atlanta newspaperman Ralph McGill in 1960, the "conflict between the states." Ike even referred to the "War Between the States" in his December 1960 meeting with members of the Civil War Centennial Commission, to give them his charge and a pat on the back, a month before leaving office.[14]

There are three possible explanations for this choice of words. Growing up in Kansas, he was likely steeped in a culture that remembered the special animosity between the states of Kansas and Missouri. Locally, it really was a

"War Between the States." It would not be surprising if that was the phrasing he grew up hearing, and thus it would be the phrasing that would sound most natural to him to say. Another possibility is that Ike was trying to suggest a certain psychological complicity with southerners' perspective on the war, to win sympathy and perhaps build opportunities for mutual understanding, as well as support for his civil rights program, which was irritating to southern sensibilities. The problem with this logical explanation lies in the fact that Ike used the locution in public and in conversation with northern correspondents as well. A third explanation could more usefully elucidate Ike's ongoing references to the "War Between the States" and also something more important than word choice: his *sensibility.* Eisenhower was preternaturally oriented to moderation, compromise, promotion of unity, and—the hallmark of his administration—the "middle way." In this context, Ike's reverence for Lincoln was matched by an equivalent respect for General Lee.

Contemporary historiography about Robert E. Lee runs the gamut between adoration in some quarters to condemnation in others.[15] But in the 1950s, the Age of Eisenhower, that was not the case. Lee was almost unassailable. The well-known incident in May 1957, when British field marshal Bernard Montgomery visited Ike in Gettysburg, toured the battlefield, and provoked a controversy, sheds light on Lee's status as an American icon and hero. Lee certainly was that for Eisenhower.

It was inevitable that Montgomery would insist on a battlefield tour while in Gettysburg. Ike complied. Trailed by a flock of reporters, the two generals traversed the battlefield over two days, stopping at the major locations where fighting occurred. Eisenhower expressed his admiration for the Iron Brigade and his criticism of General Daniel Sickles, whose controversial orders on the second day of the battle were a natural subject for discussion. No one seems to have taken any offense at the comments about Sickles.[16]

On day two of Montgomery's visit, the old warriors went out again before attending church. They climbed the tower at Culp's Hill in order to get a better view of the terrain. As they were walking down the steps of the tower, a reporter asked Montgomery about General Lee and Pickett's Charge and whether this was a major blunder. Montgomery said he'd have conducted himself "differently than Lee," and asked what Ike thought. If you had acted the same as Lee did, Ike said, I'd have "sacked" you. By some accounts this comment evoked nervous laughter among the entourage following the two generals. The tour continued to the usual places, including Confederate Avenue and the Virginia Memorial. The reunion had been tense but successful—until, that is, southern newspapers picked up on Ike's comment about Lee. Editorials from Virginia to Alabama defended Lee's honor and questioned Ike's good sense. "Southern blood boils" ran the headline in a Mississippi newspaper. A cheeky headline in the *Washington Star* put it this way: "the cotton really hit the fan."[17]

Inevitably, mail from outraged "Lost Cause" advocates streamed into the White House. Lee loyalist G.S.P. Holland of Miami, Florida, laid it out for Eisenhower. "Mr. President—am afraid that you are wrong. Don't let the shades of Thad Stevens—we hear [he] is buried in a negro cemetery by his request near Gettysburg—[mislead you]. . . . Poor old Abe [Lincoln] was pushed into the most unholy slaughter of all ages. You are a great guy. But you are getting fouled up by South haters and Constitution rapers." Another angry correspondent, Paul Courson of Albany, Georgia, observed that "your remark [about General Lee]. . . placed yourself in the same category with the thousands of yankees before you who saw fit to criticize Gen. Lee—that of a small dog yapping at the heels of a giant." Lee, he added, "did an outstanding job" and "there can be nothing said by any yankee to change that." Mayrene Garrett of Houston quoted a Texas state senator, Dorsey Hardeman, contending that Ike was "not worthy to have laced Gen. Robert E. Lee's shoes. I agree," she wrote. B. W. Middlebrook of Barnesville, Georgia, enclosed with his letter to the president a razor strop and hone, along with "the suggestion that at any time you feel inclined to speak disparagingly of Gen. Robert E. Lee, the Confederacy, or the 'Lost Cause,' that you kindly get someone to apply this razor strop." Middlebrook noted that he was also sending the same apparatus to members of the US Supreme Court.[18]

It is doubtful Ike was overly troubled by these letters, which he tasked Chief of Staff Sherman Adams and his secretary, Ann Whitman, with handling. But he did address the Lee criticism issue directly at a press conference on May 15. In that session Ike observed to the assembled media, "no doubt you have noticed on the walls [in the Oval Office] there are prints of four men, men that I consider in my book are about the four top Americans of the past. They are Franklin, Washington, Lincoln and Lee." "Anybody who ever tries to put me in any other relationship with respect to Gen. Lee is mistaken."[19]

Equally telling was Eisenhower's response to a letter from New Yorker Leon Scott, who was displeased that Eisenhower went out of his way to praise Robert E. Lee as an exemplary American. "I do not understand how any American can include Robert E. Lee as a person to be emulated and why the President of the United States of America should do so is certainly beyond me," Scott wrote. "The most outstanding thing that Robert E. Lee did was to devote his best efforts to the destruction of the United States government, and I am sure you do not say that a person who tries to destroy our government is worthy of being hailed as one of our heroes." Scott closed by asking Eisenhower to "tell me just why you hold him in such high esteem."[20]

Several aides to the president determined that Scott's letter would provide a good opportunity for Eisenhower to make his case, yet again, for Robert E. Lee as a great American. The president agreed to let them draft a reply, which he would edit and sign. The burden of his defense of Lee related to Lee's high character, his leadership skills, his selflessness and personal nobility. "From deep conviction," Ike concluded, "I simply say this: A nation of men of Lee's caliber would be unconquerable in spirit and soul. Indeed, to the degree that present-day American youth will strive to emulate his painstaking efforts to help heal the nation's wounds once the bitter struggle was over, we in our own time of danger in a divided world, will be strengthened and our love of freedom sustained."[21]

Lee's ownership of slaves and the Confederacy's foundation on slavery as a positive good remained unmentioned in Ike's letter. For Eisenhower—and for that matter, for many if not most American historians at this time—the notion that Robert E. Lee was a role model was a given, not subject to debate. Sparking sectional discord over Lee, slavery, and racial questions was not on Eisenhower's agenda. Lincoln's task as president was to thwart the Slave Power and save the Union, which he did. Eisenhower felt *his* job as president was to keep that Union safe and prosperous in thwarting international communism.[22] It could even be argued that Eisenhower deliberately highlighted his admiration for Lee as a means of advancing his notion of American civil religion at a time when maintaining national unity during the Cold War seemed imperative. Talking about the bad effects of white supremacy, past and present, would not serve Eisenhower's purpose.[23]

The so-called "Lee affair" was serious business at a time when Eisenhower was trying to keep a lid on any disruptive narrative focused on the black struggle for civil rights. This is not to say Ike could not get a "good laugh" out of the "sacking Lee" episode. That is exactly what he got when *New York Times* reporter Bill Lawrence sent him a *New Yorker* cartoon alluding to the incident. In the cartoon, two elderly white men are sitting on a verandah, with one of them observing, "And I tell you this, suh. If General Lee had had seventy-one billion dollars to play around with, Ike wouldn't even *be* in the White House today." The cartoon seems to have tickled the funny bone of Ike's brother Milton, since he also sent it to the president, through Ike's secretary, Ann Whitman. Whitman later told Milton, "the president loved the General Lee cartoon, but if I may be personal, I shudder every time another letter on his now famous remarks [about Robert E. Lee] comes into my hands."[24]

Four months after the Lee controversy flamed up and out, Eisenhower faced a much more momentous challenge to his middle way governance: defiance of federal court orders for the integration of Central High School in Little Rock, Arkansas. This subject is one of the great set pieces of modern American history, and it continues to factor into ongoing revisionist interpretations of Eisenhower's presidency. When Arkansas governor Orval Faubus, to maintain his political standing in his home state, repeatedly defied federal court orders in the summer of 1957, Eisenhower nationalized the Arkansas Guard unit in Little Rock and, further, sent in the 101st Airborne to ensure the nine African American students' safety as they integrated the school and attended classes. Eisenhower had failed to act when similar defiance of court mandated integration occurred previously in Mansfield, Texas, in 1956. In the case of Little Rock he *was* decisive, much as he would have preferred to let the issue be resolved at the local level.[25]

At the same time he sent the 101st Airborne to Little Rock—a statement of federal power if ever there was one—Ike delivered an eloquent address on national television explaining how he had no choice but to uphold the laws of the land in fulfilling his oath of office. Not surprisingly, he was subjected to considerable abuse from white southerners, including many who had voted for him and, in Congress, supported many of his initiatives. Georgia's US Senator Richard Russell, with whom he had long enjoyed cordial relations and regularly done business, blasted Ike's actions at Little Rock and went so far as to liken the 101st Airborne to "Hitler's storm troopers," an analogy which did not sit well with the president. In his response, which laid out the basis for his actions, Ike told Russell that he "completely fail[ed] to comprehend your comparison of our troops to Hitler's storm troopers. In one case military power was used to further the ambitions and purposes of a ruthless dictator, in the other to preserve the institutions of free government."[26]

Both in public and private the president emphasized that he was acting on the basis of his constitutional duty in his actions relating to school integration in Little Rock. Eisenhower repeatedly declined to draw analogies between southern "interposition" and nineteenth-century nullification doctrine associated with John C. Calhoun. Yet the president was also disinclined to offer words of support, much less empathy, for the nine black students in Little Rock who would endure a year of abuse at the hands of their white peers before Central High was closed in order to avoid further integration. Indeed, Eisenhower continued to exploit his perspective of the Civil War—a war where good men on both sides died for causes in which they believed—as a vehicle for highlighting *national unity.*

Ike's anodyne views of the war were reflected in drafting, with the help of historian Bruce Catton, the charge for the Civil War Centennial Commission in December 1960. The lessons of this "tragic" struggle, according to Ike's proclamation, related to the "heroism and sacrifice by the men and women on both sides who valued principle above life itself and whose devotion to duty is a part of our nation's noblest tradition." The deaths of six hundred thousand during the war was a "lasting testimonial to something unconquerable in the American spirit." And what had the war wrought? "A greater, freer and happier America," serving as a source of inspiration to Americans as the centennial of the war approached. Slavery? Not mentioned. Lincoln? Not mentioned. Black struggle for freedom and equal rights? Not mentioned.[27]

Meeting with the commissioners in the Oval Office, according to a memo written by one of his own staff members, Eisenhower "admitted in many ways he was more Southern than Northern. His mother was born in Virginia and he had served many years in the South. He has many friends there." At that meeting the president pointed to the portraits of Robert E. Lee and Abraham Lincoln on either side of the door leading to the Rose Garden. Once again he indicated that Lee, Lincoln, George Washington, and Benjamin Franklin were his personal "ideals" as Americans.[28] This president was not going to be found on the front lines of civil rights battles. Neither, it needs to be said, were his leading political antagonists at the time, among them Democrats Adlai Stevenson, Lyndon Johnson, and John F. Kennedy. They were even *less* assertive on behalf of advancing legal rights for African Americans than President Eisenhower.[29]

Historians have generally called Eisenhower's enforcement of federal court decisions in Little Rock one of the signature acts of his presidency, and they have understandably given him high marks on this count. Ike's overall record in the field of civil rights remains a point of contention among scholars, with several recently published books pushing back against David Nichols's favorable interpretation of Eisenhower's policies on race. Both William Hitchcock, author of an insightful comprehensive study, *The Age of Eisenhower,* and James Simon, in a newly published book on Ike's relations with Supreme Court Justice Earl Warren, argue that the president may have done his constitutional duty at Little Rock, but his outlook toward civil rights activism was cool if not cold. Eisenhower, Hitchcock notes, found himself "caught between two powerful forces" in American society and could not resolve the tension. He believed in bedrock American values of fairness and equality under the law. But he also believed the federal government "must respect local customs, habits, laws, and desires."[30] As Ike's speechwriter Emmet Hughes observed in his memoir *The Ordeal of Power,* Eisenhower believed that force would not bring about equality in America. One could achieve it only through the "slow, gradual power of persuasion."[31] This concept of *gradual* racial progress—what some observers have called a "folkways, not state-ways," approach—was Eisenhower's mantra, as evidenced in his response to a journalist's query at a press conference in September 1956. "It is difficult through law and through force," Ike said, "to change a man's heart." He lamented the actions of "extremists on both sides"—which put him in the position of equating members of the White Citizens Council with advocates for civil rights who, according to Ike, "want to have the whole matter settled today."[32]

Another of Ike's speechwriters, Arthur Larson, observed in a book published in 1968 that the president did not like the word "discrimination" and seemed uneasy about even using the world "racial." Further, the notion of "racial mingling" was anathema to Eisenhower, as evidenced in his reported exchange with Earl Warren at a White House dinner in which Warren recalled Eisenhower telling him that it was understandable for white parents not to want to have their daughters sitting at school "alongside some big overgrown negroes."[33] Larson quotes Eisenhower as saying that equality of political and economic opportunity did not mean that everyone had to mingle socially "or that a Negro should court my daughter."[34]

Throughout his presidency, Ike sought to avoid discomforting southern segregationists on racial matters, even as he endorsed recommendations by his two attorneys general supporting substantive civil rights legislation and the appointment of moderate to liberal judges to the federal bench in key southern districts. In a confidential conversation with *New York Times* Washington bureau chief Arthur Krock, with whom Ike periodically shared candid observations about men and events, he told Krock that it was "obvious" to him that aggressive integrationists, on and off the Supreme Court, were "trying to move too fast at the expense of other rights, and that the

Southern people deserve [the] most moderate procedures in revising their deeply embedded way of life." For Eisenhower, it was the suffering of southern whites during Reconstruction, not the betrayal of southern blacks in the wake of it, that mattered most.[35]

It is difficult to uncouple these attitudes from Eisenhower's lifelong reading habits, military associations, and close friendships (as he noted himself on various occasions, heavily southern tinged), along with his preternatural instinct to find the "middle way" in politics. There is little doubt that Eisenhower's views of Robert E. Lee were shaped in good measure by his reading of Douglas Southall Freeman's work. His views on Reconstruction were almost certainly influenced by textbooks, popular histories (perhaps most notably Claude Bowers's best-selling *The Tragic Era*), and films (*Gone With the Wind*) that caricatured Reconstruction as an era of radical excess and unfair treatment of white southerners.[36] As president, perhaps his favorite author was the longshoreman philosopher Eric Hoffer, whose polemic against political extremism, *The True Believer,* Eisenhower extolled to friends and purchased as gifts.[37]

When it came to responding to the newly revived Ku Klux Klan, Eisenhower's approach was muted. He would ignore it. He did not ignore blacks, but was frequently irritated by their activism. As president, Eisenhower did engage with black organizations, mainly through intermediaries. He did speak on occasion at NAACP conventions and he met once in the White House with black leaders, on June 23, 1958. His penchant for calling members of predominantly African American audiences "you people" and urging them to be patient did not endear him to them. Eisenhower did not see African Americans in full dimension, as individuals who worked and played and laughed and cried and dealt with daily indignities, simply because of the color of their skin. Ralph Ellison's masterpiece, his 1952 novel *Invisible Man,* addresses this issue. It was not on Eisenhower's radar.[38]

When Eisenhower's attorney general, Herbert Brownell, made his pitch at a cabinet meeting on March 9, 1956, for ambitious civil rights legislation, Eisenhower urged Brownell to consider some history. "Don't take the attitude that you are another [Charles] Sumner," he told Brownell. Referring to southern hostility to the Supreme Court's decision in *Brown v. Board of Education,* Eisenhower observed, "these people in the South were not breaking the law for the past 60 years. . . . Now we cannot erase the emotions of three generations overnight. . . . People have a right to disagree with the Supreme Court decision."[39]

Insofar as Eisenhower was committed to a better day for African Americans, his goals were limited. First, enforce the laws of the land. Second, make sure that discrimination within the purview of the executive branch was eliminated. But from there, Ike did not have much more to offer. He lobbied his favorite clergyman, evangelist Billy Graham, to join with pastors around the nation to advocate minor steps to "fend off heavy handed federal action" on racial issues—such steps as encouraging black participation in the South on local school boards and in civic associations, as a pathway to growing acceptance by whites.[40]

As late as July 1963, when Eisenhower delivered a major speech in his adopted home community of Gettysburg—marking the one hundredth anniversary of the great battle—he had nothing to say about the black freedom struggle. Instead, Ike used his bully pulpit to suggest that Americans needed to discipline themselves to resist federal handouts, which were just a way of enticing them to relinquish their self-reliance and independent spirits.[41]

Contrast this with Vice President Lyndon B. Johnson's speech in Gettysburg on Memorial Day that same year, in which Johnson made black civil rights a central theme of memorializing the Civil War. Influenced by Martin Luther King's "Letter from a Birmingham Jail," wherein King expressed his frustration with the slow pace of change on racial issues, Johnson said that answering African Americans' plea for justice with a call for "patience" was no longer good enough. "As we maintain the vigil of peace," Johnson observed, "we must remember that justice is a vigil too—a vigil we must keep in our own streets and schools and among the lives of all our people—that those who died here on their native soil shall not have died in vain. One hundred years ago, the slave was freed. One hundred years later, the Negro remains in bondage to the color of his skin."[42] Powerful words, soon enough translated into transformative actions by Johnson in 1964 and 1965. By contrast, as a self-described "moderate" on race, Ike saw racial progress as an ideal, but not an ideal that could be realized in his lifetime. His views of Johnson's civil rights measures reflected his conviction that changing laws did not necessarily change hearts and minds.

And yet the Lincoln who had successfully conducted the war against the Confederacy, and the Lincoln who pronounced at Gettysburg a "new birth of freedom" as a key wartime goal, remained one of Eisenhower's four favorite Americans. In November 1963, when John F. Kennedy declined an invitation to speak in Gettysburg because of a political commitment in Texas, Eisenhower was pressed again into service as the main speaker on the one hundredth anniversary of Lincoln's Gettysburg Address. This time Ike steered away from a sermon about self-reliance. In six pithy paragraphs, Ike told a large audience what the Gettysburg Address meant to him. He noted that by standing where Lincoln had expressed his "deep dedication to freedom, *our own dedication* takes added strength" (emphasis added).

Eisenhower noted that Lincoln had "lifted his eyes to the future, the future that is our present," in calling for liberty and equality for all. Eisenhower challenged his audience to "live" Lincoln's credo, and to "subordinate self to the country's good." The work of a democracy, Ike added, is "always unfinished." And so it is today.

Ike made no explicit connection between Lincoln and the black struggle, but in Gettysburg on November 19, 1963, he got right with Lincoln. Informed by historical knowledge, Eisenhower pointed his audience to better days ahead.[43]

Notes

1. For this and subsequent quotes, see Dwight D. Eisenhower to Leonard Finder, November 6, 1964; "Statement by Dwight D. Eisenhower," November 5, 1964, both in Finder Papers, Box 1, Dwight D. Eisenhower Presidential Library and Museum, Abilene, Kansas (hereafter DDEL).

2. Jean Edward Smith, *Eisenhower in War and Peace* (New York: Random House, 2012), 8–10. Quote from William I. Hitchcock, *The Age of Eisenhower: America and the World in the 1950s* (New York: Simon and Schuster, 2018), 5.

3. For a vivid account of his growing up years in Abilene, see Dwight D. Eisenhower, *At Ease: Stories I Tell to Friends* (New York: Avon Books, 1968). Quote is from page 46 of the Avon paperback edition. Eisenhower's recollections can usefully be supplemented by Kenneth S. Davis, "The Abilene Factor in Eisenhower," *New York Times Magazine,* December 9, 1951, 12, 13, 26, 28, and the incisive account of this period in Louis Galambos, *Eisenhower: Becoming the Leader of the Free World* (Baltimore: Johns Hopkins Univ. Press, 2018), 12–25.

4. Eisenhower, *At Ease,* 46–47.

5. Ibid., 49; Smith, *Eisenhower,* 15.

6. Hitchcock, *Age of Eisenhower,* 7.

7. Regarding Eisenhower's military apprenticeship, see Galambos, *Eisenhower*, chapters 3–6; for his connections with General Marshall, see Mark Perry, *Partners in Command: George Marshall and Dwight Eisenhower in War and Peace* (New York: Penguin Books, 2008).

8. Eisenhower's reading options at home growing up in Abilene, surprisingly robust, can be captured through a list of titles compiled by the staff of the Eisenhower Presidential Library. For Ike's addiction to westerns as his leisure reading of

choice, see Tim Rives, "Eisenhower and the Remnants of the Western Past," *Great Plains Traverse* 1 (2018): 4–15.

9. Eisenhower, *At Ease,* 47–48; William Bragg Ewald Jr., *Eisenhower the President: Crucial Days, 1951–1960* (Englewood Cliffs, N.J.: Prentice-Hall, 1981), 319–20, 322; and Ann Whitman Diary Series, Box 1, October 24, 1953, entry, DDEL.

10. For Freeman's forceful public support for the general in 1952, see correspondence in Eisenhower's Pre-Presidential Papers, 1916–1952, Principal File Box 43, DDEL. In a *Richmond (Va.) News Leader* editorial included in that file, Freeman had suggested that Eisenhower had "the character and the unselfish patriotism of George Washington," and would be willing, in a period of exceptional need, to accept the presidential office as a duty, and not out of ambition. See also David E. Johnson, *Douglas Southall Freeman* (Gretna, La.: Pelican, 2002), 290–92, 335, 341–42. On Freeman's work as representing the apogee of the Lee cult, see John M. Taylor, "The General and the Historians," *Columbiad* 3 (winter 2000): 140–52.

11. Eisenhower, *At Ease,* 184; for the letter to William E. Brooks, November 12, 1946, see Louis Galambos, ed., *The Papers of Dwight David Eisenhower: The Chief of Staff,* vol. 8 (Baltimore: Johns Hopkins Univ. Press, 1978), 372–73.

12. Stephen Ambrose, *Eisenhower: Soldier, General of the Army, President-Elect, 1890–1952* (New York: Simon and Schuster, 1983), 64.

13. "Eisenhower on Lincoln as Commander in Chief," broadcast on NBC, February 11, 1963, transcript in Post-Presidential Speeches Series, Box 5, DDEL.

14. Eisenhower to Ralph McGill, February 15, 1960, in *Papers of Dwight David Eisenhower: The Presidency: Keeping the Peace,* ed. Louis Galambos and Daun Van Ee, vol. 20 (Baltimore: Johns Hopkins Univ. Press, 2001), 1826. For Eisenhower's comments, see his aide Frederic Fox's "Memorandum for the Record," of the December 6, 1960, meeting, dated December 12, 1960. For the anodyne proclamation creating the commission, and a second proclamation in January heralding the centennial, both of which Bruce Catton helped draft, see White House Central Files, Office File, 1953–1961, OF-G-1, Box 684, DDEL. On southern segregationists' skepticism about the value of a "Civil War" centennial commemoration and commitment to a "Lost Cause" historiography, see Robert J. Cook, *Troubled Commemoration: The American Civil War Centennial, 1961–1965* (Baton Route: Louisiana State Univ. Press, 2007), 52–60.

15. Serious revisionism about Lee as man and general commenced with Thomas L. Connelly's *The Marble Man: Robert E. Lee and His Image in American Society* (New York: Knopf, 1977), and continues today. A key work in Lee revisionism is Elizabeth Brown Pryor, *Reading the Man: A Portrait of Robert E. Lee Through His Private Letters* (New York: Viking, 2007). John Reeves, *The Lost Indictment of Robert E. Lee: The Forgotten Case Against an American Icon* (Lanham, Md.: Rowman and Littlefield, 2018), makes a pertinent contribution to the ongoing conversation about Lee.

16. Glenn LaFantasie, "Monty and Ike Take Gettysburg," *Quarterly Journal of Military History* 8 (autumn 1995): 67–73.

17. See May 12, 1957, Associated Press story, "Lee, Meade, Both Goofed at Gettysburg, 'Ike' Agrees," and "President, Montgomery Tour Battlefield Sunday; See Electric Map; Attended Services with First Lady," *Gettysburg Times,* May 13, 1957. For copies of these articles and others relating to the Montgomery visit, see White House Central Files, 1954–1961: President's Personal Files (hereafter PPF), 1-CC (S), Box 408, DDEL.

18. Holland to Eisenhower, May 16, 1957; Courson to Eisenhower, May 14, 1957; Garrett to Eisenhower, May 16, 1957, was quoting from an Associated Press article that ran in the *Houston Post,* May 16, 1957, under the headline "Texas Sen. Hardeman Criticizes Ike, Monty." Middlebrook to Eisenhower, June 21, 1957. Each of these letters, and other missives critical of the president, appear in PPF, 1-CC (S), Box 408, DDEL.

19. "News Conference, May 15, 1957," *Public Papers of the President, Dwight D. Eisenhower, 1957* (Washington, D.C.: Government Printing Office, 1957), 356.

20. Scott to Eisenhower, August 1, 1960, in PPF, 29-I, Box 743: File of Famous Americans, DDEL.

21. Andrew Goodpaster memo to Bryce Harlow, August 6, 1960, regarding the value of responding; and Eisenhower to Scott, August 9, 1960, both in PPF, 29-I, Box 743: File of Famous Americans, DDEL. This exchange did not remain private. A copy was sent to *Atlanta Constitution* editor Ralph McGill, who included it in a column that month. It too was quoted widely. Ibid.

22. Among many sources focused on Eisenhower's Cold War policies, see Hitchcock, *Age of Eisenhower,* chapters 5, 7, 8, 11, 13, 15, 16, 17, 18, 19; Kenneth Osgood, *Total Cold War: Eisenhower's Secret Propaganda Battle at Home and Abroad* (Lawrence: Univ. Press of Kansas, 2006); and Evan Thomas, *Ike's Bluff: President Eisenhower's Secret Battle to Save the World* (New York: Little, Brown, 2012).

23. This point derives from Jack Holl's as yet unpublished essay on Eisenhower and Lee, which Professor Holl kindly shared with me as part of an email exchange on September 20 and 29, 2017. On Eisenhower's "aboveness" regarding sectionalism and partisan conflict, see William Lee Miller, *Piety Along the Potomac: Notes on Politics and Morals in the Fifties* (Boston: Houghton Mifflin, 1964), 8.

24. Eisenhower to Lawrence, June 12, 1957; Milton Eisenhower to Ann Whitman, June 3, 1957; Whitman to Milton Eisenhower, June 7, 1957, all in PPF, 1-CC, Box 408, DDEL

25. On the controversy over desegregation in Mansfield, see Robyn Duff Ladino, *Desegregating Texas Schools: Eisenhower, Shivers, and the Crisis at Mansfield High* (Austin: Univ. of Texas Press, 1996). Among many accounts of the Little Rock crisis, David A. Nichols, *A Matter of Justice: Eisenhower and the Beginnings of the Civil Rights Revolution* (New York: Simon and Schuster, 2007), chapters 8, 9, stands out. For a less admiring assessment that nonetheless credits Eisenhower for

acting in the national interest, see Hitchcock, *Age of Eisenhower,* chapter 14. James C. Durham, *A Moderate among Extremists: Dwight D. Eisenhower and the School Desegregation Crisis* (Chicago: Nelson-Hall, 1981), endorses Eisenhower's middling course.

26. Eisenhower to Russell, September 27, 1957, in *The Papers of Dwight David Eisenhower: The Presidency: Keeping the Peace,* ed. Louis Galambos and Daun Van Ee, vol. 18 (Baltimore: Johns Hopkins Univ. Press, 2001), 462–63.

27. Catton's draft of the December 6, 1960, Centennial proclamation is in White House Central Files, OF 152-G-1 Box 684, folder 2, DDEL, as is his draft of Eisenhower's January 5 statement inaugurating the centennial, and the president's editorial work on it.

28. Frederic Fox, "Memo for the Record," December 12, 1960, OF 154-A, DDEL.

29. I am indebted to emeritus professor of history at the University of Maryland Keith Olson for his persuasive comments on this subject, in lectures at the Eisenhower Teacher Workshops held at Gettysburg College, 2010–2016.

30. Hitchcock, *Age of Eisenhower,* 229; James F. Simon, *Eisenhower vs. Warren: The Battle for Civil Rights and Liberties* (New York: Liveright, 2018), especially chapters 7–9. That said, Eisenhower's actions desegregating the military, integrating Central High School in Little Rock, and opening public facilities in Washington, D.C., to African Americans put him at odds with adherents of Ohio senator Robert A. Taft in the early 1950s and with William F. Buckley and his cohort writing for *National Review* in the late 1950s. On this point, see Heather Cox Richardson, *To Make Men Free: A History of the Republican Party* (New York: Basic Books, 2014), 237, 239–240.

31. Emmet John Hughes, *The Ordeal of Power: A Political Memoir of the Eisenhower Years* (New York: Atheneum, 1963), 201–202. Hughes credits Eisenhower with a decision of character in dealing with the Little Rock crisis, but insists that Eisenhower was displeased with the *Brown* decision and preferred on racial issues "to leave things undone" (245). Eisenhower's civil rights policy, Hughes asserts, was one of "discreet drift." For a pithy rebuttal, emphasizing deeds, not words, see David A. Nichols, "Closing Argument: The Verdict on Eisenhower and Civil Rights," in *The Eisenhower Presidency: Lessons for the Twenty-First Century,* ed. Andrew J. Polsky (Lanham, Md.: Lexington Books, 2015), 49–62.

32. "News Conference, September 5, 1956," *Public Papers of the President,* 736. Also see Hitchcock, *Age of Eisenhower,* 301.

33. Arthur Larson, *The President Nobody Knew* (New York: Charles Scribner's Sons, 1968), 126. Eisenhower's quote appears in Simon, *Eisenhower vs. Warren,* xiv. Contrary to Nichols, Simon asserts that Eisenhower was uncomfortable with the *Brown* decision, believing it "more of a political opinion than a judicial decree" (371).

34. Larson, *President Nobody Knew,* 127.

35. Krock memo as an *aide-memoire,* April 7, 1960, Krock Papers, Box 18, Seeley Mudd Library, Princeton University. Eisenhower's empathy for what southern

whites experienced in the wake of the *Brown* decision appears in Simon, *Eisenhower vs. Warren,* 142–43, and Hughes, *Ordeal of Power,* 201–2. My point about Eisenhower's perception of southern history derives from Sam Roberts's obituary of historian Willie Lee Rose, quoting a review of *Rehearsal for Reconstruction* (1964) by Henry Steele Commager. See "Willie Lee Rose, Historian Who Upended Views on Reconstruction, Dies at 91," *New York Times,* June 28, 2018.

36. "What the President Reads," *Newsweek* 47 (April 30, 1956): 32–33. See, in this context, John David Smith, *An Old Creed for the New South: Proslavery Ideology and Historiography, 1865–1918* (1985; reprint, Athens: Univ. of Georgia Press, 1991), chapters 6, 8; and Donald Yacovone, "Textbook Racism: How Scholars Sustained White Supremacy," *Chronicle of Higher Education,* April 8, 2018.

37. Anthony Leviero, "President Urging a Book [*The True Believer*] to Friends," *New York Times,* March 19, 1956.

38. Hitchcock, *Age of Eisenhower,* 373; E. Frederic Morrow, *Forty Years a Guinea Pig* (New York: Pilgrim Press, 1980), 163–64; and Michael J. Birkner, "From Hackensack to the White House: The Triumph and Travail of E. Frederic Morrow," *New Jersey Studies* 3 (2017): 78–117.

39. Hitchcock, *Age of Eisenhower,* 239–40.

40. Eisenhower to Graham, March 22, 1956, and March 30, 1956, in *The Papers of Dwight David Eisenhower: The Presidency: The Middle Way,* ed. Louis Galambos and Daun Van Ee, vol. 16 (Baltimore: Johns Hopkins Univ. Press, 1996), 2086–88, 2104–5; and Graham to Eisenhower, June 4, 1956, *Papers of Dwight David Eisenhower,* 17:2190, notes 2 and 3. Hitchcock, *Age of Eisenhower,* 298–99, provides helpful context.

41. For the reading text, see Eisenhower Post-Presidential Papers, 1961–69, Speeches Series Box 6, DDEL.

42. David M. Shribman, "L.B.J.'s Gettysburg Address," *New York Times,* May 24, 2013, and for the full text, see "Remarks by Vice President, Memorial Day, Gettysburg, Pennsylvania, May 30, 1963," www.lbjlibrary.net/collections/selected-speeches/. In fairness to Eisenhower, the same month that LBJ eloquently connected the Civil War to the black freedom struggle, Ike published an article in the *New York Herald Tribune* endorsing John F. Kennedy's civil rights bill and suggesting that no Republican running for president in 1964 who failed to do so deserved the party's nomination.

43. The reading text of Eisenhower's November 19, 1963, speech can be found in Eisenhower Post-Presidential Papers, 1961–69, Speeches Series (A70-32), Box 6, DDEL. On Eisenhower's shift in emphasis from July to November 1963, and the context for Civil War centennial commentaries, see Jared Peatman, *The Long Shadow of Lincoln's Gettysburg Address* (Carbondale: Southern Illinois Univ. Press, 2013), chapter 5.

10

Playing with History

Walt Disney's Historical Films, 1946–1966

Raymond Arsenault

Walt Disney, the acknowledged master of fantasy and animated wizardry, began his experimentation with historical filmmaking in the mid-1940s. As a young man he had practically invented a new art form, one that eventually placed him among the world's most powerful culture brokers. Now, nearly twenty years after the creation of Mickey Mouse and the seminal cartoon *Steamboat Willie,* he had a notion that he could both expand his influence and shore up his financial solvency by reinterpreting the American past with an imaginative form of popular history.[1]

Having barely survived the economic challenges of wartime, he entered the postwar era with an innovative strategy that promoted commercial success through an amalgam of animation and live action. Labeled an "integrated cartoon," this hybrid form actually originated during the war when the Walt Disney Studios produced training and propaganda films for the War Department. The first feature-length integrated cartoon, a tribute to Latin America titled *Saludos Amigos,* was released in early 1943, to be followed a few months later by the powerful propaganda film *Victory Through Air Power.* Focusing on the ideas and career of Major Alexander de Seversky, a military aviation pioneer who had recently published a book with the same title, the film had a significant historical dimension. But its primary goal was clearly advocacy, not the construction of a narrative.[2]

A more self-conscious effort to use the integrated cartoon format to explore historical questions appeared three years later with the release of *Song of the South.* A mixture of 30 percent animation and 70 percent live action, the film featured the "Negro" trickster tales collected and refashioned by the

Georgia writer Joel Chandler Harris during the three decades following the end of Reconstruction. Harris's tales had long been a staple of post–Civil War southern literature. But *Song of the South* marked the cinematic debut of Uncle Remus, Brer Rabbit, Brer Fox, and the other wily creatures of the Briar Patch.[3]

The words that appear on the screen as the film opens set the tone for a nostalgic salute to the traditional values of paternalism: "Out of the humble cabin, out of the singing heart of the Old South have come the tales of Uncle Remus, rich in simple truths, forever fresh and new." The script promoted this point with frequent folkloric allusions, but it generally avoided anything resembling evidence-based history. The cartoon sequences were charming and emotionally seductive, but the live action scenes demonstrated little awareness of the racial and class complexities of the postwar South.

Disney's initial foray into popular history was entertaining enough to draw relatively large audiences, and the film won a commendation from *Parents* magazine and two Academy Awards, one given to "Zip-a-Dee-Doo-Dah" for Best Original Song, and a second, a Special Oscar, awarded to James Baskette for his inspired portrayal of Uncle Remus. Baskette's Academy Award was the first Oscar ever presented to an African American man, but this milestone did not assuage Disney's dual disappointment that the black star failed to receive a nomination for Best Actor and that *Song of the South* received no consideration for Best Picture.

The press's response to the film was also disappointing. Southern critics embraced the film as a tribute to the region's best traditions, but in the rest of the nation the reviews were decidedly mixed. Many northern critics, especially those representing the black press, wrote scalding denunciations of the live action section, which they found to be backward looking and implicitly racist. Others did not know what to make of the film, with its mixture of clever animation and hackneyed dialogue and plot lines. But even for those who fell under the spell of the Briar Patch, the film did not live up to the Disney Studios hype touting it as "an epochal event in screen history."[4]

Song of the South was, however, an important first step in what eventually became a determined march toward a Disneyfied version of American history. In the short run, the racial and regional politics surrounding the film—especially the NAACP's loud objections to the film's reliance on racial stereotypes—left Disney reluctant to produce additional films that tackled sensitive issues or episodes from the American past. For a time he steered away from potentially controversial subjects such as race, limiting the studio's historical productions to films that focused on embattled individual heroes and empowering stories. Reflecting Disney's increasingly conservative politics, they were, as the historian Steven Watts has argued, moralistic tales conceived as "libertarian Populist" expressions of individualism versus collectivism. Such prescriptive tales, in Disney's view, were just what the American public needed in the perilous times of the Cold War.[5]

He began with *So Dear to My Heart* (1949), an integrated cartoon based on Sterling North's popular children's book *Midnight and Jeremiah,* which depicted the virtues of early twentieth-century farm life in Indiana. He then followed with four off-shore classics that demonstrated the ability of heroes to triumph in the face of extreme adversity: *Treasure Island* (1950), a charming live action rendition of Robert Louis Stevenson's swashbuckling epic; *The Story of Robin Hood* (1952), an elaborate costume drama filmed in England; *The Sword and the Rose* (1953), a fictionalized dramatization of Mary Tudor's romantic adventures in the age of Henry VIII; and *Rob Roy, the Highland Rogue* (1954), a biopic on the eighteenth-century Scottish rebel Rob Roy MacGregor.[6]

Disney's largely European detour lasted until December 1954, when the studio returned to the American history track with a five-part television serial on the life of the legendary frontiersman Davy Crockett. Loosely based on Crockett's 1834 memoir, *A Narrative of the Life of David Crockett of the State of Tennessee,* the serial followed the same folkloric formula used in *Song of the South.*

No professional historians were consulted during the script development, and the studio staff all but ignored the extensive historical literature on the 1830s. Crockett was portrayed as a folk hero, plain and simple, rendering serious contextual and biographical research unnecessary. Bill Walsh, the producer of the studio's new *Disneyland* television series, recalled the origins of Disney's Crockett: "I thought it might be a good thing to do a series on vaunted American heroes, and we mulled over subjects like Johnny Appleseed, Daniel Boone, Windwagon Smith, Big Foot Wallace, and Davy Crockett. The first one we picked, by dumb luck, was Davy Crockett, who was someone at the time nobody had ever heard of."

Disney took a deep personal interest in the production and frequently visited the set to attend to various details, especially after the first episode, "Davy Crockett, Indian Fighter," became an overnight sensation. Faced with an unexpected hit, the studio scrambled to mount a national campaign that targeted children and teenagers, the first such effort organized around a television show. By early 1955, the "Crockett craze" was in full swing as millions of youngsters across the nation donned coonskin caps and buckskin jackets, while singing along with "The Ballad of Davy Crockett," the almost irresistible anthem that opened each episode.

By the time the long-awaited Disneyland theme park opened in June, Disney merchandisers were hawking more than two hundred Crockett-related items, ranging from pajamas to school lunch boxes. The popular Frontierland section of the park highlighted and magnified the Crockett phenomenon, as did frequent personal appearances by the stars of the show, Fess Parker as Davy, and Buddy Ebsen as his sidekick, George Russel. "Davy Crockett is bigger even than Mickey Mouse," *Time* magazine reported, acknowledging Disney's mastery of marketing to the nation's first generation of television viewers.

It all had little to do with legitimate history, but Davy's identification with virtues widely associated with the nineteenth-century frontier—notably courage and self-reliance—made him a national icon of historic importance. Whether he was fighting the Red Sticks, running for Congress, jousting with the roguish keelboat captain Mike Fink, or defending the Alamo against marauding Mexicans, he represented the ideal American. Indeed, as Disney and others pointed out, he also served as a model for stalwart Cold War citizenship, the kind the nation needed to counter the Soviet threat to democracy. For many enthusiasts, the frontier hero's favorite saying said it all: "Be sure you're right, then go ahead." There would be no retreat in Davy's world, or Disney's.[7]

Boosted by the Davy Crockett craze and the opening of Disneyland, and by the studio's unprecedented financial bonanza, Disney became bolder and more confident about his plans for the future. For starters, he promptly put Davy on the big screen. Splicing together large sections of the first three television episodes, he created a feature film, *Davy Crockett, King of the Wild Frontier,* released with great fanfare in May 1955.

The movie was a huge success at the box office, so much so that Disney followed up a year later with a second film adaptation, *Davy Crockett and the River Pirates.* Even more fictional than the first Crockett film, the tongue-in-cheek sequel featured a rollicking keelboat race from the Ohio River to New Orleans, with Davy and Mike Fink serving respectively as hero and antihero. Once again Disney made a killing at the box office, confirming that fictionalized historical adventures, whether dramatic or comedic, were commercially viable in 1950s America.[8]

If *Davy Crockett and the River Pirates* had little to do with historical reality, Disney's next venture represented a sharp turn toward nonfiction filmmaking. Without apologizing for the artistic license he had exercised in the past, he set out to beat the historical purists at their own game, to prove that the vaunted Disney magic was not necessarily bound by the worlds of fantasy and folklore. "Disney realism" had already shown what it could do in the genre of nature films—*The Vanishing Prairie* had just won an Academy Award as the best documentary of 1954—and he was confident that if he put his mind to it he could do the same for the art of historical filmmaking, particularly if he were dealing with a subject close to his heart.[9]

Disney wisely chose a historical project that combined two of his favorite subjects: the Civil War and railroads. The latter was perhaps his greatest passion, and he could not resist a project that, as one biographer put it, provided "the chance for him to play with full-sized trains." In August 1955, a month after the opening of Disneyland, the Disney Studios announced plans to produce a feature film entitled *The Great Locomotive Chase.* With Fess Parker in the lead role, the film would reenact the Andrews Raid, a "Civil War spy story" that included "the wildest railroad race in history."

On April 12, 1862, a band of twenty-two Union marauders, disguised as civilians and led by secret agent James J. Andrews, snuck into the Confederate railroad depot at Big Shanty, north of Marietta, Georgia, and commandeered a Rebel train hitched to the locomotive *The General.* Except for Andrews, a Kentuckian, and one other civilian, the raiders were all volunteers from Ohio, headquartered in Nashville, Tennessee. The raiders' mission was to disrupt Confederate lines of supply and communication by steaming northward along the Western & Atlantic Railroad, blowing up tracks and trestles along the way. But, unfortunately for the Union war effort, they ran afoul of William A. Fuller, a determined Confederate conductor who chased them up the line, "first on foot, then by push car and finally with another locomotive."

Fuller's extraordinary exploits slowed the raiders' progress, and after eight hours and eighty-seven miles of pursuit *The General* ran out of fuel. The raiders then scattered into the north Georgia woods, where they were soon captured by a band of Confederate cavalry. After three months in an Atlanta prison, Andrews and seven other raiders were convicted of espionage and executed. In October, eight of the surviving raiders escaped, making their way to the Union lines, but six others remained in prison until March 1863, when they were repatriated in a prisoner exchange. Later in the month the six became the first American soldiers to receive the Medal of Honor, a new medal authorized by President Lincoln the previous July. Eventually nineteen of the raiders were so honored, six posthumously.[10]

Buster Keaton parodied the Andrews Raid in his 1927 silent comedy *The General,* but Disney was the first filmmaker to attempt a straightforward, factual treatment of the incident. Disney admired Keaton's silent classic, but the primary inspiration for the making of *The Great Locomotive Chase* came from Wilbur Kurtz, an Atlanta artist and historian who served as a technical adviser during the filming of *Gone with the Wind* and *Song of the South.*

Kurtz's late wife, who died in 1946 just prior to the release of *Song of the South,* was the daughter of conductor William Fuller. As a young man, Kurtz had interviewed his father-in-law and several other survivors of the raid, and he never tired of telling Disney or anyone else about the drama and heroism of the great chase of 1862. During the filming of *Song of the South,* Kurtz persuaded Disney, who as a fellow railroad buff needed little convincing, that a cinematic version of the Andrews Raid would make great entertainment. Disney was intrigued, but it would take him a decade to act on the idea.

Interestingly enough, Disney was reluctant to credit Kurtz's background as the original inspiration for the making of the film. Just prior to the movie's release in 1956, he told a television audience that the decision to put the Andrews Raid on film was rooted in his own Middle Border childhood and in his lifelong passion for railroads. "When I was a boy in Missouri," he recalled, "I liked to listen to old soldiers who had fought in the Civil War. We had both Confederate and Union veterans in our town and my loyalties would go from General Lee to General Grant and back again depending upon which side told the most exciting tale."

His interest in the Andrews Raid, he insisted, began when he stumbled upon an eyewitness account of the raid in his family's library. Written by William Pittenger, a participant in the raid and one of the six original Medal of Honor winners, *Daring and Suffering: A History of the Great Railroad Adventure* transported a wide-eyed young boy from the mythic uncertainty of veterans' yarns to the comforting security of factual history. Here, at last, Disney exclaimed, was "a Civil War story that did full justice to both sides."

Disney's personal account of the project's conception is probably apocryphal. But, whatever its origins, *The Great Locomotive Chase* was an inspired choice for a Disney film. In a nation still sharply divided along regional lines—a nation experiencing the aftershocks of the *Brown* decision and the early rumblings of the modern civil rights movement—the Civil War remained a delicate and potentially explosive subject. From a marketing standpoint, it was fortunate, and hardly accidental, that Disney chose a Civil War story that would play in Peoria as well as Atlanta.

Despite the underlying themes of civil war and regional conflict, *The Great Locomotive Chase* offered a reassuring and balanced complement of regional heroes. As told by Disney, it was a story with no villains and no losers. Although the raid failed, the Union raiders performed heroically, emerging with Congressional Medals of Honor; by the same token, the Confederates lost the war, but in this instance they carried the day, foiling the raiders' plans. All Americans, regardless of regional persuasion, could leave the theater with a heightened sense of pride. And they could watch the film from start to finish without ever encountering the contentious issues of slavery and race, or even states' rights. Who cared what the two sides were fighting for when bravery, honor, and character were so much in evidence?

The film essentially provided entertainment and factual information without mentioning the major political controversies of the Civil War era. Combining a saga of intrigue and pursuit with the drama of old-time railroading, *The Great Locomotive Chase* promised to reawaken the historical imagination of all red-blooded Americans, even those who harbored painful memories of schoolbook history lessons. "That old Civil War story simply related as factual history," Disney insisted, "has all the elements of the wildest romance." Quoting from an 1862 Atlanta newspaper that called the Andrews Raid "the most thrilling railroad adventure that has ever occurred on the American continent," the man who had resurrected Davy Crockett and Mike Fink assured his fans that the Disney version of American history would never be boring.[11]

As the narrator of a revealing television documentary on the making of the film, Fess Parker left no doubt that the Disney Studios regarded James J. Andrews as a Crockett-style hero who exemplified the ideals of American patriotism and democratic virtue. Here was "another real American," a citizen soldier who "belongs to the hundreds of brave and dedicated men who have had their day of glory and since been forgotten." Parker's Texas twang added an ironic twist to this opening tribute to a Union hero, but the script soon turned to a glorification of the southern countryside, thus dispelling any potential confusion or nervousness on the part of southern viewers.

Allegedly sparing no effort or expense in his search for historical accuracy, Disney transported his film crew to an authentic locale "in the heart of the Deep South." Although it proved impossible to recreate the ambiance of nineteenth-century railroading on the actual site of the Andrews Raid, where narrow-gauge railroading and wooden trestles had long since given way to modern technology and urban sprawl, Disney found an acceptable substitute in the isolated mountains of northern Georgia, seventy miles northeast of Atlanta.

The town of Clayton, population three thousand, and the nearby Tallulah Falls Railroad provided a near perfect backdrop for Disney's Civil War epic. Here he found not only the remnants of a historic railroad line but also a part of the South almost untouched by the intrusions of urban development and social change. With the strains of "Dixie" playing in the background, Parker extolled "this romantic country" as a bucolic paradise.

"On every side," he intoned, "there were echoes of another century. In this rustic setting life goes on much as it did in Civil War days, and often the old ways are still the best. There's a peacefulness to this country that's hard to beat . . . nature's critters are right at home. Seems like this, in fact, was the favorite haunt of Brer Rabbit and Brer Fox of the Joel Chandler Harris stories. And good 'coon country too."

The Disney scriptwriters could not resist this allusion to *Song of the South,* which had just been rereleased, but they were careful to remind the audience that *The Great Locomotive Chase* was history, not folklore. During most of the filming, Walt Disney himself was on hand "to check every factual detail." Indeed, according to Parker, "to get into the spirit of things Walt wore a Confederate hat all the time he was on location." Presumably, having the boss wear a Union hat would have unnerved local onlookers, especially the "genuine Georgians" that Disney hired as extras.

The bit players included the mayor of Clayton, several local businessmen, and even a black waitress and a black porter. "We wanted real Southerners," Parker explained, "looks, language, and all." From the selection of the cast and locale to the refitting of nineteenth-century locomotives to the detailing of costumes, Disney was determined to replicate "historical fact—the way it happened in real life." To ensure accuracy in every detail, he hired a special staff of Civil War and railroad "experts" led by Wilbur Kurtz, and he even consulted with William Fuller's eldest son, who was on location during part of the filming. What more could anyone ask for?

Despite a measure of hyperbole, the Parker documentary accurately reflected Disney's intentions. Although no academic historians were involved in the project—an oversight that seemingly went unnoticed at the time—Disney's search for historical authenticity was genuine, and he was justifiably proud of the final product when it was released in the summer of 1956.[12]

By Hollywood standards his search for historical accuracy was reasonably successful, though knowledgeable train buffs detected that the locomotives used in the film were not entirely true to the Civil War period. For example, the studio replaced one of Fuller's pursuit locomotives, the *Texas,* with a later model, the *Inyo,* built in 1875. The stand-in for *The General*—the *William Mason* built in 1856—was more accurate. But the overall authenticity of the film's train stock fell short of Disney's outsized claims.[13]

For the most part, Lawrence Edward Watkin's script represented a faithful rendering of Pittenger's memoir, the action scenes were both entertaining and believable, and the leading members of the cast gave solid performances, especially Jeffrey Hunter in the role of William Fuller. Some Crockett enthusiasts found Parker's portrayal of a Union spy a bit unsettling, but most theatergoers seemed to like the film. As Richard Schickel, the author of *The Disney Version,* later commented, "the film had a zestful inventiveness about it, as well as a drive and a tension that one did not often find in the Disney product of this time—possibly because there was no time to pause over the antics of children and animals as so many of his other pictures did."

Upon its release, the film drew a number of positive reviews, including one from Bosley Crowther of the *New York Times,* who called it "great entertainment for youngsters and anybody who had a yen for trains." Disney, however, was underwhelmed by the critical response to what he considered to be a minor masterpiece. Some reviewers, although appreciative of Disney's effort at historical reconstruction, were disappointed with the narrative arc of the story. As even Crowther observed, "The excitement is over when they abandon the trains." Burdened with an anticlimactic ending, the film did not excite most reviewers or theatergoers to the extent that Disney had foreseen. The anticipated box office buzz never developed, and the film's gross earnings proved disappointingly modest.

Perhaps worst of all, professional historians greeted the film with polite silence. Despite Disney's best efforts, no one in the academic community was ready to recognize him as a serious historian. Unable to transcend his image as a purveyor of fantasy and commercialized popular culture, he felt unappreciated as a valid interpreter of the past.[14]

This disappointment prompted a change in strategy that returned the studio to its fictional roots. While Disney's commitment to historically based, live action entertainment remained strong, he turned away from traditional history. During the next three years, the Disney Studios made six live action films, only one of which, *Davy Crockett and the River Pirates,* involved actual historical figures. The other scripts were all works of historical fiction: *Westward Ho the Wagons* (1956), an episodic tale of wagon train life punctuated by frontier songs; *Johnny Tremain* (1957), an adaptation of Esther Forbes's novel about a teenaged patriot living in Boston during the American Revolution; *Old Yeller* (1957), a sentimental "dog and boy" story set in Texas in 1869 and based on Fred Gipson's young adult novel; *The Light in the Forest* (1958), a 1760s Indian captivity narrative based on Conrad Richter's popular 1953 novel; and *Tonka* (1958), an adaptation of David Appel's *Comanche,* a fictional account of a Native American boy's devotion to his horse.

All of these films touched on legitimate and important historical themes: westward migration, civilians affected by civil war, homesteading, frontier violence, and conflict between Native Americans and whites. But they did so outside the bounds of historical truth telling and careful contextual framing. Indeed, as biographer Neal Gabler has argued, these nostalgic, youth-oriented films "turned history into boyhood adventure." *Old Yeller,* for example, contains only one brief reference to the Civil War, no mention at all of Reconstruction, and no way of telling which side the family supported during the war. The touching story of the boy and his dog offers several moral lessons but not much history.[15]

Disney obviously felt more comfortable in the world of historical fiction than in the factually constrained world of history. As the anthropologist Stephen Fjellman has written, he preferred "Distory" to straightforward history, developing a form of "Disney realism" in which "the past was to be cleaned up." As expressed at Disneyland and in live action films, his "Norman Rockwell view of history" leapt "back across two world wars and a depression to more distant and hazy times. Colonial America, the American West, and the turn-of-the-century echoes of Main Street USA were meant to tap nostalgia and sneak past whatever grim realities attended those times and places."[16]

This was an emotionally satisfying and commercially viable formula that would take the Disney empire to once unimaginable levels of popularity and influence in the decades to come. For the most part, this success with live action fare rested on a creative blend of fiction and folklore. But as the 1950s drew to a close, Uncle Walt, as he was known at the studio, continued to experiment with television serials based on the adventures of actual historical figures. The urge to repeat the Davy Crockett phenomenon was simply too tempting to resist.

In October 1958, Disney returned to nonfiction with two television series, *The Nine Lives of Elfego Baca* and *The Tales of Texas John Slaughter.* Elfego Baca (1865–1945), a gunfighter, lawyer, and sheriff from Socorro, New Mexico, was the studio's first Hispanic hero, presaging the fictional Zorro that first appeared on television two years later. As played by Robert Loggia, Baca, like Zorro, was a fiercely combative champion of the underdog. His Anglo counterpart in the second series was John Horton Slaughter (1841–1922), a former Texas Ranger who became a sheriff, cattleman, and politician in Cochise County, Arizona. At one point, he pursued and apprehended the Apache firebrand Geronimo, an incident recreated in one of the series's later episodes, "Geronimo's Revenge." Both series drew large television audiences, but they had little commercial or cultural impact other than a repackaging of several episodes for limited European theatrical release.

The studio also produced a four-part serial on the legendary Kentucky frontiersman Daniel Boone (1734–1820), broadcast in December 1960 and March 1961, but once again the Crockett-like magic failed to materialize. Ironically, several years later (1964–1970) Fess Parker of Crockett fame would star in a popular NBC television series on Boone produced by 20th Century Fox, not Disney.[17]

The studio's most successful follow-up to the Crockett craze was a six-part television series on Colonel Francis Marion of South Carolina, the Revolutionary War hero better known as the Swamp Fox. The introduction to the opening episode of *Swamp Fox,* which aired on October 23, 1959, invited the American public to rediscover yet another lost hero from "Frontierland." Looking much like a high school history teacher and flanked by a sprawling Revolutionary War battle map, Disney extolled the virtues of "America's Robin Hood of the Revolution." In the spring of 1780 the Revolution seemed lost, but "in the darkest hour of his country's need, the Swamp Fox had been born." Leading a "hardy band of freedom fighters" skilled in guerrilla-style hit-and-run tactics, the pesky Marion disrupted

Lord Cornwallis's lines of supply and communication and paved the way for the ultimate Patriot victory at Yorktown.

According to Disney, in the months and years that followed, "the legend of the Swamp Fox was told and retold around a thousand campfires," making Marion "a hero second only to George Washington." Many in the television audience were undoubtedly puzzled, and probably somewhat ashamed, that they had never heard of this towering hero, but then again many of them had never heard of Davy Crockett until Fess Parker appeared in their living room in 1954.[18]

Disney's desire to repeat the successful Crockett formula was obvious from the start. According to Forrest Powers, the movie critic of the *Minneapolis Star,* everyone recognized the Swamp Fox as "Davy Crockett-1959." This was welcome news in the South Carolina lowcountry, where tourist dollars and celebrity status were rare commodities.

Writing several months before the airing of the first episode, one impatient South Carolina reporter began his story with the jingle "Fran-cis, Francis Marion, King of the Wild Pee Dee." "Don't look now," he warned his adult readers, "but that may well be the song that your youngsters are singing when Walt Disney gets through with the 'Swamp Fox.' He's out to make General Marion, the South's and particularly this area's Revolutionary War hero, as popular a national hero as Davy Crockett." Although the reporter's lyrics were a bit off, the actual Swamp Fox theme song bore a striking resemblance to "The Ballad of Davy Crockett":

> Swamp Fox, Swamp Fox
> hides in the glen
> Runs away so's he kin fight
> again.[19]

Armed with a catchy tune, the Swamp Fox could follow safely in Davy's footsteps, opening the hearts and perhaps even the wallets of America's youth. Accordingly, the Disney Studios touted Leslie Nielsen, the unknown twenty-six-year old Canadian actor who played Marion, as the new Fess Parker. The handsome, broad-shouldered Nielsen cut a striking figure as a dashing war hero, particularly when he wore his distinctive tricornered hat. Although more than one South Carolina historian complained that no evidence existed that that Marion ever wore such a hat, the Disney marketeers made a valiant attempt to sell the Swamp Fox's plumed tricorner as a worthy successor to Davy's coonskin. The intended Swamp Fox craze never materialized, but it was not for the want of trying.

Following the Crockett model, Disney publicists emphasized the historical authenticity of the Swamp Fox series, but they exaggerated their claims. Although the Disney Studios spent more than $800,000 on the first two episodes, a staggering figure for a 1950s television production, the attention to detail was haphazard at best. The research for the *Swamp Fox* series fell far short of the standard set by *The Great Locomotive Chase,* even though the scriptwriters had access to several historical works on Marion, including William Gilmore Simms's 1844 classic, *The Life of Francis Marion,* and a recently published biography by Robert Bass, a professor of history at Furman University who had been researching Marion's life since 1929.

The tone of the script was faithful to Simms's hagiographic portrait, but not always to the facts of Marion's life. At times, the details and sequencing of the Disney script adhered to the historical record, but the overall dramatization of the Swamp Fox contained more folklore than history. Because Disney had chosen a mythic historical character susceptible to caricature, it was not surprising that the scriptwriters and the director regularly blurred the line between fact and fiction.[20]

The die was cast when Leslie Nielsen was selected to play the role of Francis Marion. A fine actor, Nielsen was nonetheless badly miscast as the Swamp Fox. Even if one could get by Nielsen's pronounced Canadian accent, there was the problem of physical appearance. Disney's original choice for the starring role, the diminutive war hero Audie Murphy, would have been appropriate, but the six-foot, three-inch Nielsen was nearly a foot taller than the real Swamp Fox. Such miscasting was a common and perhaps forgivable practice in Hollywood, but Disney's distortions of the Swamp Fox saga went well beyond physical stature. In a revealing interview with the *Milwaukee Sentinel,* Nielsen acknowledged that Disney's characterization of the Swamp Fox was partly fiction. Asked if the Disney stories were "historically factual," Nielsen replied:

> Well, they are to a great extent. . . . Some changes had to be made of course. Names had to be changed in some instances because descendants of some of the people involved might not be pleased by the way their kin are portrayed. On the whole, the story idealizes Marion. To stick to the facts, entirely, however, would make for very dull watching.

> Even the life of Napoleon would make a dull TV series. Marion was introspective. He was a dedicated man, too. But he was not the most colorful character. They didn't want me to play him as he was. Actually, we picture him as a sort of Robin Hood of the South.[21]

John Sutton, the British actor who played Marion's archenemy Colonel Banastre Tarleton, was equally candid about the fictionalization of his character. According to Sutton, the Disney scriptwriters deliberately softened Tarleton's on-screen persona after they learned that the series might be replayed on British television. "In the opening adventure, I played Tarleton according to his actual reputation—a butcher," Sutton admitted, but "by the time the third and fourth episodes are shown in January and the fifth and sixth in March, you will almost feel sorry for the old boy."

Despite the appearance of unrehearsed candor, it is unlikely that Nielsen and Sutton were speaking on their own initiative. In the Disney empire such matters were rarely left to chance. The two actors were almost certainly speaking for Disney, who wanted to avoid a personal admission of error but who wanted to retreat nonetheless. Of course, like the Swamp Fox, Disney only retreated so that he would live to fight another day. Replenished in the familiar territory of fantasy and folklore, Uncle Walt would ultimately seize the high ground of historical truth as he defined it.[22]

During the next seven years, the Disney Studios released nine more historical films: *Kidnapped* (1960), based on Robert Louis Stevenson's 1886 historical novel set against the backdrop of the eighteenth-century Jacobite rising in Scotland; *Ten Who Dared* (1960), a dramatization of Major John Wesley Powell's exploration of the Colorado River and the Grand Canyon in the 1870s; *Swiss Family Robinson* (1960), the fictional story of an America-bound Swiss family shipwrecked on a Caribbean island; *The Sign of Zorro* (1960), the adventures of a fictionalized Mexican avenger in 1820s California; *Greyfriars Bobby* (1961), based on the true story of a Skye terrier who kept watch over his master's grave in Edinburgh from 1858 to 1872; *In Search of the Castaways* (1962), an adaptation of Jules Verne's 1867 adventure novel *Captain Grant's Children*; *Miracle of the White Stallions* (1963), an account of a renowned Vienna riding school's survival amid the turmoil of post-1945 Europe; *The Fighting Prince of Donegal* (1966), an adaptation of Robert T. Reilly's 1957 historical novel about sixteenth-century Ireland; and *Follow Me, Boys!* (1966), a small-town, mid-twentieth-century melodrama based on MacKinlay Kantor's novel *God and My Country.*

Disney released the last of these films two weeks before his death on December 15, 1966. It was the end of an era, and Walt's commanding influence on the studio would soon give way to a more dispersed form of corporate control. But while he was alive Disney put his personal stamp on virtually every creation that came out of the studio. He did not just lend his name to the Disney brand; he did things his way, with a clear sense of purpose and proprietary interest. The nine historical films listed above—those released during his last years—tell us a great deal about his evolving approach to the place of history in the Disney empire.

With one exception—*Ten Who Dared*—these nine films clearly represent a departure from the straightforward historical treatment seen in *The Great Locomotive Chase.* The turn to historical fiction was emphatic, as was his decreasing emphasis on American history. Only three of the nine had anything to do with the United States, and not one focused on a major or controversial issue.[23]

The studio's turn away from fact-based American history during the 1960s undoubtedly stemmed from multiple factors related to script acquisition and development, staff priorities, and perceived shifts in popular culture. But one of the primary factors dictating the change was almost certainly Disney's newly elevated status as an iconic figure. After years of hypersensitivity to highbrow criticism, he had begun to relax and enjoy success on his own terms. Accordingly, he no longer apologized for his personal attachment to historical dramas grounded in fiction and folklore. He had never been all that interested in historical accuracy and factual verification, and now he felt secure enough to be himself. While he had earned an enviable reputation as a perfectionist overseer of the studio's animation, his attention to detail in live action features generally focused more on costuming and sets than on the historical veracity of the script.

Disney knew that he was first and foremost an idea man, an "imagineer" who cared more about promoting a social agenda based on traditional American values than maintaining a purity of form. This disregard for the conventions of historical study was, of course, partly a matter of ego. He was, after all, the creator of new worlds—from the Magic Kingdom to Tomorrowland—a cartoon, film, and theme park maven who could blend the past, present, and future at will. In the mature Disney version of human experience, good popular history had become whatever he said it was. As long as he was able to satisfy and educate his fans with uplifting films that provided moral lessons and happy endings, he was not concerned about realism or factual accuracy.[24]

In 1937, long before the studio turned to live action and integrated cartoons, Disney assured a *Time* reporter that his approach to filmmaking was simple: "We just try to make a good picture. And then the professors come along and tell us what we do." But by the 1960s, this calculus was no longer in effect; Disney no longer cared what the professors thought. He got away with this blasé attitude because his capacity to influence mass culture on a national and even global scale had reached a level unimaginable earlier in the century. His natural bent had always favored a cultural populism suspicious of intellectual sophistication, and now he could create films and attractions in the Distory mode without fear of damaging criticism or commercial failure. In effect, he was free to play with history in an imaginative way without worrying about the tyranny of facts.[25]

In the decades following his death, the legacy of his approach to history had a profound impact on popular culture. As the Disney Studios entertainment empire spread across the globe, Distory became an almost unrivaled source of historical education. The commitment to present the Disney version of the past was manifest in the studio's expanding film production, most notably in several rereleases of *Song of the South, Million Dollar Dixie Deliverance* (1978), *The Liberators* (1987), *The Ernest Green Story* (1992), *Quiz Show* (1994), *Jefferson in Paris* (1995), *Remember the Titans* (2000), *Pearl Harbor* (2001), *Lincoln* (2012), and *Bridge of Spies* (2015). Without Walt's singular direction, the films produced with the studio's imprimatur or collaboration became more varied, including films intended primarily for adults. But, with only a few exceptions, the emphasis on "happy history" remained in force.[26]

Perhaps even more important, the commitment to history was on full display at Disneyland and Disney World, and even at the international Disney parks in France and Asia. At Disney World's Liberty Square, millions of visitors a year encountered the patriotic messages in the Hall of Presidents, and at Frontierland carefully crafted images of pioneer life introduced new generations of children to the mythic virtues of Davy Crockett and Daniel Boone. At the nearby Dixie Landings Resort, there was historical pageantry presenting southern scenes with no mention of slavery or poverty to disturb the ambiance of quaint folks and frontier chic.

The overarching message here—that history is a good-natured journey with a happy ending—was consistent with the traditions established by

Disney in the 1940s and 1950s. As Stephen Fjellman observed in 1992, the park designers took their cues from the original "imagineer," reinforcing his belief that "the world would be a better place if history could be rewritten, leaving in only the parts that 'should have happened.'"

Though seemingly illogical, this cheerful vision has captured the imagination of millions of individuals exposed to Disney's seductive magic. Indeed, as the historian Mike Wallace concluded in 1996, "one might fairly say that Walt Disney has taught people more history, in a more memorable way, than they ever learned in school." For better or worse, the historical enterprise that began with *Song of the South* in 1946 has evolved into a cultural force powerful enough to challenge the best efforts of traditional historians. No one can be certain about the future of popular history in a culturally diverse nation susceptible to changing tastes and innovations in media technology. But one thing is clear: the legacy born in the Briar Patch poses a serious problem for anyone hoping to educate the public with a balanced and nuanced view of the past.[27]

Notes

1. Steven Watts, *The Magic Kingdom: Walt Disney and the American Way of Life* (Boston: Houghton Mifflin, 1997), 5, 30–40, 51, 228–73; Neal Gabler, *Walt Disney: The Triumph of the American Imagination* (New York: Vintage, 2007), xii–xiii, 111–64, 375–447; Richard Schickel, *The Disney Version: The Life, Times, Art and Commerce of Walt Disney* (New York: Simon and Schuster, 1968), 115–35, 263–77; 3–10, 57–73; Leonard Maltin, *The Disney Films,* 3rd ed. (New York: Hyperion, 1995); Marc Eliot, *Walt Disney: Hollywood's Dark Prince* (New York: Birch Lane Press, 1993), 36–38, 44–47, 159–183; Leonard Mosley, *Disney's World* (New York: Stein and Day, 1985), 101–18, 199–210.

2. Maltin, *The Disney Films,* 57–67; Watts, *The Magic Kingdom,* 234–37, 243–48; Gabler, *Walt Disney,* 382–95, 401–5, 407, 410, 412, 433, 436. See Alexander P. de Seversky, *Victory Through Air Power* (New York: Simon and Schuster, 1942).

3. Watts, *The Magic Kingdom,* 274–80; Maltin, *The Disney Films,* 73–78; Publicity Scrapbook on *Song of the South,* PS-21, and Uncle Remus Story Research Folder, both in the Disney Archives (hereafter DA), Burbank, California. For an idiosyncratic "insider's" history of the *Song of the South* saga, see Jim Korkis, *Who's Afraid of the Song of the South? And Other Forbidden Stories* (Orlando: Theme Park Press, 2012). On Joel Chandler Harris (1848–1908), see R. Bruce Bickley Jr., *Joel Chandler Harris: A Biography and Critical Study* (Athens: Univ. of Georgia Press, 2008); and Joel Chandler Harris, *The Complete Tales of Uncle Remus* (Boston: Houghton Mifflin, 2002).

4. Maltin, *The Disney Films,* 74 (quotations), 75–78; Watts, *The Magic Kingdom,* 273–80; Gabler, *Walt Disney,* 432–39, 442, 463, 468–70; Korkis, *Who's Afraid of the Song of the South?* 19–80; Schickel, *The Disney Version,* 276–77; Eliot, *Walt Disney,* 183–84. For correspondence on controversies surrounding the script and casting, see Uncle Remus Story Research Folder, DA. For a broad sample of reviews, see the clippings in PS-S21, DA.

5. Thomas Cripps, *Slow Fade to Black: The Negro in American Film, 1900–1942* (New York: Oxford Univ. Press, 1977), 383–86; Thomas Cripps, *Making Movies Black: The Hollywood Message Movie from World War II to the Civil Rights Era* (New York: Oxford Univ. Press, 1993), 179, 187–94; Maltin, *The Disney Films,* 78; Korkis, *Who's Afraid of the Song of the South?* 31, 65–71, 78; Watts, *The Magic Kingdom,* 276–79, 283–302; PS-S21, and Uncle Remus Story Research Folder, DA.

6. Maltin, *The Disney Films,* 85–89, 97–100, 104–7, 110–12, 115–17; Watts, *The Magic Kingdom,* 5–6, 285–91, 296; Gabler, *Walt Disney,* 439, 468–72, 489, 491, 614–15. On *So Dear to My Heart,* and *Treasure Island,* see the clippings in PS-S2, -S3, and -T3, DA. For an insightful discussion of Disney's effort to influence popular conceptions of American history, see Mike Wallace, *Mickey Mouse History and Other Essays on American Memory* (Philadelphia: Temple Univ. Press, 1996), 133–74.

7. David Crockett, *A Narrative of the Life of David Crockett of the State of Tennessee* (Lincoln: Bison Books, 2011); Mark Derr, *The Frontiersman: The Real Life and the Many Legends of Davy Crockett* (New York: William Morrow, 1993); Michael Wallis, *David Crockett: Lion of the West* (New York: William Morrow, 2012); Paul F. Henderson, *The Davy Crockett Craze: A Look at the 1950s Phenomenon and Davy Crockett Collectibles* (Hillside, Ill.: R and G Productions, 1996); Mosley, *Disney's World,* 245 (first quotation), 249; Eliot, *Walt Disney,* 228–29; "The Wild Frontier," *Time* (May 23, 1955), 92 (second quotation); "Davy's Time," *Time* (May 30, 1955), 9–10; Watts, *The Magic Kingdom,* 286, 313 (third quotation), 314–19, 322, 366, 373, 379, 391, 452; Maltin, *The Disney Films,* 122–24, 135–36, 351–52, 357–59; Gabler, *Walt Disney,* 513–18, 520, 530, 603, 615; and Schickel, *The Disney Version,* 300. See also the voluminous clippings in PS-D10, -D11, and -D12, DA. On Frontierland, see Stephen M. Fjellman, *Vinyl Leaves: Walt Disney World and America* (Boulder: Westview Press, 1992).

8. Maltin, *The Disney Films,* 122–24, 135–36; PS-D11 and -D12, DA.

9. Fjellman, *Vinyl Leaves,* 59 (quotation); Watts, *The Magic Kingdom,* 303–13, 365; Maltin, *The Disney Films,* 113–15, 117–19, 128–30, 137–38, 142–44, 148–49.

10. August 1955 press release (quotations), and numerous *Atlanta Constitution* clippings, *The Great Locomotive Chase* publicity scrapbook, PS-G, DA. On the Andrews Raid, see William Pittenger, *Daring and Suffering: A History of the Andrews Railroad Raid into Georgia in 1862* (Nashville, Tenn.: Cumberland House, 1999); Samuel Epstein and Beryl Epstein, *The Andrews Raid; or The Great Locomotive Chase* (New York: Coward-McCann, 1956); Russell S. Bonds, *Stealing the General: The Great Locomotive Chase and the First Medal of Honor* (Yardley, Pa.:

Westholme, 2008); Gordon L. Rottman, *The Great Locomotive Chase: The Andrews Raid 1862* (Oxford, UK: Osprey Publishing, 2009); and James G. Bogle and Stan Cohen, *The General and the Texas: A Pictorial History of the Andrews Raid, April 12, 1862* (Missoula: Pictorial Histories Publishing Company, 1999). On Disney's fascination with trains (especially miniature trains) and the effort to use historically accurate locomotives in the film, see Mosley, *Disney's World,* 215–19; Watts, *The Magic Kingdom,* 264–65; Gabler, *Walt Disney,* 465–68, 473–76, 478, 481–84, 488, 498, 520, 543, 545; and Maltin, *The Disney Films,* 133–34.

11. *Buster Keaton: The General* (DVD, American Pop Classic studio, 2015). On Keaton (1895–1966), see Edward McPherson, *Buster Keaton: Tempest in a Flat Hat* (New York: Newmarket Press, 2007). On Wilbur G. Kurtz (1882–1967), see David O'Connell, *The Art and Life of Atlanta Artist Wilbur G. Kurtz: Inspired by Southern History* (Mt. Pleasant, S.C.: Arcadia, 2013); Wilbur G. Kurtz, *Technical Advisor, The Making of Gone with the Wind: The Hollywood Journals of Wilbur G. Kurtz* (Atlanta: Atlanta Historical Society, 1978); Wilbur G. Kurtz, interview by Richard Doud, June 5, 1965, transcript in the Archives of American Art (Smithsonian Institution); and Cripps, *Making Movies Black,* 19. *Behind the Scenes with Fess Parker, Disneyland* television broadcast, May 30, 1956, transcript in DA (quotations); Maltin, *The Disney Films,* 132–34, 358. Gabler, *Walt Disney,* 11, notes that "Sometimes Walt would tag after Erastus Taylor, a Civil War veteran, who would relive his battle exploits."

12. *Behind the Scenes with Fess Parker* (quotations); Maltin, *The Disney Films,* 132–34.

13. https://en.wikipedia.org/wiki/The_Great_Locomotive_Chase.

14. Maltin, *The Disney Films,* 133–134; Watts, *The Magic Kingdom,* 296; Schickel, *The Disney Version,* 301 (quotation); Bosley Crowther, "Saga of Rails," *New York Times,* June 27, 1956 (quotations). See the various reviews in *The Great Locomotive Chase* publicity scrapbook, PS-G, DA.

15. Maltin, *The Disney Films,* 134–36, 138–45 (first quotation), 148, 150–52; Watts, *The Magic Kingdom,* 286, 290–95, 299–300, 328, 331, 372–73, 379; Gabler, *Walt Disney,* xiii (second quotation), 548–49, 585, 614–15; *Old Yeller* publicity scrapbook, PS-O1, DA.

16. Fjellman, *Vinyl Leaves,* 59–60 (quotations). On Disneyland as an expression of Disney's passion to create an imaginary or fictional world, see Gabler, *Walt Disney,* 497–99.

17. Maltin, *The Disney Films,* 353–54, 358–60; Watts, *The Magic Kingdom,* 292–93, 295, 300, 369. See *The Nine Lives of Elfego Baca* publicity scrapbook, PS-N; The *Tales of Texas John Slaughter* publicity scrapbook, PS-T14; and *Daniel Boone* publicity scrapbook, PS-D, all in DA. See also Howard Bryan, *Incredible Elfego Baca: Good Man, Bad Man of the Old West* (Santa Fe: Clear Light Publishing, 1993); Allen E. Erwin, *The Southwest of John Horton Slaughter, 1841–1922* (Glendale, Calif.: Arthur Clarke, 1965); and John Mack Faragher, *Daniel Boone: The Life and Legend of an American Pioneer* (New York: Henry Holt, 1992).

18. Maltin, *The Disney Films,* 292, 353, 359–60; Watts, *The Magic Kingdom,* 291 (last quotation), 292, 295, 300, 369; "The Birth of the Swamp Fox," episode 1 of the *Swamp Fox* serial, broadcast on *Walt Disney Presents,* October 23, 1959, copy in DA (quotations); *Swamp Fox* publicity scrapbook, PS-S15.

19. *Minneapolis (Minn.) Star,* n.d. (quotation), *Charleston (S.C.) News and Courier,* circa August 1959 (quotation), clippings in *Swamp Fox* publicity scrapbook, PS-S15; "The Birth of the Swamp Fox," all in DA. The series featured two episodes broadcast in late October 1959 ("The Birth of the Swamp Fox" and "Brother Against Brother") and four episodes ("Tory Vengeance," "Day of Reckoning," "Redcoat Strategy," and "A Case of Treason") broadcast in January 1960. Maltin, *The Disney Films,* 359.

20. *Swamp Fox* publicity scrapbook, PS-S15, contains numerous clippings and press releases on the show. See especially Norman Shavin, "Ex-Canadian to Portray 'Robin Hood of the South,'" *Atlanta Journal,* September 1, 1959; and "Swamp Fox," *Los Angeles Times,* October 25, 1959. See William Gilmore Simms, *The Life of Francis Marion* (New York: G. F. Cooledge and Brother, 1846); and Robert D. Bass, *Swamp Fox: The Life and Campaigns of General Francis Marion* (New York: Henry Holt, 1959). For a more recent study of Marion, see John Oller, *The Swamp Fox: How Francis Marion Saved the American Revolution* (Cambridge, Mass.: Da Capo, 2016).

21. *Milwaukee (Wisc.) Sentinel,* circa October 1959 (quotations), clipping in *Swamp Fox* publicity book, DA; Simms, *The Life of Francis Marion,* 26–27.

22. Unidentified clipping in *Swamp Fox* publicity scrapbook (Sutton quotation). On General Tarleton, see Robert D. Bass, *The Green Dragoons: The Lives of Banastre Tarleton and Mary Robinson* (New York: Henry Holt, 1957), which the Disney scriptwriters consulted during the production of *Swamp Fox.* For a revisionist view of the man known as "Bloody Tarleton," see Anthony J. Scotti Jr., *Brutal Virtue: The Myth and Reality of Banastre Tarleton* (Berwyn Heights, Md.: Heritage Books, 2002).

23. Maltin, *The Disney Films,* 167–69, 174–80, 192–93, 204–6, 208–10, 243–47; Watts, *The Magic Kingdom,* 293, 296, 300, 302, 342, 369–73, 391–92, 400, 404–5; Wallace, *Mickey Mouse History,* 134–135; Gabler, *Walt Disney,* 505, 563, 568–69, 630–33; MacKinlay Kantor, *God and My Country* (Cleveland, Ohio: World Publishing Company, 1954). On John Wesley Powell (1834–1902), see Wallace Stegner, *Beyond the Hundredth Meridian: John Wesley Powell and the Second Opening of the West* (Boston: Houghton Mifflin, 1954); and Don Worster, *A River Running West: The Life of John Wesley Powell* (New York: Oxford Univ. Press, 2001).

24. Schickel, *The Disney Version,* 339–427; Watts, *The Magic Kingdom,* 425–53; Mosley, *Disney's World,* 263–307; Eliot, *Walt Disney,* 247–81.

25. "Cinema: Mouse and Me," *Time* (December 27, 1937); Watts, *The Magic Kingdom,* 404–45; Gabler, *Walt Disney,* 562–617.

26. Maltin, *The Disney Films,* 247–325. For a list of Disney movies made between 1937 and 2018, see http://disneymovielist.com or http://movies.disney

.com/all-movies. *Million Dollar Dixie Deliverance* (historical fiction featuring a wounded black soldier, Confederate kidnappers, and five children from a Union family), *The Liberators* (loosely based on a true story of black-white Underground Railroad collaboration in antebellum Kentucky), and *The Ernest Green Story* are made-for-television movies. Based on the life of one of the Little Rock Nine students involved in the desegregation of Central High School, *The Ernest Green Story* won a Peabody Award. *Quiz Show,* a dramatization of the 1950s quiz show scandal involving Charles Van Doren, received four Academy Award nominations, including one for Best Picture. *Quiz Show* was distributed by Disney-owned Buena Vista Pictures, as were *Jefferson in Paris* (produced by Touchstone Pictures), *Remember the Titans,* and *Pearl Harbor* (produced by Touchstone Pictures). *Lincoln* and *Bridge of Spies,* a Cold War spy thriller based on true events surrounding a 1964 prisoner exchange, were directed by Steven Spielberg, produced by Dreamworks, and distributed by Walt Disney Studios, the successor to Buena Vista Pictures. *Lincoln* received twelve Academy Award nominations, and *Bridge of Spies* received six.

27. Fjellman, *Vinyl Leaves,* 59, 60 (first quotation), 61–107; Wallace, *Mickey Mouse History,* 134 (second quotation), 155.

Acknowledgments

This collection of essays, conceptualized by Paul A. Cimbala and John David Smith six years ago, has benefited greatly from the encouragement and advice offered by a number of knowledgeable editors. We are especially grateful to William A. Link and Michele Gillespie, who went out of their way to find a place for our book in the University Press of Kentucky's New Directions in Southern History book series, and to Anne Dean Dotson, Suzanne La Rosa and Randall Williams of NewSouth Books, and Fredric Nachbaur and Andrew L. Slap of Fordham University Press.

We would also like to thank the following historians for graciously sharing their ideas and expertise with us: Richard Fusco, Malcolm J. Harkins III, Angela Howard, James Kopaczewski, Francis Graham Lee, and Marion W. Roydhouse. The editors of this volume are also indebted to Linda Patterson Miller, Stephen J. Whitfield, Sylvia Angelika Smith, and Kathleen Hardee Arsenault for their timely advice and words of encouragement. Gloria Davenport of the University of North Carolina at Charlotte's Department of History provided valuable secretarial support. We were also very fortunate to work closely with Patrick O'Dowd of the University Press of Kentucky, a consummate professional. Derik Shelor proved to be a highly competent and thoughtful copyeditor. Daniel Buck offered invaluable technical support. The John Hope Franklin Professorship of Southern History research fund and the University of South Florida Foundation graciously provided financial support for the indexing of this volume.

Finally, we want to thank Professor Randall M. Miller of St. Joseph's University, whose long and distinguished career as a scholar and teacher inspired this volume. The editors and contributors hope that their efforts have come reasonably close to meeting Randall's extraordinarily high standards of scholarship and intellectual engagement—and that every page of this book reflects some aspect of his wise and humane approach to history, and life.

Contributors

Raymond Arsenault is the John Hope Franklin Professor of Southern History at the University of South Florida. One of the nation's leading civil rights historians, he is the author or editor of ten books, including *Freedom Riders: 1961 and the Struggle for Racial Justice* (2006), *The Sound of Freedom: Marian Anderson, the Lincoln Memorial, and the Concert That Awakened America* (2009), and *Arthur Ashe, A Life* (2018). The 2011 PBS *American Experience* documentary *Freedom Riders,* based on his book, won three Emmys and a George Peabody Award.

Michael J. Birkner is a professor of history at Gettysburg College, where he has taught since 1989, chairing the department from 1993 to 2003 and serving as the Benjamin Franklin Professor of Liberal Arts from 2001 to 2016. Birkner is the author or editor of fourteen books and many articles on nineteenth- and twentieth-century American social and political history. He has written and lectured extensively on the Eisenhower presidency and in 2018 led a Gilder-Lehrman seminar for secondary school teachers at American University focused on the nation's thirty-fourth president.

Paul A. Cimbala is a professor emeritus of history at Fordham University in the Bronx, New York. He has edited several essay collections with Randall M. Miller and recently coauthored with him *The Northern Home Front during the Civil War* (2017). He is writing a history of the Veteran Reserve Corps during the Civil War and Reconstruction.

Stanley Harrold recently retired as a professor of history at South Carolina State University. His most recent book is *American Abolitionism: Its Direct Impact on Politics from Colonial Times into Reconstruction* (2019).

James R. Hedtke is a professor of history and political science at Cabrini University, where he has taught for forty-seven years. Hedtke received his bachelor's from St. Joseph's University, his master's from Villanova University, and his Ph.D. from Temple University. He is the author of four books, including two on the American Civil War: *Civil War Professional Soldiers, Citizen Soldiers, and Native American Soldiers of Genesee County, New York: Ordinary Men of Valor* (2006) and *American Civil War: Facts and Fictions* (2018).

James Oliver Horton (1943–2017) was the Benjamin Banneker Professor of American Studies and History at George Washington University, where he also directed the George Washington University Center for Public History and Public Culture. He was active in public history, was nationally recognized for excellence in teaching, and was president of the Organization of American Historians (2004–2005). **Lois E. Horton** is a professor emerita of history at George Mason University. The Hortons' coauthored works include *Black Bostonians* (1979), *In Hope of Liberty* (1997), *Hard Road to Freedom* (2001), and *Slavery and the Making of America* (2005). They also coedited *Slavery and Public History* (2006). Lois Horton's most recent book is *Harriet Tubman and the Fight for Freedom* (2013).

Daniel Kilbride is a professor of history at John Carroll University in Cleveland, Ohio. He is the author of *Being American in Europe, 1750–1860* (2013). He currently is writing a book on American engagement with Africa in the nineteenth century.

John David Smith, the Charles H. Stone Distinguished Professor of American History at the University of North Carolina at Charlotte, is the author or editor of thirty books, including *An Old Creed for the New South: Proslavery Ideology and Historiography, 1865–1918* (1985), *The Dictionary of Afro-American Slavery* (1988) (with Randall M. Miller), *Black Judas: William Hannibal Thomas and* The American Negro (2000), *Lincoln and the U.S. Colored Troops* (2013), and *Dear Delia: The Civil War Letters of Captain Henry F. Young, Seventh Wisconsin Infantry* (2019) (with Micheal J. Larson). Smith has received The Gustavus Myers Center Award for the Study of Human Rights in North America and The Mayflower Society Award for Nonfiction.

Diane Miller Sommerville is a professor of history at Binghamton University, SUNY. A historian of the nineteenth-century South, she has authored two monographs, *Rape and Race in the Nineteenth-Century South* (2004) and, most recently, *Aberration of Mind: Suicide and Suffering in the Civil War–Era South* (2018). That work was a finalist for the Lincoln Prize and recipient of the Willie Lee Rose Prize, awarded annually by the Southern Association for Women Historians for the best book on southern history written by a woman. She is currently working on a project on postpartum disorders in the nineteenth-century South.

Stephen J. Whitfield is a professor emeritus of American studies at Brandeis University, where he taught for forty-four years. He is the author of nine books, including most recently *Learning on the Left: Political Profiles of Brandeis University* (2020). Whitfield served as a Fulbright visiting professor at the Hebrew University of Jerusalem and at the Catholic University of Leuven (Belgium), and also taught at the Sorbonne and at the University of Munich.

Index

New Directions in Southern History

Series Editors

Michele Gillespie, Wake Forest University
William A. Link, University of Florida

The Lost State of Franklin: America's First Secession
Kevin T. Barksdale

The Civil War Guerrilla: Unfolding the Black Flag in History, Memory, and Myth
edited by Joseph M. Beilein Jr. and Matthew C. Hulbert

Bluecoats and Tar Heels: Soldiers and Civilians in Reconstruction North Carolina
Mark L. Bradley

Becoming Bourgeois: Merchant Culture in the South, 1820–1865
Frank J. Byrne

Willis Duke Weatherford: Race, Religion, and Reform in the American South
Andrew McNeill Canady

Cowboy Conservatism: Texas and the Rise of the Modern Right
Sean P. Cunningham

Confederate Citadel: Richmond and Its People at War
Mary A. DeCredico

A Tour of Reconstruction: Travel Letters of 1875
Anna Dickinson (J. Matthew Gallman, ed.)

Raising Racists: The Socialization of White Children in the Jim Crow South
Kristina DuRocher

Rethinking the Civil War Era: Directions for Research
Paul D. Escott

Marriage on the Border: Love, Mutuality, and Divorce in the Upper South during the Civil War
Allison Dorothy Fredette

Lum and Abner: Rural America and the Golden Age of Radio
Randal L. Hall

A Higher Mission: The Careers of Alonzo and Althea Brown Edmiston in Central Africa
Kimberly D. Hill

The New Southern University: Academic Freedom and Liberalism at UNC
Charles J. Holden

Entangled by White Supremacy: Reform in World War I–era South Carolina
Janet G. Hudson

Bloody Breathitt: Politics and Violence in the Appalachian South
T. R. C. Hutton

Cultivating Race: The Expansion of Slavery in Georgia, 1750–1860
Watson W. Jennison

De Bow's Review: *The Antebellum Vision of a New South*
John F. Kvach

Remembering the Battle of the Crater: War as Murder
Kevin M. Levin

My Brother Slaves: Friendship, Masculinity, and Resistance in the Antebellum South
Sergio A. Lussana

The Political Career of W. Kerr Scott: The Squire from Haw River
Julian Pleasants

The View from the Ground: Experiences of Civil War Soldiers
edited by Aaron Sheehan-Dean

Reconstructing Appalachia: The Civil War's Aftermath
edited by Andrew L. Slap

The Long Civil War: New Explorations of America's Enduring Conflict
edited by John David Smith and Raymond Arsenault

A Rape in the Early Republic: Gender and Legal Culture in an 1806 Virginia Trial
Alexander Smyth (Randal L. Hall, ed.)

Blood in the Hills: A History of Violence in Appalachia
edited by Bruce E. Stewart

Moonshiners and Prohibitionists: The Battle over Alcohol in Southern Appalachia
Bruce E. Stewart

The U.S. South and Europe: Transatlantic Relations in the Nineteenth and Twentieth Centuries
edited by Cornelis A. van Minnen and Manfred Berg

Southern Farmers and Their Stories: Memory and Meaning in Oral History
Melissa Walker

Law and Society in the South: A History of North Carolina Court Cases
John W. Wertheimer

Family or Freedom: People of Color in the Antebellum South
Emily West